PEARSON
mysocialworklab

MySocialWorkLab offers:

- A complete **Pearson eText** of the book
- A wealth of engaging **videos**
  - **Brand-new videos**—organized around the competencies and accompanied by interactive assessment—that demonstrate key concepts and practices
  - **Career Exploration videos** that contain interviews with a wide range of social workers
- Tools for **self-assessment and review**—chapter specific quizzes tied to the core competencies, many written in the same format students will find on the licensing exam
- A **Gradebook** that reports progress of students and the class as a whole
- **MySocialWorkLibrary**—a compendium of articles and case studies in social work, searchable by course, topic, author, and title
- **MySearchLab**—a collection of tools that aid students in mastering research assignments and papers
- **And much more!**

Save time and improve results!

MySocialWorkLab is a dynamic website that provides a wealth of resources geared to help students develop and master the skills articulated in CSWE's core competencies—and improve their grades in their social work courses.

MySocialWorkLab is available at no extra cost when bundled with any text in the **Connecting Core Competencies Series.** Visit **www.mysocialworklab.com** to learn more.

> **"I would require [MySocialWorkLab]—especially if there were a way to harvest the results for program assessment."**
>
> —Jane Peller, *Northeastern Illinois University*

In recent years, many Social Work departments have been focusing on the CSWE Educational Policy and Accreditation Standards (EPAS) to guide their accreditation process. The current standards, issued in 2008, focus on mastery of the CSWE's ten core competencies and practice behaviors. Each of the ten core competencies now contains specific knowledge, values, skills, and the resulting practice behaviors as guidance for the curriculum and assessment methods of Social Work programs.

In writing this text, we have used the CSWE core competency standards and assessment recommendations as guidelines for structuring content and integrating the pedagogy. For details on the CSWE core competencies, please see www.cswe.org.

For the core competencies highlighted in this text, see page iv.

CSWE EPAS 2008 Core Competencies

Professional Identity

2.1.1 Identify as a professional social worker and conduct oneself accordingly.

Necessary Knowledge, Values, Skills

- Social workers serve as representatives of the profession, its mission, and its core values.
- Social workers know the profession's history.
- Social workers commit themselves to the profession's enhancement and to their own professional conduct and growth.

Operational Practice Behaviors

- Social workers advocate for client access to the services of social work;
- Social workers practice personal reflection and self-correction to assure continual professional development;
- Social workers attend to professional roles and boundaries;
- Social workers demonstrate professional demeanor in behavior, appearance, and communication;
- Social workers engage in career-long learning; and
- Social workers use supervision and consultation.

Ethical Practice

2.1.2 Apply social work ethical principles to guide professional practice.

Necessary Knowledge, Values, Skills

- Social workers have an obligation to conduct themselves ethically and engage in ethical decision-making.
- Social workers are knowledgeable about the value base of the profession, its ethical standards, and relevant law.

Operational Practice Behaviors

- Social workers recognize and manage personal values in a way that allows professional values to guide practice;
- Social workers make ethical decisions by applying standards of the National Association of Social Workers Code of Ethics and, as applicable, of the International Federation of Social Workers/International Association of Schools of Social Work Ethics in Social Work, Statement of Principles;
- Social workers tolerate ambiguity in resolving ethical conflicts; and
- Social workers apply strategies of ethical reasoning to arrive at principled decisions.

Critical Thinking

2.1.3 Apply critical thinking to inform and communicate professional judgments.

Necessary Knowledge, Values, Skills

- Social workers are knowledgeable about the principles of logic, scientific inquiry, and reasoned discernment.
- They use critical thinking augmented by creativity and curiosity.
- Critical thinking also requires the synthesis and communication of relevant information.

Operational Practice Behaviors

- Social workers distinguish, appraise, and integrate multiple sources of knowledge, including research-based knowledge, and practice wisdom;
- Social workers analyze models of assessment, prevention, intervention, and evaluation; and
- Social workers demonstrate effective oral and written communication in working with individuals, families, groups, organizations, communities, and colleagues.

Adapted with the permission of Council on Social Work Education

Diversity in Practice
2.1.4 Engage diversity and difference in practice.

Necessary Knowledge, Values, Skills	Operational Practice Behaviors
• Social workers understand how diversity characterizes and shapes the human experience and is critical to the formation of identity. • The dimensions of diversity are understood as the intersectionality of multiple factors including age, class, color, culture, disability, ethnicity, gender, gender identity and expression, immigration status, political ideology, race, religion, sex, and sexual orientation. • Social workers appreciate that, as a consequence of difference, a person's life experiences may include oppression, poverty, marginalization, and alienation as well as privilege, power, and acclaim.	• Social workers recognize the extent to which a culture's structures and values may oppress, marginalize, alienate, or create or enhance privilege and power; • Social workers gain sufficient self-awareness to eliminate the influence of personal biases and values in working with diverse groups; • Social workers recognize and communicate their understanding of the importance of difference in shaping life experiences; and • Social workers view themselves as learners and engage those with whom they work as informants.

Human Rights & Justice
2.1.5 Advance human rights and social and economic justice.

Necessary Knowledge, Values, Skills	Operational Practice Behaviors
• Each person, regardless of position in society, has basic human rights, such as freedom, safety, privacy, an adequate standard of living, health care, and education. • Social workers recognize the global interconnections of oppression and are knowledgeable about theories of justice and strategies to promote human and civil rights. • Social work incorporates social justice practices in organizations, institutions, and society to ensure that these basic human rights are distributed equitably and without prejudice.	• Social workers understand the forms and mechanisms of oppression and discrimination; • Social workers advocate for human rights and social and economic justice; and • Social workers engage in practices that advance social and economic justice.

Research Based Practice
2.1.6 Engage in research-informed practice and practice-informed research.

Necessary Knowledge, Values, Skills	Operational Practice Behaviors
• Social workers use practice experience to inform research, employ evidence-based interventions, evaluate their own practice, and use research findings to improve practice, policy, and social service delivery. • Social workers comprehend quantitative and qualitative research and understand scientific and ethical approaches to building knowledge.	• Social workers use practice experience to inform scientific inquiry; and • Social workers use research evidence to inform practice.

Human Behavior
2.1.7 Apply knowledge of human behavior and the social environment.

Necessary Knowledge, Values, Skills	Operational Practice Behaviors
• Social workers are knowledgeable about human behavior across the life course; the range of social systems in which people live; and the ways social systems promote or deter people in maintaining or achieving health and well-being. • Social workers apply theories and knowledge from the liberal arts to understand biological, social, cultural, psychological, and spiritual development.	• Social workers utilize conceptual frameworks to guide the processes of assessment, intervention, and evaluation; and • Social workers critique and apply knowledge to understand person and environment.

CSWE EPAS 2008 Core Competencies *(continued)*

Policy Practice   2.1.8 Engage in policy practice to advance social and economic well-being and to deliver effective social work services.

Necessary Knowledge, Values, Skills

- Social work practitioners understand that policy affects service delivery and they actively engage in policy practice.
- Social workers know the history and current structures of social policies and services; the role of policy in service delivery; and the role of practice in policy development.

Operational Practice Behaviors

- Social workers analyze, formulate, and advocate for policies that advance social well-being; and
- Social workers collaborate with colleagues and clients for effective policy action.

Practice Contexts

2.1.9 Respond to contexts that shape practice.

Necessary Knowledge, Values, Skills

- Social workers are informed, resourceful, and proactive in responding to evolving organizational, community, and societal contexts at all levels of practice.
- Social workers recognize that the context of practice is dynamic, and use knowledge and skill to respond proactively.

Operational Practice Behaviors

- Social workers continuously discover, appraise, and attend to changing locales, populations, scientific and technological developments, and emerging societal trends to provide relevant services; and
- Social workers provide leadership in promoting sustainable changes in service delivery and practice to improve the quality of social services.

Engage, Assess, Intervene, Evaluate   2.1.10 Engage, assess, intervene, and evaluate with individuals, families, groups, organizations, and communities.

Necessary Knowledge, Values, Skills

- Professional practice involves the dynamic and interactive processes of engagement, assessment, intervention, and evaluation at multiple levels.
- Social workers have the knowledge and skills to practice with individuals, families, groups, organizations, and communities.
- Practice knowledge includes
  - identifying, analyzing, and implementing evidence-based interventions designed to achieve client goals;
  - using research and technological advances;
  - evaluating program outcomes and practice effectiveness;
  - developing, analyzing, advocating, and providing leadership for policies and services; and
  - promoting social and economic justice.

Operational Practice Behaviors

(a) Engagement
- Social workers substantively and affectively prepare for action with individuals, families, groups, organizations, and communities;
- Social workers use empathy and other interpersonal skills; and
- Social workers develop a mutually agreed-on focus of work and desired outcomes.

(b) Assessment
- Social workers collect, organize, and interpret client data;
- Social workers assess client strengths and limitations;
- Social workers develop mutually agreed-on intervention goals and objectives; and
- Social workers select appropriate intervention strategies.

(c) Intervention
- Social workers initiate actions to achieve organizational goals;
- Social workers implement prevention interventions that enhance client capacities;
- Social workers help clients resolve problems;
- Social workers negotiate, mediate, and advocate for clients; and
- Social workers facilitate transitions and endings.

(d) Evaluation
- Social workers critically analyze, monitor, and evaluate interventions.

C O N N E C T I N G C O R E C O M P E T E N C I E S **Chapter-by-Chapter Matrix**									
Chapter	Professional Identity	Ethical Practice	Critical Thinking	Diversity in Practice	Human Rights & Justice	Research Based Practice	Human Behavior	Policy Practice	Practice Contexts	Engage Assess Intervene Evaluate
1	✔	✔				✔				
2	✔	✔							✔	
3	✔	✔								✔
4	✔	✔		✔						
5	✔			✔	✔					
6		✔					✔			✔
7				✔		✔				✔
8		✔							✔	✔
9		✔							✔	✔
10	✔						✔			✔
Total Chapters	6	7	0	3	1	2	2	0	3	6

THIRD EDITION

The Practicum Companion for Social Work

Integrating Class and Field Work

Julie Birkenmaier
Saint Louis University

Marla Berg-Weger
Saint Louis University

Allyn & Bacon

Boston   Columbus   Indianapolis   New York   San Francisco   Upper Saddle River
Amsterdam   Cape Town   Dubai   London   Madrid   Milan   Munich   Paris   Montreal   Toronto
Delhi   Mexico City   Sao Paulo   Sydney   Hong Kong   Seoul   Singapore   Taipei   Tokyo

Editor in Chief: Dickson Musslewhite
Executive Acquisitions Editor: Ashley Dodge
Editorial Product Manager: Carly Czech
Executive Marketing Manager: Jeanette Koskinas
Senior Marketing Manager: Wendy Albert
Marketing Assistant: Patrick M. Walsh
Production Manager: Kathy Sleys
Associate Production Project Manager: Maggie Brobeck

Editorial Production and Composition Service: Joseph Barnabas Malcolm/PreMediaGlobal
Interior Design: Joyce Weston Design
Cover Designer: Kristina Mose-Libon/Suzanne Duda
Cover Image: David Burch/UpperCut Images/Getty Images
Creative Director: Jayne Conte
Printer/Binder: Edwards Brothers, Inc.
Cover Printer: Lehigh-Phoenix

Credits appear on Page 243, which constitutes an extension of the copyright page.

Library of Congress Cataloging-in-Publication Data

Birkenmaier, Julie.
    The practicum companion for social work : integrating class and field work / Julie Birkenmaier, Marla Berg-Weger.—3rd ed.
        p. cm.
    Includes bibliographical references and index.
    ISBN-13: 978-0-205-79541-3
    ISBN-10: 0-205-79541-2
    1. Social work education.   2. Social service—Fieldwork.   I. Berg-Weger, Marla, 1956–   II. Title.
HV11.B44 2011
361.3'2071—dc22

                                                                                    2010010676

    10 9 8 7 6 5 4 3   EB 14 13 12 11

Allyn & Bacon
is an imprint of

www.pearsonhighered.com

ISBN-10: 0-205-79541-2
ISBN-13: 978-0-205-79541-3

Contents

3. Safety in Social Work Settings   51

4. Making the Most of Your Practicum Supervision   68

Preface

The Practicum Companion for Social Work: Integrating Class and Field Work is designed to accompany bachelor-level (BSW) and master-level (MSW) social work practicum students through their initial experiences in the field component of the social work education process.

Each unit covers issues pertinent to the social work field placement. Practice applications are woven throughout each unit to provide an avenue for student integration of the material into their practica. Each unit ends with a summary, student scenario postscripts, and one or more practice applications.

In addition to providing information on applying social work knowledge and skills in the field through practice, each unit contains several case scenarios and practice applications. The case scenarios constitute situations relevant to the topic presented. Students may encounter similar situations in their field placements. Some case scenarios end with discussion questions that lead into the topic and are resolved at the end of the unit. The practice applications are discussion questions, role-plays, and exercises that will help students integrate the material covered in each unit and apply the material to their experiences. Both the case scenarios and the practice applications may be used to stimulate critical thinking and discussion in field supervision or the classroom.

You will follow the progression of five fictitious students—Ben, Cameron, Corina, Lauren, and Rosa—through their practicum experiences. These students will encounter situations in their practica that may mirror your experiences or those of your classmates. In addition, these students' stories will help other students apply the knowledge, skills, and values through issues presented in this text and help spur discussion. Postscripts to most of the scenarios are presented at the end of each unit.

It is our sincere hope that this book will differ from the other texts you have read for your social work courses. This text is designed to aid you in your integration of theory with practice, where the "rubber hits the road."

Connecting Core Competencies Series

The new edition of this text is a part of Pearson Education's new *Connecting Core Competencies* series, which consists of foundation-level texts that make it easier than ever to ensure students' success in learning the ten core competencies as stated in 2008 by the Council on Social Worker Education. This text contains:

- ▶ **Core Competency Icons** throughout the chapters, directly linking the CSWE core competencies to the content of the text. **Critical thinking questions** are also included to further students' mastery of the CSWE's standards. For easy reference, page iv displays which icons are used in each chapter, in a chapter-by-chapter matrix.
- ▶ **An end-of-chapter Practice Test,** with multiple-choice questions that test students' knowledge of the chapter content and mastery of the competencies.

▶ **Additional questions pertaining to the videos and case studies found on the new MySocialWorkLab** at the end of each chapter to encourage students to access the site and explore the wealth of available materials. If this text did not come with an access code for MySocialWorkLab, you can purchase access at: **www.mysocialworklab.com.**

Acknowledgments

We would like to recognize the valuable input made to this book by the following reviewers, contributors, and supporters: Gary Behrman, PhD, MSW; Ellen Burkemper, PhD; Melford Fergusen, MSW; Jason Garay; Janelle George, MSW, MPA; Marian Hartung, MSW; Pam Huggins, MSW; Heidi Jaeger, MSW; Dana Klar, MSW, JD; Lisa Knapp, MSW; Suzanne LeLaurin, MSW; Don Linhorst, PhD; Claire McCown, PhD; Jan McGillick, MA; William Padberg, PhD; Carole Price, MSW; Robert Sontag, MSW; Jane Sprankel, MSW; Susan Tebb, PhD; Cheryl Waites, PhD; Stephen Wernet, PhD; Doris Westfall, MSW; Jan Wilson, PhD.

We would also like to thank the reviewers who have provided excellent guidance over the years: Kay Carolyn Brooks, University of Southern Mississippi (emerita); Kathleen V. Heltzer, University of Minnesota, Duluth; Patricia Kolar, (retired, formerly at the University of Pittsburgh); Vicki Gardine Williams, Tennessee State University; Arlene Kaplan, Florida Atlantic University; and Arturo Acosta, El Paso Community College.

We would especially like to thank Katie Terrell, MSW student at Saint Louis University for her invaluable help with this edition.

J. B.
M. B.-W.

Before You Head into the Field: A Prepracticum Guide

If you have not already received information from your social work program about practicum and prepared for the practicum placement/seeking process, the following information will assist you as you make arrangements.

WHAT IS PRACTICUM?

Practicum (or *field placement*) is a social work internship served within an agency or organization affiliated with your social work program that provides a type of social work service. The focus of practicum is gaining supervised social work experience in order to enhance the knowledge and skills gained from your coursework. The process by which students secure a practicum site varies widely.

ASK YOURSELF

Questions to ask yourself as you begin the practicum placement/selection process include the following:

1. What client system(s) interest me (social work with individuals and families, groups, organizations, and communities)?
2. What client populations interest me (children, older adults, teen mothers, etc.)?
3. What client issues interest me (homelessness, mental health, child abuse/neglect, troubled adolescents, etc.)?
4. What setting would I prefer (school, community-based health clinic, public child welfare, advocacy organization, etc.)?
5. What size agency would I prefer (large, midsized, or small)?
6. What knowledge and skills do I want to gain as a result of this practicum experience?
7. What area or field of social work practice do I see myself involved in after I graduate?
8. What social work knowledge and skills do I need to achieve both my short term and long-term professional goals? What practice behaviors do I need to demonstrate in the upcoming practicum?
9. What mentor qualities best assist me in learning? How can I assess for those qualities when interviewing potential field instructors?

REASONABLE EXPECTATIONS FOR THE FIELD EXPERIENCE

Although educational models of the field program vary across social work programs, students in all programs are required to demonstrate practice behaviors and competencies. There are general expectations of the field experience that stem from the Educational Policy and Accreditation Standards issued by the CSWE, to which accredited social work programs are required to adhere. These standards include the following (CSWE, 2008):

1. A structure that facilitates the integration of coursework with the experiences in the field. Models include a class taught on campus,

periodic face-to-face seminars, online seminars and agency-based group learning experiences.

2. A structured admission procedure to field education.

3. A planned and structured learning experience with opportunities for student to demonstrate competencies at the appropriate (i.e., BSW or MSW) level.

4. Policies, procedures, expectations, and appropriate support for field instructors and agencies.

5. Policies and procedures for placing and monitoring students; maintaining field liaison contacts with agencies; and evaluating student learning and field setting effectiveness congruent with the program's competencies.

TIPS FOR THE PRACTICUM INTERVIEW

The extent to which students interview for a practicum position varies among social work programs. If you will interview with an agency representative, your preparation for the interview may include obtaining background information about the agency so that you can engage in a knowledgeable dialogue with the interviewer about the agency and anticipating questions similar to the following and preparing answers to them.

Questions That May Be Asked of You at the Interview

1. Why are you interested in working with this particular population/ agency/field supervisor?

2. What courses have you completed that may be relevant to this setting/work?

3. What are your strengths related to social work skills and knowledge? Your areas for growth?

4. What are your strengths related to professional work habits? Your areas for growth?

5. What are your career goals? Goals for this practicum? How could this practicum help you achieve your long-term goals?

6. Under what type of supervision do you learn best?

7. What is the most effective way in which you learn (by watching and modeling others, by listening to others talk about their work, by jumping in and learning from your mistakes, etc.)?

8. What experience/interest/skills do you have that set you apart from other candidates for this practicum slot?

9. What practice behaviors do you need to learn at your next practicum to master the relevant social work competencies?

An interview often includes time for questions to be asked of an agency representative that will aid you in determining whether a practicum within a particular setting meets your goals.

Questions to Consider Asking an Agency Representative

1. What is the history of the organization?

2. Will I be able to demonstrate the specific practice behaviors and competencies required by my program at this setting? What has been the range of learning experiences for previous students at this agency?

3. What are some possible tasks/activities with which I will be involved?

4. What style of supervision is used by the field instructor?

5. Does the agency have a formal training procedure/orientation for students?

6. What are the expectations of the field instructor regarding logistics (i.e., hours at the practicum, flexibility of hours, availability of the student to clients, dress code, meetings, parking, travel, etc.)?

7. Will other students be working in the agency during my practicum? How many students does one field instructor supervise at one time?

8. Will the person interviewing me become my field instructor? If not, will I have an opportunity to meet with my field instructor before I begin my practicum?

9. Will I have the opportunity to have contact with all aspects of the agency and learn more about the overall functioning of the agency?

10. Will the work entail any health or safety risks? Will I need any health tests or immunizations to work at the agency?

11. Does the work at the agency pose any legal liability risks? Do I need to arrange for my own professional liability coverage, or would the agency or social work program policy also cover me?

12. If needed, does the agency offer Health Insurance Portability and Accountability Act (HIPAA) training? Does the agency require a criminal background check or drug screening? If so, does the university, college, or agency handle the logistics (to include payment), or is the student responsible for completing them and supplying the agency with the information?

Getting Started on Your Social Work Practice Career

Core Competencies in this Chapter (Check marks indicate which competencies are covered in depth)				
✔ Professional Identity	✔ Ethical Practice	☐ Critical Thinking	☐ Diversity in Practice	☐ Human Rights and Justice
✔ Research Based Practice	☐ Human Behavior	☐ Policy Practice	☐ Practice Contexts	☐ Engage, Assess, Intervene, Evaluate

For the things we have to learn before we can do them, we learn by doing them.

—Aristotle

That long-awaited point in every student's social work training has finally arrived. The semester in which you begin practicum has begun. The hours that you, your practicum site, and the social work program faculty spent in developing practicum plans have resulted in a placement. Everyone is ready to begin. With the implementation of the 2008 Council on Social Work Education (CSWE) Educational Policy and Accreditation Standards (EPAS), social work education embraces competency-based education that emphasizes 10 core competencies. Competencies are defined as "measurable practice behaviors that are comprised of knowledge, values, and skills" (Council on Social Work Education [CSWE], 2008). The 10 competencies are as follows:

- Identify as a professional social worker and conduct oneself accordingly
- Apply social work ethical principles to guide professional practice
- Apply critical thinking to inform and communicate professional judgments
- Engage diversity and difference in practice
- Advance human rights and social and economic justice
- Engage in research-informed practice and practice-informed research
- Apply knowledge of human behavior and the social environment
- Engage in policy practice to advance social and economic well-being and to deliver effective social work services
- Respond to contexts that shape practice
- Engage, assess, intervene, and evaluate with individuals, families, groups, organizations, and communities

The field experience component of social work education is designated by CSWE as the "signature pedagogy" of social work education because it "represents the central form of instruction and learning in which a profession socializes its students to perform the role of practitioner" (EPAS Policy 2.3, CSWE, 2008). Simply put, signature pedagogy emphasizes the social work practice behaviors of thinking, performing, and acting with integrity (Shulman, 1999). Signature pedagogy, however, encompasses individual and collaborative components, including observation, performance, analysis, interpretation, inquiry, and responses that become internalized as part of a professional's practice (Shulman, 1999). This designation not only denotes field education as a critical facet of social work education but clearly stipulates that field education (i.e., the demonstration of practice behaviors) is a required component of the preparation of competent and effective social work practitioners and is equally as important as classroom experiences (Holloway, Black, Hoffman, & Pierce, 2009; Zastrow & Petracchi, 2009).

The field practicum experience is the integration of the theoretical knowledge you have gained in the classroom with the skills you will learn in the field. You will obtain supervised practice experience in which you can apply the knowledge, skills, values, and ethics that you have learned in the classroom to achieve the purpose of social work, which is to "promote human and community well-being" (CSWE, 2008). The practicum experience has long been considered a significant factor in the professional development of social work practitioners (Shaffer, 2008). Along with an educationally focused, community-based approach, the field experience provides an opportunity for you to conceptually explore and work with the theories, practice models, areas of knowledge and skills, and fields of social work practice. The practicum will be unlike any other academic experience you have had to date, as you are required to apply your learning through practice behaviors, develop and maintain professional autonomy, and represent yourself as a social work professional. While you continue to be a "consumer" of learning, the practicum enables you to be a "provider" of social work services.

The readings, exams, role-plays, case vignettes, papers, and recordings you completed as preparation for social work practice will be put to the test in the next weeks and months. This text is intended to help, guide, and support you through this exciting, stimulating, and, sometimes, challenging learning experience. This chapter will address the issues to consider when beginning your practicum: developing relationships, learning styles, expectations for the practicum (including competencies and practice behaviors), and the integrative practice field seminar.

GETTING STARTED IN YOUR PRACTICUM

Cameron has accepted a practicum at a substance abuse treatment facility. He has completed the orientation and is contemplating his first day of practicum. However, he has begun to question his choice of a practicum site because he is unsure whether he can separate his role as a social worker from his status as a recovering person and Alcoholics Anonymous sponsor. He is concerned about the stresses that this practicum may create for him and wonders whether he may be tempted to begin drinking again. Should he raise these issues and fears with his field instructor?

Cameron's ethical dilemma is not an uncommon one. Many social workers have had life experiences that strengthen them as social work professionals but have concerns that these same experiences will impede their ability to be competent practitioners. The dilemma, as in Cameron's situation, focuses on the student's ability to blend the personal with the professional. These are important issues to consider as you begin to plan for your first day at practicum.

Following the all-important self-reflection process and the negotiation of your practicum arrangements—start date, schedule, and supervisory assignment—the real work begins. You must begin by preparing emotionally and practically for your field experience. Areas for you to consider in anticipating the practicum include the following:

Professional Identity

Critical Thinking Question

Professionalism involves ongoing self-reflection. What are your thoughts and feelings about practicum expectations and opportunities?

- ▶ Developing relationships with your field instructor, staff, and client systems and the agency or social work program person(s) so you can turn to them with questions, problems, and crises.
- ▶ Identifying and understanding practicum expectations, time and role management, and your niche within the agency.
- ▶ Planning your practicum goals—including competencies to be mastered and the practice behaviors you will engage in to gain these competencies—in order to develop learning plan and evaluative criteria.
- ▶ Identifying your learning style and role.
- ▶ Beginning to consider the amount and type of personal disclosure you may want to share with your field instructor and staff. (Helping professionals are often personally familiar with life traumas; if this is the case for you, consider whether you feel it appropriate to share your life experiences—and how much.)

Developing Relationships at Your Practicum Site

Relationships with co-workers, field instructors, and fellow practicum students that begin in the practicum may become lifelong personal and professional associations.

Building relationships is essential to a successful and meaningful learning experience during your practicum. Relationships with co-workers, field instructors, and fellow practicum students that begin in the practicum may become lifelong personal and professional associations. Many social workers go on to work, collaborate, and become friends with colleagues met during practicum. Social workers typically report that the practicum and the field instructor relationships, in particular, are powerful and influential experiences that can also be challenging (Fox, 2004; Giddings, Vodde, & Cleveland, 2003).

The relationships that emerge as meaningful for you may evolve for a variety of reasons. Even the student–field instructor relationship, though rooted in a formal mentoring structure, may result in a sharing of common interests and goals, and in mutual learning. You may also establish relationships with staff because you share mutual interests and experiences. However, you should not assume that all meaningful, even powerful, learning needs to be based on positive experiences. You may find that skills and knowledge can be gained from relationships with agency staff, even clients, that are not always pleasant; the most memorable and valuable learning may result from the most difficult, challenging, and (what seemed at the time) unsuccessful encounters that you experience. You should therefore remain open to all potential relationships and consider each encounter an opportunity for learning. Do you recall any memorable learning that did not feel valuable at the time but proved powerful in retrospect?

In the development of relationships within the practicum setting, you can call on skills learned in your prerequisite coursework. For example, applying the rapport-building skills practiced through role-plays can be a first step toward integrating oneself into the community of the agency. You are encouraged to employ such additional engagement skills as initiating contact with others by introducing yourself, using others' names, and inquiring about staff roles and responsibilities and agency culture, history, and tradition.

The Adult Learner: What Is It and Am I One?

Social work education is based on the assumption that each student brings a lifetime of experiences to the practicum learning process and assumes responsibility for optimizing the learning potential of the classroom and field experiences. This conceptualization is known as the *adult learner model* of education (Knowles, Holton, & Swanson, 2005). Along with using their life experiences to motivate themselves to gain further knowledge and enhance skill building, adult learners seek to determine and have control over their own learning (Knowles et al., 2005, p. 174).

The social work practicum is an excellent opportunity for you to develop and utilize the adult learner model. By taking responsibility for your own professional growth and development in social work practice, you can explore and deepen your knowledge and skills for future practice. This approach enables you to build on the strengths previously developed through employment, volunteer/community service, coursework, other educational experiences, and life in general. Incorporating adult learner concepts into your practicum experience will prepare you for future social work employment, in which you will have to function autonomously and professionally.

Three areas affect the adult learner's ability to gain from the learning environment (Memmott & Brennan, 1998): (1) personal characteristics, (2) cognitive development, and (3) learning style. You and your field instructor must be aware of and identify your individual traits and patterns in each of these areas. Personal characteristics (e.g., gender, age, ethnicity) influence the way in which you will perceive the learning experience. Your phase of cognitive development determines your capabilities for learning, and each student possesses a unique learning style.

Learning style refers to the way in which you most effectively receive, process, and integrate information. Your learning style determines your ability to perceive and process information and to translate that information into behavior. Identifying your learning style is particularly relevant for you and your field instructor as you develop the tasks and activities required for the learning agreement (e.g., the learning plan/contract that you negotiate with your field instructor) and the strategies for implementing and evaluating these activities. Although numerous frameworks are available for identifying your learning style, you may opt simply to consider your learning style, communicate your assessment to your field instructor, identify the field instructor's teaching style, and discuss the fit between the two.

What Kind of Learner Am I?

Corina knows from her practicum orientation that the social work program expects her to be an "adult learner," but she is unsure exactly what this means in terms of her behaviors and performance at her practicum. She is feeling lost, overwhelmed, and intimidated by the staff and clients at the detention facility. She feels that she needs more direction than her field instructor seems to want to provide. She senses that her field instructor expects immediate independence. Corina is unsure whether other students feel this way, and she is reluctant to raise her fears with others. Should she ignore her feelings and dive into her work, or should she voice her anxiety to others (if so, to whom)?

Corina's fears are not unusual, particularly for students in their first practicum experiences. Think of other new ventures on which you have embarked during your life. Until you have had the opportunity to familiarize yourself with the setting, the expectations, and the people involved, you may naturally question your decisions and abilities.

Learning is a process; moreover, the way in which we learn varies, but learning typically encompasses four basic elements (Fox, 2004, p. 121): (1) cognition—the student's ability to perceive and gain knowledge; (2) conceptualization—development of ideas and thoughts; (3) affect—the meaning (e.g., values, judgments, and feelings) attached to information; and (4) behavior—actions that result from new learning. Utilizing these four elements to frame the way in which we learn, consider now the variations in our *learning styles*. The concept of experiential learning is particularly relevant for social work field education as it is a "process whereby knowledge is created through the transformation of experience" (Kolb & Kolb, 2005, p. 194). In collaboration with their field instructors, social work students build on the knowledge learned in the classroom to their practice experience, thus transforming themselves from students to practitioners. The experiential learning model frames learning as a cycle that begins with *experiences* that are *observed* and *reflected* upon. The reflections are *assimilated* as abstract concepts and implications from which *actions are tested*. The tested actions become the basis for new experiences, and the cycle continues (Kolb & Kolb, 2005, p. 194). Social work field experiences enable students to observe activities, to reflect upon them with colleagues and the field instructor, to assimilate and integrate these reflections into the knowledge previously gained, and, finally, to apply (test) the new information into their own practice behaviors. Although learning may be viewed as a cycle, consider the unique ways in which you learn. There are multiple learning styles inventories and assessments that will help you to identify your particular learning style. One that may be of interest to you as a social work practicum student is the VARK, a learning styles tool that has been in use for nearly two decades (Fleming & Mills, 1992). VARK is an acronym that delineates learning preferences into four categories that help us to understand information preferences and strengths within the learning context. The four categories suggest that information is preferred as follows: visual (V)—diagrams, charts, and so on; aural (A)—lectures, discussions, and so on; read/write (R)—text-based (words); and kinesthetic (K)—action (e.g., demonstrations, simulations, videos).

Adult learning can be both a process and an outcome. Although you are expected to function as an adult learner, the field experience can aid you in your development in that role. Students typically perceive field instructors as being educators as well as role models (Papadaki & Nygren, 2006). Your field instructor will both facilitate structured learning opportunities that are designed to allow you to experience the application of social work theory to practice and demonstrate competencies. Structured learning experiences may occur in the form of receiving an assignment from your field instructor, carrying out the assignment, and processing the experience with your field instructor. For example, after observing several intake assessments at the detention facility, Corina is assigned to conduct an intake interview for a new client. Armed with the knowledge of the intake process, she completes the assessment, documents the information gathered, submits the written assessment to her field instructor, and discusses the experience as well as the content with her field instructor. This structured process enables Corina to apply her knowledge and skills, reflect on the experience, and obtain feedback regarding her performance.

Practice Application 1.1 Learning and Teaching Style Exercise

The VARK Questionnaire is available online at www.vark-learn.com/english/index.asp. You and your field instructor each can take a few moments to complete the 16-item questionnaire to learn more about your individual learning styles. Ask your field instructor how he or she perceives himself or herself as (1) a learner, (2) a teacher (and how his or her learning style influences his or her approach to teaching), and (3) a supervisor. Most of us will adapt our learning style to create our approach to teaching; your field instructor's teaching style may therefore be simply an extension of his or her approach to learning.

How do your learning style and that of your field instructor fit and how can the two of you negotiate the inevitable differences? Patience, creativity, and respect will be the keys to a successful negotiation. The following chart may help you make a comparison between the two of you.

Learning Style	Student	Field Instructor (as a learner)	Field Instructor (as a teacher)
Visual			
Aural			
Read/Write			
Kinesthetic			
Multimodal			

When problems arise in practicum between students and their field instructors, they may be rooted in the interaction of the students' and instructors' learning styles. Should you encounter a problem in your practicum experience, consider re-evaluating the fit between your learning–teaching styles and those of your field instructor. When you have reconsidered the learning style issues, you may want to describe your perception of your learning style and needs to your field instructor.

You may find yourself learning differently at different points in your life and professional development. Students and field instructors often prefer learning through concrete experience because students can actively engage in the experience, which then provides the basis for discussion and processing of that experience. However, there is no one right learning style. The key is to gain awareness of your individual style and then build on its characteristics as strengths. Despite the fact that your specific learning style will not determine a successful or unsuccessful practicum outcome, the optimal learning situation occurs when you and your field instructor adapt your teacher–learner styles for maximum fit.

Whether you consider yourself a new or a seasoned adult learner, the field practicum experience provides an excellent opportunity for you to assume responsibility for applying your previous and ongoing social work learning. As an adult learner, you must take the initiative to optimize your learning experience by integrating your existing knowledge and skills with newly learned skills in order to prepare for social work practice. The following discussion provides some suggestions that you may consider when using the adult learner model to enhance your practicum learning.

What Is My Role as a Student Learner?

Embedded in developing relationships in the field site are the critical tasks of determining your role and integrating yourself into the overall functioning of the agency. The practicum may be some students' first professional

---

Practice Application 1.2   Self-Assessment: What Do I Know and What Do I Need to Know?

In developing an understanding of your place as a student learner within this practicum experience, you can engage in a thorough self-assessment prior to its onset. This self-assessment can become a practice that continues throughout the entire learning experience and beyond. Your self-assessment should include consideration of such issues as these:

- What do I know about this agency—mission, services, population/community served, policies, funding, history, and reputation?
- What is the dominant culture of the organization [i.e., what disciplines and service(s) are the primary focus]?
- What knowledge, skills, and values do I bring to this experience?

- What knowledge and skills do I want to acquire from this experience?
- What are my strengths, particularly as they relate to the mission and services of this agency or organization?
- What role have students traditionally had at this site? If I am the first practicum student at this site, what do I think the student role might entail?

Think about other questions you would like to add to this list, and then share it with your field instructor. Beginning the process of role identification by raising these questions brings you to consider the area of expectations. The following discussion will focus on the many and varied expectations that will be imposed on you as you move through this field experience.

experience. It may be others' first time in a social work setting or as a social work professional. For still others, it may just be one of many experiences in a social service setting. No matter where you are in your personal or professional life, the practicum is a new beginning. This is the first time you have functioned as an undergraduate- or graduate-level social worker. Such a new beginning requires you to devote time and attention to gaining a clear understanding of your role within the unit/department, agency, and community.

What Can I Expect from My Practicum?

Practicum is an interactive and structured learning process that places multiple expectations on you. The social work program will communicate educational expectations for students, agencies, and field instructors. As an adult learner, you, too, must develop expectations for your agency and your field instructor. Establishing a clear understanding of mutual expectations enhances your ability to determine goals, roles, and performance standards. A quality field experience is influenced by clarity of expectations, opportunities to integrate theory and practice and have diverse experiences, supervisory quality, and the university–agency relationship (Todd & Schwartz, 2009, p. 392). In a recent review of field education research, Bogo (2006b) reports that an optimal field experience includes a supportive field instructor who provides balanced feedback and regular supervision, has appropriate learning activities and role models, and engages in reflection and self-critique.

Depending on your level of training and experience, the first two to three weeks of your practicum may begin with more passive learning activities (e.g., orientation, observing others, and reading manuals and literature). This passive learner role may stifle your enthusiasm for beginning social work practice. The normal progression of learning social work practice is to move from passive to active learning. Although reading and observing others are essential to learning, you should begin engaging in more active learning activities within the first month of your practicum (depending on previous experience and current knowledge and skill level). Guided by ongoing assessment of your skills and comfort level, you and your field instructor should consistently infuse challenges into your work. You should transition from passive learning to active learning by engaging in such activities as assuming responsibility for another worker's case, co-facilitating a group or meeting, and being observed by others. Your ultimate goal is to progress to competence at a higher level of autonomy at which you are solely responsible for cases or projects and group or meeting facilitation.

You will begin your practicum with a wide range of learning needs and goals, including demonstrating practice behaviors. In addition to accepting the objectives, competencies, and practice behaviors established by the social work program, you are encouraged to identify your individual educational agenda for supervision. For example, are you interested in learning general social work skills to be used with a broad population or in developing expertise in a specific area (such as working with children who are sexually abused, grantwriting, or group facilitation)? Practicum-related anxiety is not uncommon, particularly in areas of preparation, safety, working with clients, and supervision, and can even have positive impact on learning (Gelman, 2004; Gelman & Lloyd, 2008). To optimize the experience, the following are suggestions for you and your field instructor as you develop and negotiate your practicum experience (Gelman, 2004; Gelman & Lloyd, 2008; Munson, 2002):

- Seek opportunities to discuss your questions and concerns
- Gain information about your site by talking with current and former practicum students and your field instructor before beginning your practicum
- Observe the work of others
- Gain exposure to specialized cases, practice approaches, and practice behaviors
- Engage in collaborative co-facilitation activities
- Invite and accept feedback and critiques of your work
- Request more direct supervision
- Develop more self-awareness and self-care strategies (e.g., stress management, yoga, meditation)
- Welcome support and encouragement (e.g., peer mentoring, integrative seminars, and online support groups or chat rooms)
- Obtain training in group work
- Improve diagnostic skills

What Will the Social Work Program Expect from Me?

Each accredited social work program must adhere to the requirements set forth by CSWE (2008). The program has flexibility in determining how best to deliver the practicum curriculum. The program will inform you and your fellow students of the expectations for fulfilling the field component of the social work degree.

Each student must fulfill a number of administrative and curricular requirements to initiate and finalize arrangements for completing the field experience. As an adult learner, you are responsible for ensuring full awareness of all program requirements, which may include the following tasks:

- Completion of practicum forms required by the school and agency
- Verification of your health status and completion of any health-related requirements (e.g., immunizations, physical examination, tuberculosis skin test, and orientation and/or certification related to bloodborne pathogens, universal precautions, and HIPAA regulations)
- Verification of malpractice coverage
- Completion of personal information, which may include background criminal records and child and adult abuse checks, health insurance information, and/or drug screening

The Learning Plan

In Ben's practicum orientation, the social work program faculty described the completion of the learning plan as a process mutually negotiated between the field instructor and the student. Ben approached his field instructor, stating that they needed to develop his learning plan. The field instructor responded by asking Ben what he wanted to do in his practicum. She suggested that Ben complete the learning plan and that she would sign off on it. What do you think Ben should do at this point?

Although Ben's experience is (one hopes) unusual and unfortunate, his situation presents him with an opportunity to respond as an adult learner. Ben should not accept sole responsibility for completing the learning plan.

Your social work program will provide the processes and procedures for completing a practicum learning plan that is intended to be a collaboration between your social work program, the agency, and you. The completed learning plan then serves as a contract among all parties for the learning experience. The development of the learning contract should occur in a stepwise progression. As an adult learner, you are responsible for initiating and coordinating the learning contract development process. Figure 1.1 outlines a general plan for completing your learning contract. The development of your learning contract may have begun during the interviewing and placement process, possibly even before you or the agency made a commitment to the specific practicum arrangement. After you confirm your practicum site, further consider your expectations for learning at the agency. Begin by reviewing the agency's mission and services, and discuss your specific practicum roles and responsibilities with your field instructor. At

---

Step 1: Conceptualization (the "Big Picture")
- Identify goals and competencies for the social work program.
- Identify goals for the agency and field instructor.
- Identify goals and competencies for yourself.
- Identify actual learning opportunities available and possible at the practicum site.

Step 2: Developing Tasks, Activities, and Practice Behaviors
- Using the social work program expectations as a guide, you and your field instructor can develop a list of competencies, tasks, activities, and practice behaviors to be included in the learning plan.

Step 3: Draft
- Develop a draft of planned tasks and activities (using format/form provided by the social work program), identifying the following:
- Specific competencies, tasks, activities, and practice behaviors
- Timeframe
- Evaluative criteria for each competency, task, activity, and practice behavior
- Persons and resources required for each area

Step 4: Draft Review
- All relevant persons (field instructor, task instructor, other staff who will be responsible for any of your activities, faculty liaison, and, of course, you) should review the draft of the learning plan.

Step 5: Revision
- Using the input obtained from the review, revise your learning plan.

Step 6: Finalization
- Complete a final version, obtain needed signatures, and submit (by the social work program's due date).

Step 7: Integration
- Regularly integrate your learning plan into your supervisory session as a checklist for progress and evaluation.

Figure 1.1
Steps in Completing Your Practicum Learning Plan

this point, you can develop a list of potential tasks and activities to be completed throughout the practicum and consider how the potential tasks and activities would fulfill the educational objectives, competencies, and practice behaviors required by your social work program. Also consider whether and how your field instructor will evaluate your progress toward the competencies.

After developing the practicum learning plan and activities, move on to inviting ideas for new learning and consider tasks, activities, and practice behaviors to include in the learning contract. Because the development of this document is a collaborative process, you can engage in ongoing discussion and negotiation with your field instructor and faculty liaison in anticipation of its finalization.

The learning agreement should delineate a plan that will fulfill the practicum goals established by the social work program that articulate student roles, tasks and activities, and practice behaviors planned for the practicum along with the evaluation criteria by which your progress and performance will be assessed. In order for the learning contract to be an effective tool for your growth, the tasks, activities, and practice behaviors outlined within the contract should be competency based; specific; challenging; relevant; appropriate to the setting, your level of experience, interests, and goals; and measurable. You and your field instructor should determine items for inclusion that are realistically achievable given your schedule, timeframe, skill level, and access to supervision and resources.

Students often feel ill prepared to assert themselves in the development of specific tasks and responsibilities to be completed in the practicum. Being an adult learner, you are responsible for conveying to your field instructor and practicum faculty your skills, interests, values, and goals. Students' satisfaction and perceived skill are shown to relate to the value, pleasure, and self-efficacy (Fortune, Lee, & Cavazos, 2005). Although the agency, field instructor, and social work program may have far more experience in developing learning contracts, the document becomes individualized only with the input provided by your unique perspective as a student learner. You will be able to own the educational experience if you feel invested through active participation in the process.

Keep in mind the possibility that your goals and interests will not always mesh with the structure and limitations of the practicum site. The agency may have conflicting policies, inadequate resources, and other constraints that will prohibit you from engaging in all potential learning experiences. The learning plan should also serve as a mechanism to ensure that you are learning social work skills and practice behaviors, as opposed to fulfilling a needed role at the agency (e.g., typing, filing, childcare, or transportation). Should either of these situations arise, discuss with your field instructor the possibility of gaining the desired experiences outside your practicum agency. For instance, if you are interested in developing your group work skills in a way the agency cannot accommodate, you may want to explore group opportunities in a related agency setting. If you feel your self-advocacy efforts have been unsuccessful in negotiating with your field instructor, you may consider discussing the issues with your faculty liaison.

Key to the development of the learning agreement/contract is the evaluative component. Students and field instructors should always be vigilant about the primary purpose of the practicum: You are working at the agency to learn competencies, practice behaviors, and skills to enable you to be an effective social work practitioner. Your goal is to acquire, learn, and demonstrate social work skills for your future as a social worker. Although your goal is to be a competent practicum student and, eventually, an effective employee, these are not the only aims of this

---

Practice Application 1.3 Watch Your Body

Electronically recording your social work practice can be a valuable experience (if a somewhat painful one, at least in the beginning). When possible, audio- or videotape yourself engaged in your practicum activities. If you have the opportunity to videotape yourself, review the recording and then review again with the audio muted. Critically examine your body language and nonverbal behavior and the client's body language and nonverbal behavior in reaction to *your* behavior. Do you see things during this review that you did not see before? Record your perceptions in a journal entry, and share them with a member of your practicum team.

Developed by Ellen Burkemper, PhD, LCSW, MFT

---

experience. Therefore, initiate each task, activity, role, and responsibility by considering its learning value based on the evaluation criteria to be used.

Integrating evaluation from the beginning provides you and your field instructor the opportunity to engage in an ongoing evaluative process throughout the learning experience. Having clear and diverse strategies for measuring each task, activity, and practice behavior enables you and your field instructor to engage in assessment and to modify the learning contract, as needed, to reflect your growth, progress, and agency realities. To integrate intermediate benchmarks and feedback, actively use the learning contract to guide discussions with your field instructor *throughout* the practicum experience. Do not wait for all assessments to be made and conveyed at the end of the practicum.

Using a range of evaluative techniques will provide you and your field instructor with comprehensive and helpful feedback on your learning and performance. These techniques include direct observation by your field instructor or other staff of you performing your practicum tasks and activities, review of written work, audio- or videotaping of you in action, process/summary recording of your encounters with clients, group supervision/case conferences in which you present and discuss your work, and the maintenance of daily log of the ways in which you spend your time. When the time comes for the formal evaluation forms to be completed, you and your field instructor will have ample data from which to evaluate your progress and performance.

Incorporating evaluative standards into the learning agreement phase maintains your and your field instructor's focus on the goals of the field experience and establishes the basis for supervisory sessions over the course of the practicum. Thinking forward to the evaluation of your experience provides you and your field instructor with an opportunity to discuss the legacy that you hope to leave as a result of the time you have spent at the agency. Your legacy might be a project you completed, a program you developed and/or implemented, a grant proposal you wrote, a resource directory you compiled, or a practicum student orientation you created. Emphasizing evaluation built on competency-based student learning outcomes as part of the learning environment provides an appropriate and valuable indoctrination for you into the real world of contemporary social work practice, in which considerable attention is paid to evaluation and outcomes.

What Can I Expect from My Practicum Site?

When agencies and field instructors volunteer to work with practicum students, they devote considerable time and resources to the endeavor. At the same time, agencies and field instructors derive a number of benefits from the experience, including professional development; new ideas, perspectives, and work from a student; links to a college/university; challenges to agency practice; and enhancement of agency profile (Barton, Bell, & Bowles, 2005). Recognizing the importance and value of the practicum experience, individual field instructors and agencies develop and maintain differing standards of professional social work behavior and practice for practicum students. Agency and supervisor expectations may range from well defined and structured to open ended and informal. As an adult learner, you are responsible for ensuring that you have a thorough knowledge and understanding of both agency and field instructor expectations.

You can expect that your field instructor will initiate and facilitate an orientation at the outset of the practicum experience. Some agencies provide students the opportunity to participate in new employee orientation, whereas other agencies develop orientations specific to practicum students. Some agencies do not provide formal orientations but instead engage in an informal orientation process with each student. You should inquire about the type of orientation process your agency provides. Regardless of the type of orientation format, you should obtain information on the agency's and field instructor's expectations of you and clarify your expectations of the agency and the field instructor. Some general guidelines for agency orientation include the following:

- Completion of required agreements with the social work program regarding practicum expectations, precautions, and opportunities
- Agency tour (including your assigned workspace) and introductions of key staff with whom you will have contact
- Clarification of rules for use of office space (e.g., is it to be shared, used for client interviews, locked?)
- Information regarding agency policies and practices (e.g., schedule, time cards/clocks, parking, breaks [times, locations, restrictions], identification, credentials, sick/vacation leave, confidentiality, dress code, management of client/case information, and documentation)
- Information on equipment and communication systems (e.g., telephone, fax, computer, mailboxes, messaging), clarification regarding student use of equipment, and instructions for use (to include passwords and codes)
- Information on policies regarding reimbursement for practicum-related expenses (e.g., personal vehicle mileage incurred as a result of practicum-related travel)
- Information concerning your responsibilities for after-hour emergencies involving your clients
- Safety information—procedures within the agency, with clients, in the community, and on home visits

What Can I Expect from My Field Instructor?

Ethical Dilemma: To Confront or Not to Confront

Shortly after starting her practicum, Rosa celebrated her twenty-first birthday. On that occasion, she decided that she would no longer take the medication that she had been taking since age 10 to control her attention-deficit disorder (ADD). She believed that she had outgrown the problem. She did not consult or share with anyone about discontinuing the medication. Within the first weeks of her

Ethical
Practice

Critical Thinking Question

Utilizing the NASW *Code of Ethics* to guide your social work practice, which standards in the *Code of Ethics* are relevant in Rosa's situation?

practicum, Rosa began to experience a variety of problems, including difficulties focusing her attention on assigned orientation materials, following instructions, completing tasks, missing social cues, demonstrating obstinate and confrontive behaviors, and monopolizing conversations. Having considerable personal and professional knowledge of ADD, Rosa's field instructor suspected that Rosa experienced ADD and that the changes in her behaviors were the result of her discontinuing medication.

▶ *Does this situation present an ethical dilemma? If so, why? If not, why?*
▶ *Would it be ethically appropriate for Rosa's field instructor to confront Rosa with her suspicions, or would doing so be an infringement of personal boundaries?*
▶ *What would you do if you were Rosa and your field instructor addressed this issue with you?*

"Students should expect their instructors to create learning environments in which they are challenged by ideas just far enough beyond their grasp that they must struggle to learn, but not so far that they become frustrated and disillusioned" (Groccia, 1997). According to students, field instructor qualities that enhance learning include being available, respectful, responsive, supportive, fair, objective, and knowledgeable (Barretti, 2009). Being able to observe professionals in practice, receiving regular and balanced feedback, and having reflective activities that allow for self-critique are considered by students to be important to the learning process (Barretti, 2009; Bogo, 2006b). You should feel that your field instructor is pushing the limits of your abilities but supporting your growth in the process through such strategies as:

▶ Committing to your educational growth and development
▶ Serving as a mentor who will provide ongoing, balanced feedback that includes your strengths and areas for growth
▶ Supervising the practicum and evaluating areas such as teaching style, performance expectations, formal and informal availability (and contacts if she or he is unavailable), and supervision schedule and format
▶ Developing a plan for learning, including orientation approach (schedule, activities, staff involvement, and student preparation), opportunities to observe ("shadow") field instructors or other staff and students, case/project assignments, and staff and student collaborations
▶ Sharing student-related information, including practicum structure and parameters, organization's formal and informal strategic plans that guide programming, agency culture, and student roles as distinct from volunteer roles
▶ Clarifying physical and emotional boundaries as they relate to the practicum experience
▶ Providing information you need to learn and function as a practicum student within the department, agency, and community, including the following:
    ▶ Agency/professional information and resources—policy/procedure manuals, resource directories, readings, and staff orientation materials
    ▶ Administrative/logistical information—attendance policy, parking, and identification of self as a student

- Providing community resource information, including referral/referring groups, provision of information for referrals, and contact information
- Encouraging learning opportunities, including annual meetings, conferences, fundraising events, or lobby days
- Providing information regarding appropriate behavior, dress, and interaction with clients, staff, administration, and community professionals, including information regarding such activities as identifying yourself as a student, seeking out assignments from the field instructor and other staff, reading during practicum hours, completing homework during practicum hours, and collaborating with staff and community professionals
- Outlining expectations and providing balanced feedback regarding writing and speaking behaviors and skills
- Encouraging your critical thinking about practice by, in turn, encouraging questions and providing multiple sources of knowledge

What Can I Expect from My Faculty Liaison?

Your social work program practicum faculty can be a valuable resource as you plan and complete your field experience. Although the role of the practicum faculty member assigned as your resource or liaison varies among programs, you can generally expect the faculty member(s) to:

- Serve as a liaison between your social work program, the practicum site, and you to promote achieving the competencies and practice behaviors defined by your program (CSWE, 2008)
- Orient you to the practicum process and social work program expectations of you, the field instructor, and the agency
- Provide information on and assistance in developing the learning agreement/contract, including suggestions for tasks and activities, evaluation criteria, and outcomes
- Offer support regarding practicum issues by responding to questions, mediating conflicts, implementing changes, and advocating as needed on your behalf
- Be actively involved in the selection, orientation, training, and support of practicum sites
- Monitor the practicum experience to ensure that you and your field instructor are meeting the goals and learning the competencies and practice behaviors established by you and the social work program (Note: Most social work practicum faculty will conduct at least one on-site visit each semester to the practicum site to meet with you and your field instructor to discuss tasks, activities, progress toward goals, and any problems or concerns.)
- Be available throughout the practicum experience to assess and reassess your interests, goals, skill development, and professional aspirations
- Be available to provide you with a safe space to process your practicum experiences and challenges

What Should I Expect from Myself?

As you move through your practicum, establishing high standards of performance and learning for yourself can result in valuable learning. Bogo et al. (2006) report that field instructors value students' abilities to demonstrate procedural skills

---

Practice Application 1.4 Becoming a Reflective Practitioner

Even before you begin your practicum, you can begin to develop your reflective practice skills by journaling about the experience. Your journal can include your thoughts and feelings about your practicum experience as well as reflections on your learning, progress toward goals, successes and challenges faced within the practicum, and questions for your field instructor, faculty, and yourself. Before making your daily entry, review your previous entry to enable you to reflect on progress, setbacks, and changes. Be sure that, at the end of your practicum experience, you return to your journal to assess your growth.

(e.g., assessment, intervention, documentation, and communication) along with their approach to learning, professional behavior, and ability to conceptualize practice and relational capacities.

A key aspect of self-expectations is a commitment to reflective practice, a thoughtful, yet critical processing of your practice experiences. Engaging in reflection can help you interpret meaning, develop understanding, and clarify actions (Furman, Coyne, & Negi, 2008). Such reflection can allow you to view yourself within the larger context of your practicum and the profession (Mailloux & Whitten, 2009). Strategies for reflective practice may include maintaining a practicum journal or log, developing a professional social work portfolio (paper, electronic, or web-based selection of materials from your practicum experience, which includes but is not limited to assessments, evaluations, samples of your written and oral work, and your résumé), and a personal resource file.

In addition to reflection, the following list offers guidelines for self-expectations (Grise-Owens, 2008):

- Take responsibility for your own learning and choices by setting realistic goals and expectations, defining your own success, pursuing your own learning, and proactively seeking out learning opportunities
- Familiarize yourself with the competencies and practice behaviors that you will be working toward for your practicum experience
- Commit to practicing critical thinking by using multiple sources of knowledge, including practice knowledge and analyzing models of practice
- Anticipate opportunities to establish collaborative relationships with others, including fellow students, faculty, your field instructor, and practicum liaison
- Maintain a balanced and healthy lifestyle, including self-care strategies
- Be prepared to engage in ongoing evaluation of your practice, beginning with an assessment of your practice skills and including feedback from yourself and others
- Commit to leaving a legacy for the agency by completing a needed project or resource
- Take advantage of all formal and informal resources offered by the social work program, the agency, friends, and family
- Learn to prioritize your professional responsibilities and work

INTEGRATIVE PRACTICE FIELD SEMINAR

Integrating theory with social work practice has been an emphasis of social work educators since the beginning of formalized social work education. Focusing on the integration of theoretical knowledge with the application of competency-based

social work practice enables you to maintain a perspective on the evolution of our profession and to link contemporary field instruction issues to the profession's historical development.

To integrate theory with practice, begin by absorbing conceptual information, translate that knowledge into concrete, interventive strategies, apply the strategies through practice behaviors, and evaluate your practice. To effectively integrate theory and practice, you must synthesize the contribution of all members of your social work practicum team. Each member of your team contributes a unique and valuable perspective that promotes the desired integration: The educator provides the substantive theory; the field instructor brings practice wisdom; and you possess the ability to reflect and critically analyze the information received and to act on it.

One strategy for facilitating integration is the *integrative practice field seminar.* Many social work programs require an integrative practice field seminar concurrently with the field experience. There is variation in the structure, format, and delivery of this practicum-related curriculum. The following discussion offers insights and suggestions for maximizing the learning potential of the integrative practice field seminar.

What Can I Expect from the Integrative Practice Field Seminar?

Social work educators recognize the value and learning potential of the opportunity to share and engage in mutual support and problem solving while addressing practice-related issues. The integrative practice field seminar may blend structured and unstructured activities aimed at supporting you and your colleagues while providing the opportunity for theoretical frameworks to be applied to actual social work practice. Focusing on the common experiences and concerns of the students can create an environment truly suited to stimulation and integration. You should be challenged to translate and apply the theoretical concepts and knowledge you have learned into behavioral social work practice competencies and behaviors. Such a transformation will require you to engage regularly and frequently in self-assessment, risk taking regarding new ideas and practice techniques, and ongoing evaluation of your knowledge, skills, and values.

A part of the integrative seminar experience may be to incorporate evidence-based practice into discussions. As social workers, we are bound by our *Code of Ethics* (National Association of Social Workers, 2008a) to maintain awareness of current social work practice and ethical knowledge through published literature and continuing education. Utilizing the findings from systematic, empirical research and involving the client system as a collaborator to develop appropriate interventions is known as *evidence-based social work practice* (EBP) (Jenson & Howard, 2008). Evidence-based practice incorporates and values not only findings from published research but the practitioner's experience and expertise along with input from the client system regarding preferences and situational information (Thyer, 2009).

Developing the routine of consulting the literature for evidence to guide and support practice interventions complements the use of the social worker's intuitive and critical-thinking skills. You can use your intuitive skills and practice wisdom to assess the client system's situation and then critically evaluate the evidence presented within published articles and books to determine the optimal course of intervention for the client and you to pursue. Reviewing research and meta-analysis articles and practice guidelines can provide a wealth of information.

The challenge in becoming an evidence-based practitioner and applying theory to practice lies in determining the information that you need from the literature, evaluating the research-based literature, determining the best way to utilize the evidence, and applying strategies for empowering the client system to collaborate in deciding the most effective intervention for the situation. The essential steps of EBP include converting information needs into answerable questions, locating evidence to answer questions, appraising and applying evidence to practice and policy decisions, and evaluating processes (Jenson & Howard, 2008). Integrative practice seminars can provide the opportunity for students and faculty to explore practice competencies and behaviors from an evidence-based perspective.

Gaining comfort with reading research-based literature is key to becoming an evidence-based social work practitioner. A reputable peer-reviewed research article or book will be organized into five sections: (1) introduction; (2) literature review; (3) methods and theory; (4) findings and implications; and (5) summary. Folaron (2001) provides a helpful guide to understanding and evaluating published research. Applying the structure can aid you in being able to critically evaluate the literature as well as the practice concept or intervention being presented.

The integrative practice field seminar provides an opportunity to hone your evidence-based practice skills. General objectives appropriate for an integrative practice field seminar include the following:

▶ Integration of content on social work issues (history, policy, human behavior, diversity, practice, research, and evaluation) with practicum experiences
▶ Networking and processing with your peers and instructor
▶ Development of your knowledge of the community and its resources

Research Based Practice

Critical Thinking Question

Evidence is critical for effective social work practice. What strategies are appropriate for practicum interventions?

- Professional socialization and a deepening of your knowledge of the breadth of the social work profession
- Creation of a safe environment for developing your own self-awareness
- Exploration of practice issues and behaviors, particularly ethical dilemmas and use of self in practice
- Inventory and comparison of diverse social work settings within which social work practice occurs
- Discussion of organizational and policy issues

What Can I Expect from My Seminar Instructor?

The integrative practice field seminar may be unlike any other course you have completed during your academic career. In the seminar, the instructor will utilize a variety of teaching techniques but will serve primarily as a *facilitator* for your learning. The seminar will be a learning space in which you can openly discuss practice situations and challenges with your fellow students and the faculty. Students report that seminars that promote group processing and problem solving are key to the learning experience (Barretti, 2009). Generally, you should anticipate that the seminar instructor will:

- Communicate clearly his or her expectations for the course, students, and the practicum sites
- Stimulate discussions focused on peer support, values, and ethically related issues and dilemmas
- Facilitate respectful but challenging discussions of social work practice issues, the social work practice community, and professional development issues
- Emphasize the importance of maintaining confidentiality
- Consult with students and practicum sites regarding practicum questions, concerns, and dilemmas
- Challenge students in areas of practice behaviors, skills, and issues

What Can I Expect from the Other Students?

In an effort to process practice situations and support your peers, you should approach the integrative practice field seminar with high expectations of fellow students. Often, the most valuable learning results from input from other students, with facilitation provided by the seminar instructor. Therefore, you should expect the following from your seminar classmates:

- **Attendance.** As process is an ongoing aspect of seminars, students should be in regular attendance so that other students feel respected and valued and do not have to repeat information and so that each contributor's input is relevant and consistent.
- **Active preparation and participation.** To achieve the goal of mutual and reciprocal interaction, all students must be able and willing to actively engage in seminar discussion.
- **Respect.** Students will be taking risks in presenting and exploring ideas, values, and newly acquired skills; therefore, it is critical to respect one another's rights to take such risks in practicum and to articulate opinions, fears, frustrations, and experiments. Students must also offer support for each other's willingness to share and must respect each other's right to reject input or suggestions.

▶ **Confidentiality.** Due to the potentially confidential nature of the information shared in the seminar, all students must rigidly adhere to a high standard of confidentiality—specifically, discussing clients only with the field instructor's approval and no identifying information and maintaining compliance with HIPAA, particularly in situations involving taped and/or presented information.

▶ **Balanced feedback.** As students provide input to colleagues, each should try to provide positive, strengths-based ideas along with comments on areas for growth and change.

What Should I Expect from Myself?

As an adult learner, you can optimize the learning potential of the integrative practice field seminar by maintaining the same expectations of yourself that you have of others. You can also:

▶ Commit to learning through constantly challenging your knowledge, skills, and values

▶ Commit to the learning of others by modeling strengths-based interactions

▶ Actively interact with other students and the instructor through ongoing exchanges and explorations of issues

---

Practice Application 1.5 Seeing My Practicum Site and Field Instructor with Different Eyes

On your third or fourth visit to your practicum site following your initial orientation, approach the setting visualizing yourself as a client of this agency. When you arrive on the premises and enter the building as a client, identify and assess the following facets of your experience:

▶ Do your perceptions of the agency and staff change? If your perceptions do change, how do they change?

▶ What are your first impressions in terms of the sights, sounds, smells, client–client interactions, client–staff interactions, and staff–staff interactions, and agency culture?

▶ How do your impressions make you feel about the agency? Yourself? Your profession?

After completing this exercise, reflect on your experience by journaling your impressions and explanations for your feelings. You may then want to share your reflections with your field instructor and other students.

You may want to repeat this exercise later in your practicum and record how, if at all, your perceptions and observations have changed and the reasons for these changes. This activity enables you to discuss with your field instructor your impressions and any recommendations for the agency.

Now that you have seen your practicum site through different eyes, consider a similar exercise related to your field instructor. During one of your early supervisory sessions with your field instructor, take the opportunity to learn more about the professional socialization that your field instructor experienced. The following questions can serve as a springboard for this discussion:

▶ Where did you complete your practicum (practica)?

▶ What do you recall about the experience(s)— positive, negative, and meaningful aspects?

▶ What was most helpful/least helpful about your field instructor's teaching style?

▶ Regarding your experiences as a field instructor, what have been your most/least successful experiences with students (without disclosing confidential/specific information)?

A discussion centered on these and other related issues can serve to open a dialogue about values, work styles, and expectations. You can also learn about your field instructor's perception of supervision and accountability. From this discussion, develop with your field instructor a list of at least three strategies for structuring your practicum to optimize the benefit for you (as a learner), your field instructor (as a teacher), and your practicum site.

Developed by Jan McGillick, MA

- ▶ Be willing to challenge, question, and take risks
- ▶ Invest in the value of the input of others
- ▶ Be willing to follow up on viable suggestions, questions, and areas of concern

SUMMARY

This chapter established the foundation for the remainder of this book. We encourage you to consider yourself an adult learner in the practicum setting, in the integrative practice field seminar, and in the use of this text as a learning tool. This unit addressed the beginning phases of the practicum experience, enabling you to move from the first days of the practicum and the first seminar meeting to the orientation and, finally, to the development of the learning agreement/ contract. While the social work faculty, seminar instructor, and other students are there to support and guide you, you have the opportunity and responsibility to embrace the challenges that lie ahead in your practicum, the seminar, and beyond, with a grounding in social work competencies and practice behaviors.

Cameron discussed his concerns with his practicum liaison. His liaison validated his fears, commended him for recognizing a potential ethical dilemma, and acknowledged that these issues are normative for students with Cameron's life experiences. The liaison encouraged him to consider that the stresses of beginning a practicum and transitioning from a consumer of services to a provider of services may have heightened his vulnerabilities regarding his own recovery process. Second, with the liaison's urging, Cameron initiated a discussion with his field instructor. His field instructor assured him that his response to the situation was normal, stating that many new substance abuse treatment professionals question their ability to work effectively with abusers/addicts while maintaining their own abstinence and recovery. The field instructor suggested that Cameron pay particular attention in the upcoming weeks to his feelings and reactions to client situations and identify any situations/remarks that raise unresolved issues for him. The field instructor asked Cameron to maintain a journal, focusing particularly on his ongoing feelings about working with a recovering population, and raise the issue during supervision sessions as he felt necessary.

Corina raised the issue of autonomy (and her fears about not having attained autonomy yet) in her integrative practice field seminar. With the support of the seminar instructor and fellow students, she chose to approach her field instructor with her concerns. Her field instructor had no idea that Corina was feeling the way she was and commended her for taking responsibility for confronting the autonomy issue. The field instructor then initiated a discussion of his expectations regarding her performance, during which he recognized that he may have been pushing Corina too fast given her comfort level. They agreed to check in with each other at each supervisory meeting to determine Corina's status. This situation could easily have evolved into a less satisfactory outcome, but Corina's willingness to take the initiative in her learning experience led to a positive one.

Ben confronted his field instructor at a supervision session, stating that he felt that she was not interested in his learning, as evidenced by her cavalier attitude toward his learning plan. The interaction was quite strained and resulted in both Ben and the field instructor independently contacting the social work program faculty to state that they did not believe the practicum would work out. The practicum liaison initiated a three-way meeting to discuss the problem. Both Ben and the field instructor had the opportunity to present their perspectives on the situation, and with negotiation facilitated by the liaison, they agreed to continue the practicum. The field instructor agreed to commit more time to Ben's learning, and the three discussed ways in which Ben could handle difficult situations in a calmer, more diplomatic manner.

Succeed with PEARSON **mysocialworklab**

Log onto **MySocialWorkLab** to access a wealth of case studies, videos, and assessment. (*If you did not receive an access code to* **MySocialWorkLab** *with this text and wish to purchase access online, please visit* www.mysocialworklab.com.)

1. **Click on Career Explorations. Select one of the social worker videos to review that is of interest to you.** While watching the video, identify the areas that are consistent with your professional interests and goals. What additional information would you like to have about this field of practice? Develop a strategy for obtaining more information about this field of practice.

2. **Click on Core Competency Videos. Select Professional Identify and watch the video on Professional Demeanor.** What knowledge and skills do you need to prepare yourself for a first professional encounter with a client?

PRACTICE TEST The following questions will test your knowledge of the content found within this chapter. For additional assessment, including licensing-exam type questions on applying chapter content to practice, visit **MySocialWorkLab.**

1. Core social work competencies do not include:
   a. Developing your professional identity
   b. Utilizing your intuitive skills for assessment
   c. Incorporating new practice techniques and methods
   d. Having knowledge of current policies

2. The first activity a practicum student should do when beginning a practicum experience is:
   a. Complete the learning plan
   b. Ask for work assignments
   c. Meet staff members
   d. Set up your workspace

3. The experiential adult learner model includes the following steps:
   a. Observe, reflect, assimilate, and test experience
   b. Observe, test, assimilate, and reflect experience
   c. Test, assimilate, reflect, and observe experience
   d. Reflect, observe, assimilate, and test experience

4. Your practicum experience should include learning opportunities in all of the following areas except:
   a. Observe other professionals
   b. Develop self-awareness
   c. Videotape practice
   d. Sole responsibility for work assignments

5. If you identify an area or skill you would like to experience, the most appropriate strategy is to:
   a. Research area in the social work literature
   b. Ask field instructor if experience is appropriate
   c. Ask faculty liaison if experience is appropriate
   d. Arrange experience and present information to field instructor

6. Appropriate evaluation strategies to include in your learning plan include all of the following except:
   a. Direct observation of practice
   b. Audio- or videotape of practice
   c. Document experiences
   d. Obtain feedback from other practicum students

Ethical Practice

7. If you observe a staff member engaged in a possible unethical practice, your first response should be to:
   a. Review NASW *Code of Ethics*
   b. Take no action, but continue to observe for future occurrence
   c. Talk with your field instructor about concerns
   d. Ask staff member to explain behavior/action

Professional Identity

8. At times, the faculty liaison and field instructor roles may overlap. Which of the following is the role of the field instructor only?
   a. Provide balanced feedback about student performance
   b. Serve as a mentor
   c. Share information on community resources
   d. Provide information on agency culture and practices

9. Practicum students should:
   a. Write learning agreement and present to field instructor for approval
   b. Accept any practicum assignment
   c. Be familiar with CSWE Educational Policy and Accreditation Standards
   d. Wait for field instructor to suggest learning opportunities

10. The Integrative Practice Field Seminar is an appropriate arena for all of the following activities except:
   a. Integration of theory and practice
   b. Discussion of concerns about field instructor
   c. Discussion of ethical dilemmas
   d. Exploration of practice methods

Log onto **MySocialWorkLab** once you have completed the Practice Test above, to access additional study tools and assessment.

Answers

Key: 1) b 2) c 3) a 4) d 5) d 6) d 7) c 8) d 9) c 10) b

2

Socialization into the Social Work Profession

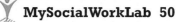
Core Competencies in this Chapter (Check marks indicate which competencies are covered in depth)				
✔ Professional Identity	✔ Ethical Practice	☐ Critical Thinking	☐ Diversity in Practice	☐ Human Rights and Justice
☐ Research Based Practice	☐ Human Behavior	☐ Policy Practice	✔ Practice Contexts	☐ Engage, Assess, Intervene, Evaluate

Socialization is a concept often discussed in terms of establishing one's identity within a particular group. *Socialization* can be considered "the process by which you learn all that you need to know in order to get along in the world in which you live" (Russo, 1993, p. 70). Central to the 10 core competencies required for social work practice is the concept of professional socialization. The first core competency ("Identify as a professional social worker and conduct oneself accordingly") establishes the need for social work students to be socialized into the profession (CSWE, 2008). Through your socialization into a group, you informally, and possibly formally, learn the rules, roles, norms, customs, traditions, and value and philosophical bases of that group. If you opt to continue as a member of the group, you determine which of the group's qualities and characteristics you accept and which you reject. In the final analysis, you establish your identity within and affiliation to that group.

Through your socialization into a group, you informally, and possibly formally, learn the rules, roles, norms, customs, traditions, and value and philosophical bases of that group.

The practicum is just one phase of your socialization as a social work professional. The decision to become a social worker began your socialization process. You may have had an experience with a social worker or have a family member or friend who is a social worker. Think for a moment about your decision to become a member of the social work profession.

Now that you have reflected on your initial decision to join the social work profession, consider how your socialization process has evolved thus far. You have completed part of the required coursework, and you may even have had volunteer or paid social work–related experiences. The coursework and volunteer or employment experience you have gained was the beginning of your formal socialization as a social worker. You have learned of our profession's history, achievement, challenges, values, and ethical stances. You have learned that some social workers emphasize a generalist approach and others, building on the generalist perspective, develop specialized expertise in a particular area of practice. As you learned, social work is a discipline comprising an extremely diverse membership. The profession includes differences on many fronts—political views, religion, and ethnicity, to name a few. In fact, social work is a profession that prides itself on embracing diversity, both that of those we serve as well as that of our own members. Therefore, socialization into this profession can and should be an individualized process unique to each person that takes into account his or her culture and ethnicity, personal and professional experiences, values, and personality.

Part of your socialization process requires you, as a new social worker, to find your niche within the profession. Because the social work profession is a broad, demanding, and complex discipline, you must learn to juggle and balance the many and diverse demands placed on you in virtually any setting in which you practice social work. You are required to maintain objectivity while staying committed to the profession. You are required to exhibit empathy—but not sympathy—and you must confront the ethical dilemmas that will surely arise. While aspects of these issues are skill based, much of your competence in these areas will emerge through your socialization into the profession.

Your professional socialization process will never end. You will find that you change, grow, and evolve throughout your life and learn new knowledge, skills, and competencies as you progress through your social work career. There are two (often concurrent) avenues of socialization that

Professional Identity

Utilize this chapter to compile professional socialization activities that you can develop as a social worker.

will occur as you develop your social work identity. First, you will become socialized into the social work profession, in general. This phase of socialization involves learning the knowledge, skills, values, competencies, and practice behaviors of the profession as a whole. Second, your basic social work socialization process will be enhanced by the knowledge, skills, values, competencies, and practice behaviors gained that are specific to your area(s) of interest, field of practice, and practice setting. For example, you will develop your identity as a social worker, but you may also identify yourself as having particular interest and expertise in one area, such as domestic violence or health. Your challenge is to blend and balance these two potentially conflicting processes.

This chapter will aid you in identifying yourself as a social work practitioner; learning to balance the multiple, often conflicting, roles you will assume as a social worker; establishing professional and personal boundaries; managing the inevitable stressors that emerge; and anticipating the transitions that will occur as you move through your life as a social worker. We hope that you will use this information to enhance your socialization experience and to contribute to the positive image of the social work profession.

ME? A SOCIAL WORKER?

Ben was certain about his decision to change his career plans from medicine to social work—that is, he was until he had completed the coursework that precedes practicum. During class discussions, Ben frequently felt as though he was missing something. He marveled at his fellow classmates who seemed to understand intuitively the subtleties of a client situation. He found that these nuances often escaped him. Now, he is growing increasingly concerned about his ability to be a member of the social work profession, particularly now that he has started his first practicum. He knows he wants to work with people but wonders if his "missing it" is what prevents him from being as intuitive as his peers. He questions whether this is due to his innate skills, his upbringing, his Asian heritage, being male, or being a biology major. What do you think about Ben's perceived ethical dilemma? Are his fears realistic? What would you suggest he do to resolve the ethical dilemma of whether to continue to pursue a social work career or switch to another field?

Practice Application 2.1 Often-Asked Client Questions

Clients make a significant contribution to your ability to perceive yourself as a professional social worker—both positive and negative. Role-play with your field instructor or other seasoned social work professional the following scenarios, in which clients present you with questions and comments:

1. "You're just a student. I want a real professional (or social worker)."
2. "Do you have children?"
3. "What is your success rate with treatment?"
4. "I'm here today because I don't know where to turn. What can you do for me?"

5. "You know, it's really hard for me to be here, but here I am. What do I have to do to get through this, and how can you (just a student) help me?"
6. "It's hard to describe my situation because, very frankly, I don't understand how it happened. It seems like this situation has taken on a life of its own. You're an expert, so I know you'll know what to do."

Process with your field instructor your thoughts and feelings regarding these potential situations. Can you think of other questions or situations that might jar your confidence? _____

Developed by Ellen Burkemper, PhD, LCSW, MFT

Many social work students find themselves in the dilemma that Ben is facing and ask themselves, "How can I possibly understand the clients' problems and be helpful to them?" Students often become intimidated when observing more experienced social work students, practitioners, and field instructors, questioning whether they will ever be that skillful and effective. Beginning to define oneself as a social work professional is one step toward achieving the practice wisdom that is so critical to the competent practice of social work. *Practice wisdom* is defined as "accumulation of information, assumptions, ideologies, and judgments that have seemed practically useful in fulfilling the expectations of the job" (Barker, 2003, p. 370). Practice wisdom encompasses all the aspects of a social worker's socialization into the profession—knowledge, values, principles, and experiences. Such expertise is refined over time through evaluation and reflection of practice behaviors (Chu & Tsui, 2008). Considered a key component of evidence-based practice, practice wisdom brings the social worker's experience and expertise into the development of an intervention and practice behaviors. The practicum experience signals the beginning of the development of practice wisdom as a part of the social worker's repertoire of knowledge and skills. This developmental process then continues throughout one's career.

STRATEGIES FOR YOUR SOCIALIZATION AS A SOCIAL WORKER

We have defined professional socialization and emphasized the necessity for the process. The questions that need to be addressed now are, How does professional socialization happen? Who is responsible for it happening? Will it occur if you are passive and reactive? These issues should become an integral part of your field experience. Yes, your socialization may happen *to* you, but as with any endeavor, you will likely have a richer, more meaningful experience if you are proactive and take responsibility for initiating your socialization into your new profession. Although it is important for all individuals to approach new ventures at their own paces and in their own styles, we have compiled the following suggestions for you and the other members of your practicum team to consider as you begin your journey into social work.

Student-Initiated Strategies

▶ Join professional social work organizations at your school and in the community. Actively participate in these organizations (e.g., run for office, attend conferences, and volunteer for committees).

▶ Start a student social work organization if one does not exist in your social work program, or establish a special-interest group with other students who share your interests.

▶ Become involved with your school's alumni activities through such programs as career mentoring, student recruitment, and continuing education events.

▶ Volunteer or seek part- or full-time employment in a social service setting while you are a student.

▶ Identify your field instructor, faculty, and yourself as the learning team that is responsible for your professional socialization.

▶ Identify a social worker to serve as your mentor. This person may be a faculty member, field instructor, or other social work practitioner whose expertise you value and respect.

▶ Seek out as many and varied practicum-related experiences as you can to broaden your social work competencies and skills.

▶ Develop your professional social work portfolio, including your résumé and examples of your work.

▶ Read social work–related literature (e.g., *NASW News*, topic specific journals and books), and peruse the social work journals and websites on a regular basis for updates in your areas of interest.

▶ Form or join a peer/professional support group that focuses on supervision, licensure examination preparation, or other common interests and concerns.

▶ Participate in your community's social, cultural, and political activities, even if you do not plan to remain in the area following graduation.

▶ Seek opportunities to practice defining a social worker to others (friends, family, and clients).

▶ Put yourself in situations in which you represent the profession to non–social work professionals and community groups. (There is no better way to gain confidence in your professional identity than to portray your profession to others).

▶ Gain awareness of personal biases and values in working with diverse groups by seeking professional experiences with diverse groups and reflecting on these experiences with your field instructor.

▶ Focus on yourself by being open to new learning, being assertive, and regularly reflecting on your learning (Calloway-Graham, Mason, & Peak, 2004). Learn and refine your skills for reflective thinking and practice—process alone, in writing, and in consultation with others your thoughts, feelings, values, and actions as you encounter new social work experiences. The ability to analyze your practice behaviors, the reasons you chose that approach, the way in which the client system was affected, and your feelings about your choices is invaluable in the development of competencies, self-monitoring, self-supervision, and critical thinking.

⬧ View your field instructor not just as a supervisor or mentor but as a social work professional with whom you can and should regularly consult on practice-related issues, particularly legal and ethical issues.

We have encouraged you to be proactive in your socialization process. You are not, however, solely responsible for covering every aspect of your orientation and immersion into social work.

Another member of your learning team, your field instructor, can be an invaluable resource, guide, and mentor as you grow and develop as a professional social worker. The student–field instructor relationship can be viewed as a helping alliance in which each interaction provides an opportunity for modeling, learning, and reflecting (Fox, 2004). Field instructors can model the development and retention of skills along with interpreting the meaning of students' values and beliefs (Barretti, 2007). Consider the following strategies as you and your field instructor discuss your professional development.

Field Instructor–Initiated Strategies

Your field instructor can:

⬧ Invite you to participate in case conferences, staff meetings, inservice training sessions, continuing education events, professional meetings, events, lectures, and seminars
⬧ Recommend and discuss relevant readings with you in terms of the implications for your practice
⬧ Be a mentor or connect you to a mentor
⬧ Connect you to other social workers to broaden your perception and definition of social work
⬧ Require you to maintain a professional journal or log, read the log, and provide you with regular feedback regarding your growth as a social worker, including self-care as a normative expectation
⬧ Utilize supervisory sessions to take supervision beyond the technical/ clinical realm and help you to think *automatically* from the social work perspective
⬧ Suggest you develop your professional portfolio
⬧ Discuss values and ethical implications of practice situations and behaviors
⬧ Assist you in all areas of your practice (i.e., engagement, assessment, intervention and evaluation)

You have now had the opportunity to consider your own socialization into the social work field. Where do you think you are in the process? What have you achieved? What do you want to achieve in the future? How can you approach your goals?

A significant part of any socialization process is gaining an understanding of the group into which one is being socialized. As a practicum student, you strive to understand not only the social work profession but also your practicum site. You can begin your socialization to your practicum site by gaining familiarity with the organization, its culture, and practices. Such orientation typically occurs both formally and informally. Formal orientations involve informational sessions and reading materials and provide organizational history, mission, rules, policies, and practices, while informal orientations can include observations and discussions. The combination of formalized orientations coupled with opportunities to interact with co-workers and mentors provides the optimal organizational introduction and clarity of roles and expectations (Jaskyte, 2005).

Practice Application 2.2 Social Work from Your Own Perspective

Prepare a written statement describing your definition and philosophy of social work and your perception of the role of the social work professional in your practicum site.

Interview representatives of as many of the disciplines represented in your practicum agency as possible. Ask each person to describe social work in general, to define the role of social work in the agency, and to compare and contrast social work with his or her own discipline's philosophical, ethical, and theoretical stances. Using your prepared statement, share with the person you are interviewing your own perspective of social work and discuss the similarities and differences between your respective views of social work.

Summarize your findings, and share them with your field instructor, agency staff, fellow students, and your integrative field practice seminar. Consider the following questions:

▶ Have your perceptions of social work changed? If so, how have they changed?

▶ Who was instrumental in contributing to this changed perception?

▶ If your perceptions are not changed, have they been strengthened by this exercise?

If you find that your perceptions have, in fact, been altered as a result of this exercise, rewrite your original prepared statement on social work and use it in your discussions with others. Be certain to save your statements so that you can reference them as you move through your professional development.

Practice Application 2.3 Social Work from Many Perspectives

The following practice application is designed to strengthen your identity as a social worker as well as to aid you in understanding the professional perspectives of other disciplines. You may use the case presented here or refer to a situation that has arisen at your practicum site that involved at least three different disciplinary perspectives. You may also opt to complete this exercise as a group activity (another opportunity to gain learning from multiple perspectives). After reading the case, follow these steps:

▶ Identify the disciplines most critical to the intervention, and determine who should be in attendance at the upcoming meeting.

▶ Identify the issues you consider most relevant in developing an intervention.

▶ Develop a list of questions you would pose to a representative of each discipline.

▶ Locate a representative from each of the disciplines identified in your assessment. (These may be employees at your practicum site, colleagues of

agency staff, and faculty members at your university or college.)

▶ Ask each representative to read the case and respond to the list of questions that you have developed from the perspective of his or her discipline.

▶ Summarize your findings for presentation to your field instructor or integrative field practice seminar, including the ethical implications relevant for each discipline.

The Case

You are a social work practicum student in an elementary school. You were assigned by your field instructor to work with Danielle and her family. Danielle is a 12-year-old female who is in the sixth grade, having been retained in the third grade for poor academic performance. Her mother recently died, and Danielle is living with her stepfather and her younger half-sister from her mother's marriage to Danielle's stepfather.

Danielle receives special education services based on the recommendation of the multidisciplinary conference (MDC). In addition to a poor academic performance history, Danielle has been diagnosed with attention-deficit disorder (ADD) and reads and comprehends several levels below her grade level. You are preparing for Danielle's upcoming individual education plan (IEP), an annual review of the educational and behavioral goals established by the MDC when Danielle's eligibility for special education services was determined.

The Disciplines

Teacher: Danielle's teacher made the original referral to the school guidance counselor based on several concerns, including poor academic performance, reading deficits, truancy, and behavioral problems in the classroom (difficulty focusing on the tasks assigned, excessive talking, and difficulty staying seated). Even after Danielle began taking medication for her ADD, the teacher finds her a behavioral problem in the classroom. The teacher will be reporting on Danielle's current academic performance and classroom behavior.

Guidance Counselor: Upon receiving the referral from the teacher, the guidance counselor initiated referrals to the school psychologist (for educational testing) and social worker (for truancy and family assessment). The guidance counselor is the coordinator of the school's IEP process and will be facilitating this meeting.

Psychologist: The psychologist has completed educational testing with Danielle and will be reporting on the findings at the IEP.

Resource Room Teacher (i.e., Reading Specialist): The reading teacher has been working with Danielle for several months and will report on the reading problems identified in the MDC's initial eligibility determination, type of reading problems, and Danielle's progress in meeting her goals.

School Social Worker: Upon receiving a referral for social work services, you have completed a home visit to Danielle's family. You found the home itself to be unclean and in a state of disarray and the home situation to be chaotic. You have determined that Danielle's stepfather is immobilized by his grief over the loss of his wife, unable to provide adequate care or monitoring for either of the children, and not at all attached to Danielle. He appears to have appropriate parental feelings about his biological child, but said to you that if Danielle had "anywhere else to go, she'd have been shipped there as soon as the funeral was over."

As a part of the MDC to determine eligibility for special education services, you were involved in the completion of the social developmental study that included a family history, classroom observation, and behavioral analysis. As a result of your assessment, referrals were made for Danielle to receive services from the resource room teacher and a psychiatric evaluation to determine the presence of an attention-disorder diagnosis (resulting in the prescribing of medication).

Public Child Welfare Worker: A protective service investigation was completed based on an anonymous report to the protective service agency that included the following information: Danielle does not attend school regularly, is out late at night with older males (may be involved in substance use), and is left unsupervised for several days at a time. The protective service worker reported to you in a telephone conversation that the stepfather wants to "get rid of her as soon as somebody will take her."

The Perspectives

Obtain the perspectives of each of the disciplines, and compare and contrast your findings, focusing particular attention on the ethical implications of the perspectives.

PULLING IT ALL TOGETHER: HOW CAN I JUGGLE ALL THE ROLES?

Your professional social work socialization can be considered a slate on which you and others write the social work knowledge, skills, values, competencies, and practice behaviors that you gain during your educational experiences. This slate is not blank: You bring to the social work profession your personal and professional life experiences. Once you have begun to fill your professional slate, the next step for you, as a new professional, is to take the concepts from your slate and internalize them as part of your professional self. The slate will fill quickly, and you will begin to determine how to manage all the knowledge, roles, and interests that have affected you.

The process of filling your slate may be guided by a number of different and varied persons with whom you interact during your training. Your field instructor and social work program faculty probably have the most influence on your socialization. Increasing your self-awareness in the areas of your interests, goals, styles, values and ethics, frustrations, and needs are key to gaining balance in your social work career. Issues and tasks that seemed paramount in the beginning may recede once you have considered the realistic capabilities of your agency, your client, and most important, yourself. In fact, students who practice skills during practicum perceive a greater level of competence, are more satisfied with the field experience, and are evaluated higher by field instructors (Fortune, Lee, & Cavazos, 2007).

Your practicum provides you with the opportunity to explore and challenge your feelings, history, stereotypes, and attitudes in order to deepen your understanding of yourself and your place within the social work profession.

Your practicum provides you with the opportunity to explore and challenge your feelings, history, stereotypes, and attitudes in order to deepen your understanding of yourself and your place within the social work profession. Your mentor has the advantage of having more social work experience than you have at this point in your career. He or she can teach you the skills necessary for prioritizing the demands on you and the roles to which you have been assigned or you have chosen for yourself.

Consider the following issues as you contemplate how you can effectively juggle the many and varied roles that you want and need to fulfill and the emotions that accompany them:

- *Balance, balance, balance!* No one part of your professional or personal life should dominate the others to the detriment of other responsibilities and interests.
- While multitasking (ability to complete more than one activity at a time) is viewed as a desirable quality, do not impose this expectation on yourself if you are not comfortable with it.
- To the extent possible, tackle difficult aspects of your learning when you are at your best (i.e., mornings if you are a "morning person").
- Gain insight into your work style and patterns and build on those strengths.
- Ensure that you regularly leave your office or building for breaks, lunch, or home visits.
- Pace yourself. Spread out your obligations so that you will have time for unplanned events and demands.
- To the extent possible, diversify your work activities to provide variety in your daily routine.

To enhance your ability to manage your workload, consider these additional strategies (Sheafor & Horejsi, 2008):

- Manage, plan, and prioritize your workload with a daily work plan. Every hour spent in planning can result in a savings of three to four hours of actual work. To identify strategies for increasing your efficiency, consider documenting the way in which you spend your day.
- Assume events that you did not expect will occur often and build in time to respond (i.e., procrastinating on deadlines can mean you do not have time, energy, and resources to handle the unplanned occurrences).
- Use technological resources to your advantage to increase your efficiency and effectiveness.

SETTING PROFESSIONAL BOUNDARIES

> *Cameron had been concerned about potential overlapping conflicts that could occur as a result of his roles as a person in recovery and an Alcoholics Anonymous (AA) sponsor. Despite his heightened self-awareness and previous discussions with his sponsor and practicum team, his worst fears are being realized. He is encountering clients from his practicum at his own AA meetings, and they are approaching him before and after the meetings to discuss their recovery struggles, asking if they should re-enter treatment and even if he would see them for individual sessions. Despite being flattered by their confidence in him, several ethical dilemmas have emerged for Cameron: (1) How can he separate himself from his professional role when he is attending an AA meeting? (2) How can he set limits with former clients without the client feeling rejected? (3) How can he be certain what his student role should be? What suggestions do you have that will help Cameron be an ethical practitioner?*

Cameron's particular ethical dilemma may be unique, but this type of ethical dilemma is not uncommon for social workers. Although we may try to leave our professional lives at the office, our families, friends, neighbors, and communities may not make this an easy task for us. Social workers, in general, and new social workers, in particular, may have difficulty setting limits—that is, saying no—when people ask for help. Like many social workers, you probably joined this profession because you are a compassionate person who wants to contribute to improving others' quality of life. Without limit setting, you may find yourself in the helping mode around the clock.

Boundaries are the "regions separating two psychological or social systems" (Barker, 2003, p. 52). While it is critical to the helping process to maintain clearly delineated roles for the client and professional and personal and professional objectivity, the practitioner need not be distant or hierarchical. By maintaining an empathetic and collaborative approach with the client, the role distinctions are clear, but not oppressive (Dietz & Thompson, 2004).

The line between professional and nonprofessional behavior and activities can become blurred. One type of *dual relationship* is present in Cameron's situation. Fellow group members view him as a professional social worker in a situation in which he is attempting to function as a participating member of a self-help group. Dual relationships can occur unintentionally (e.g., being a member of the same group, organization, or community) or intentionally (e.g., engaging in a business, social, or sexual relationship with the client). While engaging in a nonprofessional relationship with a client may seem natural and comfortable because of mutual interests or issues, such a relationship can be disastrous for both the worker and the client. Along with boundary issues, dual relationships can create a conflict of interest for the social worker and must be approached with caution and forethought to the possibility of an ethical violation (Reamer, 2009).

The National Association of Social Workers (NASW) *Code of Ethics* (2008a) clearly states that social workers should not be in situations in which conflicts of interest, dual relationships, exploitation, or violation of confidentiality can occur. The *Code of Ethics* also addresses the propriety of having a dual relationship with a former client following the termination of the professional relationship.

An ethical issue related to Cameron's situation and boundary setting, in particular, is that of *self-disclosure*. The question of how much information and time to self-disclose can become a dilemma for the beginning social worker. As in the case of our student, Cameron, many social workers are drawn to the profession as the result of a powerful life experience. The inclination to share that experience and the hope that it will be helpful for the client can be overwhelming. Should this dilemma occur for you, consult with your field instructor and other seasoned practitioners. You may find that processing the issues will enable you to put them in perspective and will guide your self-disclosure choices, but you may also find that you need to seek additional support to address your past.

Engaging in appropriate interactions with clients and colleagues can be an emotional and frustrating one for helping professionals. Should you experience discomfort from your own feelings or from verbal or nonverbal messages sent by your client, immediately seek out your field instructor or a faculty member for an opportunity to process, and think and practice reflectively. These are issues that you do not have to confront on your own.

STRESS: BANE OR BOON?

At times, all helping professionals encounter professionally related stress. This is part of being in a discipline that is intimately involved in the ongoing crises of individual, family, and community life. Learning experiences are not always perceived as positive, but can be meaningful and illuminating. Three avenues are available for responding to inevitable stressors:

1. Negative response—intimidation, feeling overwhelmed, immobilization, and, ultimately, burnout
2. Positive response—reframing the stressor as a challenge or a valuable learning experience
3. Combination of the previous two responses—beginning on one avenue and moving to the other, or vacillating back and forth between the two

Generally, *stress* is considered to be a response to a positive or negative event in which one's usual coping mechanisms do not adequately address the stimulus. Even positive events (e.g., marriage, the birth of a child, or a new job) can produce stressful reactions. Social work students experience a combination of positive and negative stressors with tensions occurring in the areas of feeling competent to respond to client circumstances (particularly regarding safety issues), the field instructor relationship, and functioning appropriately within the practicum agency (Barlow & Hall, 2007). Such potential stressors point to the need for realistic expectations and awareness of self and most importantly, the willingness to identify and address stressors as they occur. Often, helping professionals believe that, with our training, we should be able to handle more than the average person and be able to treat or counsel ourselves.

Stressors can originate at the societal, community, agency, or individual levels. At the societal level, our profession has changed dramatically in recent years with the increase of family and community violence, the advent of HIV/AIDS, and the changes brought on by welfare reform and managed care. These changes have filtered down to the community level, resulting in a disintegration of neighborhoods and services in some communities. At the agency level, political and economic changes have resulted in decreasing resources, increasing workloads, and workers being responsible for tasks for which they are not adequately trained (Birkenmaier, Rubio, & Berg-Weger, 2002; Rubio, Birkenmaier, & Berg-Weger, 2002). At the individual level, we must recognize that even we, as social workers, are not immune to the stressors that befall others. Just because we develop heightened self-awareness and have the knowledge and skills needed to respond appropriately to life's stresses, we are not guaranteed the ability to stave off the effects of life events. Social work students report that interactions with clients create, by far, the most stress for them during the practicum experience, followed by staff/agency/field instructor problems and the field process (Birkenmaier et al., 2002).

HOW WELL IS YOUR WELL-BEING?

Stressful reactions can assume multiple and sometimes co-existing forms. *Secondary or vicarious trauma* (stressful response to a trauma experienced by another) and *burnout* (stress related to feeling overwhelmed and undersupported by the job) can occur separately or simultaneously (Wharton, 2008). Along with role ambiguity or conflict, disparities between professional ideals and actual outcomes can contribute to social work burnout (Lloyd, King, & Chenoweth, 2002). When stressors accumulate, *compassion fatigue* can occur. Compassion fatigue is "a state of tension and preoccupation with . . . traumatized patients . . . that results from re-experiencing the . . . traumatic events, avoidance/numbing of reminders and persistent arousal associated with the patient" (Figley, 2002, p. 1435). Such stressful responses typically manifest in physical or psychosocial symptoms. You should consider that you are experiencing a stress reaction if you note a change in your usual behaviors, thoughts, or feelings. In a recent study of NASW members (Arrington, 2008), social workers report fatigue as the most frequent concern, followed by psychological problems, work performance problems, and health-related issues. Being in tune with your physical and mental states is key to early and effective intervention. Some physical indicators that you may experience when confronted with acute or ongoing stress include the following:

- Being more clumsy or awkward than usual
- Increase in frequency or severity of physical illnesses (e.g., colds, flu, and headaches) that may result in increased absences from work, school, or social events
- Increase in frequency or intensity of crying, particularly if you find that you are crying more often than usual or that crying is triggered more easily than usual
- Regression to former, broken, or unhealthy habits (e.g., smoking, substance use/abuse, and over/undereating)
- Significant changes in eating or sleeping patterns

Stress can also present itself in less concrete ways, as evidenced by changes in your emotional status. Should you find yourself experiencing one or more of the reactions included in the following list, you may want to evaluate your life situation and investigate ways to decrease your stress levels:

- Withdrawal from or avoidance of usually enjoyable social or professional activities
- Denial that stress exists in your life or denial that you may not be coping well with the stressors in your life

- ▶ Missing deadlines, meetings, and appointments or being consistently late
- ▶ Procrastination
- ▶ Increase in the number of items that you lose or misplace
- ▶ Variability of your affect
- ▶ Feeling that you are out of control
- ▶ Changes in your usual organizational patterns (you may be less organized or overly organized)
- ▶ Feelings of hopelessness and helplessness
- ▶ Inappropriate emotional outbursts (e.g., anger, dismay, or hysteria)
- ▶ Frequent or constant complaining with no follow-up action to rectify the situation
- ▶ Persistent anger that may be inappropriate, frequent, or misdirected
- ▶ Responses that are inappropriate to the situation (e.g., over- or under-reaction)
- ▶ Overwhelming desire to flee the situation, your practicum/job, or your life in general
- ▶ Decrease in your efficiency or effectiveness, particularly regarding professional or academic performance
- ▶ Feedback from others that you seem tired, stressed, burned out, or unhappy
- ▶ Negative changes in your interactions with those close to you
- ▶ Inability to maintain your focus or attention

Consider the ways in which you respond to stressors: Do you know your "red flags" (those reactions or behaviors that prompt a negative response in your life) and what they mean when they occur? Are your stressors different based on your being in the early, middle, or late stage of the crisis situation? Think back to a particularly stressful period or event in your life, and consider these questions:

1. How did you know that the event/period was stressful?
2. What were the physical or psychosocial indicators that you were experiencing stress?
3. How did you respond to the stress? Was your response positive, negative, or a combination?
4. Was your response effective in resolving the stressful situation?
5. Would you respond to future stresses in the same way, or would you choose a different response? If the latter, what strategy(ies) would you use to handle the stress more effectively?

Stress can lead to secondary trauma, burnout, or compassion fatigue even at the beginning of your career. Such stress should not be viewed in the same vein as the typical stressors that people experience on a daily basis (Ruggles, 2004). While a heavy workload with increasingly complex individual and family situations, altercations with the people in our world, and a perceived lack of control over outcomes may be occupational stressors that come with being a social worker, you may be burning out when your attempts at coping with the stress lead you to experience negative physical and/or emotional reactions. In cases in which the stress has become severe or chronic, you may begin to experience symptoms of clinical depression, anxiety, or physical illness. In the event that you do not feel able to cope adequately with the stressors in your life, do not delay in raising the issue with your field instructor or contacting a mental health professional. Social workers are human and can periodically benefit from the very services that they provide to others. Your field instructor or social work program faculty can be excellent resources should you choose to pursue treatment options.

SELF-CARE AS PROFESSIONAL DEVELOPMENT

What does *self-care* mean to you? Take a few moments to consider the meaning of this concept and ways in which you do or do not engage in self-care. *Self-care* can be defined as the self-initiated, proactive behaviors that are intended to maintain your physical, emotional, and social health.

Promoting self-care is a common strategy that social workers encourage their clients and patients to incorporate into their lives to prevent illness, maintain their physical and emotional health and well-being, and reduce stress. Recognizing the importance of self-care, NASW (2008b) has issued a policy statement calling for social work practitioners, employers, and educators to support a range of policies and practices to enable social workers to become educated, aware, and proactive about caring for themselves. Moreover, the NASW *Code of Ethics* (2008a) mandates that social workers should not allow the impairment of self or colleagues to impede practice. Given this level of commitment by our profession, we, as social workers, are obligated to integrate the practice of self-care into our personal and professional lives as well so that we may do the following:

1. Act as role models for those we urge to accept the concept of self-care
2. Empower others to care for themselves
3. Understand the challenges that come with taking care of ourselves so we may empathize with others
4. Be healthy, balanced care providers for others

You have seen that in your role as a social work student, you will likely be confronted with numerous demands, often simultaneously. These demands may often be overlapping and conflicting. Self-care therefore becomes a necessity, as opposed to a luxury, if you are to meet these demands without paying too great a price in terms of your health, well-being, and effectiveness.

One of the most important self-care strategies that you can employ as a student and throughout your social work career is to have a professional mentor. A *mentor* is typically a more experienced professional within your field, with whom you develop a relationship in which the mentor serves as a guide, support person, and sounding board. Mentors are integral to self-care as they can aid you in processing your experiences through reflective thinking, guide you in career choices and decision making, and help you to hone your knowledge and skills and challenge and clarify ethical dilemmas. Mentoring relationships may occur naturally (i.e., a relationship that evolves around a common interest), or they may be formalized, as in the case of the assigned field instructor, supervisor, or faculty member. Strategies that will enable your mentoring relationship to aid you in self-care include assuming responsibility for your own development; remaining open to new ideas; routinely assessing with your mentor your strengths, areas for growth, and progress; and being comfortable discussing both successes and failures (Brown & Waites, 2002). Along with having a supportive mentor or supervisor, other factors that can serve to ameliorate stressful outcomes for social workers include having the support of your colleagues and a positive career orientation (Lloyd et al., 2002; Ngai & Cheung, 2009).

Professional Identity

Professional Identity

Using reflection and self-correction, what personal self-care strategies can you implement during your practicum?

Strategies for balancing your myriad roles appeared earlier in this chapter. The list provided here includes a sampling of self-care strategies that can be used to supplement your efforts to maintain a personal–professional balance. A healthy person often has a wide and diverse range of self-care strategies that are used alternately or for specific situations. In fact, NASW members report that exercise, followed by meditation and therapy are the primary strategies for addressing stress (Arrington, 2008). Consider these self-care strategies:

- Acknowledge self-care as a priority and a part of your lifestyle. You may even wish to add an addendum to your learning plan that includes your plans for self-care during your practicum.
- Attend faithfully to your physical and emotional well-being.
- Acknowledge your emotions, particularly your reactions to your work. It is sometimes necessary to allow yourself to feel anger, grief, and elation concerning your clients, your work, and social issues.
- Develop and use both personal and professional support systems. However, you are cautioned not to exploit or overuse your support network, particularly not to engage with your field instructor, faculty, or fellow students as if they are your therapists.
- Join personal and professional groups that you enjoy and that stimulate you.
- Develop a student peer-support group at your site or at your school.
- Ask for help if you need to from your field instructor, faculty, fellow students, family, or formal university and community services.
- Build into your regular schedule nonoverlapping time for completing your practicum hours, school work, fun activities, and down time.
- Stay tuned into yourself at the mind and body levels and conduct reality checks on a regular basis. (You may even want to ask others to reality check with you.)
- Develop relationships with significant others who can challenge you, if needed.
- Know and heed the signals that tell you that you are becoming stressed.
- Ask others to share their strategies for ensuring their emotional and physical health.
- If one self-care strategy does not seem to be effective for you, try something different.
- Have attainable personal and professional goals, monitor your progress in reaching them, and re-evaluate these goals on a regular basis.
- Although you want to challenge and stretch yourself consistently, do not push yourself beyond your limits over a long period. You may be able to overextend yourself successfully in the short term, but you can suffer if you push yourself over the long term.
- Use considerable caution in resorting to artificial means to maintain your energy (e.g., drugs, alcohol, diet aids, excessive caffeine, and stimulants).
- Do not expect others to take care of you. They may raise issues, but you are responsible for taking action.
- Work to your strengths and know your limitations, changing what you can.
- Avoid procrastination. The crisis of a last-minute deadline can create even more stress.
- When you elect to confront a stressor or injustice, choose your battle carefully. Your energy may be more effectively directed to another area at that time.

Ethical Dilemma: Rosa's Stress

In Chapter 1, Rosa had discontinued her ADD medication and was experiencing difficulty functioning. Her field instructor had observed problems with Rosa's functioning and discussed her observations with Rosa. Rosa admitted that she had, in fact, stopped the medication. She agreed to consult her physician, and after that discussion, Rosa was prescribed a new medication. Rosa adjusted to the new medication and was again functioning well in her practicum. Rosa was concerned that she would be perceived negatively as a result of her earlier performance, so she threw herself into her coursework and practicum. Within a few weeks, her field instructor was again concerned about Rosa, but this time, it was prompted by Rosa putting in more hours than she was scheduled for, not taking breaks during the day, eating at her desk, and taking reading home. Rosa often looked tired and explained that she was staying up late at night studying. When Rosa and her field instructor talked, Rosa admitted that she was worried about burning out but did not know what to do.

▶ *What steps can Rosa take to address the stressors that she is experiencing?*
▶ *Should Rosa admit to her field instructor that she is fearful of receiving a poor evaluation?*
▶ *What is an appropriate role for the field instructor to have in helping Rosa develop a plan for self-care?*

THE TRANSITIONS OF PROFESSIONAL SOCIALIZATION

The final area to consider as we discuss your socialization as a social worker is the *transitions* that you have experienced and will experience as you continue on your professional journey. Transitioning from one phase of an experience to the next provides the opportunity to evaluate, re-evaluate, and plan for the future. There are several natural transitions that will occur as you move into and through your social work career. Beginning with your practicum, we will highlight these transitions here and focus on issues for you to consider while you are a student. It is important to note that transitions from one "event" to the next may be compartmentalized by semesters and graduation, but your socialization as a social worker will likely be ongoing, more complex, and difficult to quantify (Barretti, 2004). Your social work socialization includes transitions that can be categorized as follows: (1) coursework to first (or first semester of) practicum, including beginning, middle, and termination phases; (2) subsequent or second semester of practicum to graduation; and (3) student to professional.

Coursework to Practicum

The transition from theory to practice is integral to your socialization as a social worker and begins with the planning of your first practicum. As you have learned, social work education emphasizes the integration of the theoretical and conceptual frameworks with the application of social work competencies, skills, and practice behaviors during field work. During this phase of your development, you move from the classroom setting in which you gained theoretical and conceptual knowledge to the competency-based field experience.

You may or may not have entered your social work program with an idea of the type/area of social work in which you are interested. By the time you began to plan your first practicum, you may have continued, focused, or changed those interests as a result of faculty/peer influence, readings, class exercises, guest lecturers, or service experiences. Despite the way in which your interests and planning process are evolving, you are making or have made the transition from classroom to field during this phase of your professionalization.

The key issues to grasp during this phase may seem basic, but are key to your social work development. During this stage, you must consider such questions as:

Practice Contexts

What are the societal issues and trends that impact the population(s) with which I am working?

- With which population(s), settings, and areas of social work do I want to develop my skills?
- Have I inventoried my knowledge and skills to determine what I know and what I do not know?
- Am I grounded in basic social work–related theory and how to begin to apply those theories to actual practice situations?

Do not be dismayed if you do not have the answers to these questions. You have hundreds of hours of field experience during which you can work on the answers.

Beginning to Middle Phase

The issues raised in the previous section may seem rudimentary. But the issues that occur in this phase are perhaps the most abstract and difficult ones you will encounter throughout your social work journey. The issues that emerge here may have overwhelmed you at times, and you may vacillate between thoughts of self-doubt and jubilation regarding your career choice. Here are some points to consider as you move through the beginning phase of your practicum:

- Identify your competency and skill level at the onset of your practicum.
- Identify your goals for this phase as well as those of your field instructor and social work program (know where you want to be at termination).
- Identify the competency and skill level for the end of your practicum.
- Periodically review your goals, and evaluate and plan the direction for the next phase of your practicum experience.
- Engage in mutual feedback with your field instructor regarding this phase of the experience.

Middle Phase to Termination Phase

By the middle phase of your first practicum, you have survived the beginning of this new experience. You have gained a working knowledge of the agency's function and operations. You have been implementing the goals, tasks, and activities outlined in your learning plan; you have been assigned a workload (cases and projects); and you are comfortably entrenched in the daily routine of your practicum organization. Now is the time to begin *actively* planning for your termination from this practicum. Some areas for you to consider and discuss with your field instructor include:

- Strategies and timeframes for termination of practicum responsibilities (e.g., case transfers and final reports)
- Areas of gain (knowledge, competency, practice behaviors, and skill growth and values clarification)
- Areas for continued growth (for the remainder of this practicum and beyond)
- A plan for the targeted areas for growth, including specific practice behaviors
- Your feelings regarding your termination from your clients, groups, co-workers, and field instructor
- Mutual feedback regarding your practicum experience
- The plan for completion of the evaluation

Subsequent Practica or Second Semester of Practicum to Graduation

Once you have successfully completed your first practicum experience, the subsequent semester(s) in which you complete practicum builds on familiar practicum activities and developing new learning opportunities and practice behaviors that enhance earlier learning objectives. In some instances, you may find that you could easily function on automatic pilot regarding your practicum experiences, particularly if you continue to work in the same or similar setting or with a comparable population. You can optimize your learning by seeking out new and challenging levels of responsibility, activities, and experiences to extend your capabilities and limits. Here are some key strategies to consider as you move along this segment of the social work path:

- Continue to engage in an ongoing evaluation of your goals, competency and skill level, strengths, and areas for growth. (You may want to use your learning plan as a tool for monitoring your progress.)
- Develop strategies to address those issues identified earlier.
- Identify new experiences desired that may or may not be required by your social work program.
- Utilize available resources to help identify future career, employment, and training directions.
- Integrate, as much as possible, your practicum experiences into your coursework.
- Discuss with your field instructor and social work program faculty their willingness to provide a reference for you. (Some agencies and individuals have a no–reference letter policy.) Before asking for a reference, inquire whether your field instructor and faculty could provide a positive reference.

Practicum Student to Professional Social Worker

The phenomenon that often occurs during this phase of a social worker's professional development is akin to a panic: One suddenly realizes how little one knows, school loans may be coming due, and the job market looms ahead. This experience may not become a reality for you or may be gradual or may come and

Social work is not something you do but something you become.
—Julie Birkenmaier

go. Regardless of how you experience this milestone, there are a number of issues to consider as you move out of the role of student and into the role of professional social worker. Some strategies for easing this transition include the following:

- Identify goals for the next chapter of your life—another degree, additional training, employment, or long-term volunteer service (e.g., Peace Corps).
- Develop your résumé using your school's career service office. This office may offer résumé development services, employment workshops, employment listings, and the opportunity to conduct practice employment interviews.
- Establish your goals and criteria for employment.
- Determine the realities for your transition—economic, geographic, and skill preparation.
- Keep your options open, particularly as you consider your first social work position at your current level.
- Maintain contact with faculty and staff at your practicum sites, including your field instructor. Many have extensive community and professional contacts.
- Be visible. Regardless of whether you have chosen to continue your training or to become employed, use your networking skills to maintain and develop your ties to the social work community.

Good luck! You have embarked on what promises to be a challenging, seldom dull, and rewarding career.

Practice Application 2.4 A Social Worker's Day

This exercise focuses on gaining further understanding and insight into the roles and responsibilities, overall job requirements, and client and agency expectations in a typical day in the work life of a social worker. You will be able to analyze and potentially change how your time is actually spent. This exercise will prove most helpful in the middle or termination phase of your practicum experience, when you are working somewhat autonomously.

Select a typical day at your practicum. Prior to arrival at your practicum site, take a piece of paper and, on the left side, write down every half-hour time slot, beginning with your start time (i.e., 8:00 A.M., 8:30 A.M., etc.) and going through to your expected ending time. Divide the rest of the paper into two columns. In the left column, write down in each half-hour slot the activities that you plan or anticipate for the day. Include the vast array of activities in which you are typically engaged, such as reading mail, collaborating with other professionals, meeting with clients (e.g., counseling, intake, and services), making telephone calls, recording assessments/notes, attending staffings, meeting with your field instructor, making a home visit (include travel time), presenting at a community meeting, and so on. Do not forget to write in breaks and lunch. Keep this list handy throughout the day and write in the actual activities that occurred.

In small student seminar groups or with your field instructor, review the completed planned and actual activity lists. Then consider these questions:

1. What was accomplished, and what was not accomplished?
2. What activities took longer or shorter time spans than expected?
3. How were priorities met or unmet?
4. How were expectations and needs of clients, your agency, community contacts, and your field instructor met or not met?
5. How did recording via computer, handwritten notes, or dictating fit into the day?
6. What happened when there was a client crisis?
7. Were you surprised, pleased, or satisfied with your results?
8. Where do you need to allocate more or less time to meet the job requirements for the day?
9. Did you spend time on activities when, in fact, you wished you were spending time on other activities?

Debriefing—As professionally trained social workers, our days are often very busy and unpredictable. Our work requires frequent communications and collaborations and the ability to change tasks continually, from answering telephone calls, to being a therapist, to collaborating with other professionals, to traveling in the community, to responding to a grieving family, to numerous other activities. Our services may be needed for longer than could be predicted. Some experienced social workers reflect that there is no typical day. Instead, their day flows with a sense of the priorities among their responsibilities and the services they provide. As many modern-day professionals remark, there is not enough time in the day to complete their work, and social work is no different.

This exercise is designed to provide insight into how you spend your time, what time may be needed to perform your professional responsibilities, and where you may want to take an active approach to managing time for your overall effectiveness and performance as a social worker. For example, finding the time to record assessments or case management goals and progress notes is often put off, and before you know it, this job has become overwhelming. Where can this fit in your day? Your field instructor will help you evaluate and plan for this situation and others that become apparent as a result of this exercise. Near the end of your practicum, try this exercise again.

Developed by Pamela Huggins, LCSW

Practice Application 2.5 Thinking Like a Social Worker

This exercise uses a case vignette to aid you in strengthening your responses to social work practice situations. You will be better able to integrate generalist social work knowledge and skills by focusing on the strengths and empowerment orientation.

This exercise is most helpful if completed in large groups (i.e., integrative practice field seminar) as many ideas can be expressed. Information on the case is provided in small increments and builds into a larger case scenario that offers several opportunities to think like a social worker. Following the completion of each section, the group is asked to share their responses to these questions:

1. What are your thoughts and impressions?
2. What questions or responses would you have in relation to assessment?
3. What individual, family, group, community, and organizational interventions (including therapeutic responses) would you suggest?
4. What social work values are relevant in this case?
5. What are the ethical implications of the case vignette, including the social work intervention?

Case Vignette
▶ A 35-year-old woman comes to your office stating that she is depressed. She tells you that her two children have been placed in foster care because the family's water and electricity were shut off due

to nonpayment and neighbors are no longer willing to help with food.
▶ The client is ineligible for public assistance because her husband works erratically as a day laborer, thus generating income for the family.
▶ Her husband is not currently working due to active alcohol dependence, past work history, and a depressed economy.
▶ The client and her family were unable to gain admittance to either a homeless shelter or a transitional housing unit because both were full, resulting in her inability to keep the children with her.
▶ The community believes that poor people are responsible for their own plight.

Debriefing

1. How would you evaluate your ability to think in terms of a strength practice approach versus focusing on problems and dysfunction? Were you aware of automatic judgmental or blaming-the-victim thoughts?
2. In what ways were you aware of empowering approaches? In what ways do you support the client's efforts to assume responsibility and gain a sense of competence, confidence, and control?
3. What social problems, policies, or programs can you identify that would be appropriate in this case?
4. What interventions did you identify?

(continued)

5. Were there aspects of this case about which you need more information to be effective (e.g., alcohol dependence, legislative impact on welfare programs)? Specify the area(s) in which you required more information. How can you obtain this information?

This case illustrates the social work profession's unique generalist approach to helping others and impacting systems. Many of our interdisciplinary colleagues are very skilled helpers, particularly in the area of treating this client's depression. Our helping orientation, however, prepares us to understand and work effectively with individuals, families, groups, and the community. This means that we approach this case by providing social services for this woman, including individual support and assistance. Other services focus on her environment (i.e., multiple systems—family, friends, religious and cultural affiliations, community, government programs, health care, economic opportunities, societal attitudes, and discrimination).

Developed by Pamela Huggins, LCSW

SUMMARY

This chapter has focused on a wide range of issues, all related to your social work journey. You are well on your way to becoming socialized as a professionally degreed social work practitioner. We have emphasized the need for a proactive approach to your socialization experience, ongoing attention to your professional goals and needs, anticipating the possible pitfalls that may occur along the way, strategies for addressing stresses, and awareness about the transitions that occur.

Ben's fears about the profession he has chosen nearly succeeded in immobilizing him. For several weeks (even after he began his practicum), he thought daily about the possibility of withdrawing from the MSW program. Because he had been too fearful about his concerns to talk with anyone, the anxiety had mounted. The turning point for Ben was a question posed to him by his field instructor during supervision. He sat down in his field instructor's office for their weekly session, and his field instructor asked, "Ben, how's it going?" Wanting desperately to talk with someone about his almost paralyzing fears, Ben immediately began to pour out his story to his field instructor. Fortunately, Ben's field instructor was able to validate and normalize his experience. The supervisor shared with Ben a similar experience (which most of us have had at some point in our social work careers) that enabled Ben to put his fears into perspective and understand that learning to practice social work is not all about intuition but about learning knowledge and skills.

Cameron considered the three ethical dilemmas that faced him regarding the distinction between his role as a social work student and his role as a person in recovery. Once he was able to realize that feeling flattered by the former clients/AA members' attention was not helpful to him or the AA members, he began to process the information from a professional perspective. Although Cameron recognized he had to convey to the AA members that his roles as a practicum student and fellow AA member could not overlap, he found that implementing his realization was an entirely different issue. On several future occasions, Cameron found himself literally cornered by former clients /AA members who were asking for his professional opinion. Cameron felt at a loss as to how to extricate himself from this dual and overlapping role. He tried several strategies:

1. *Avoidance.* He stopped attending that particular meeting and went to a meeting farther from home. (This just made him angry at the others and himself.)

2. *"Turfing."* He persistently attempted to refer the AA members to other professionals. (This was not successful.)

3. *Confrontation.* Cameron finally simply told them that he was uncomfortable with his dual role and that he would not be able to discuss their individual treatment issues with them further. This worked.

Succeed with **PEARSON mysocialworklab**

Log onto **MySocialWorkLab** to access a wealth of case studies, videos, and assessment. (*If you did not receive an access code to* **MySocialWorkLab** *with this text and wish to purchase access online, please visit* www.mysocialworklab.com.)

1. Click on the Core Competency videos and return to the Professional Identity videos depicting Sarah Harden. Review Professional Roles and Boundaries and Advocating for the Client. Consider the way in which you would ascertain if the client's motivation is compliance with her physician's recommendation

or drug-seeking behavior. What action will you take if you determine she is seeking drugs?

2. Click on the Core Competency videos. Select Diversity in Practice and review the video entitled, Building Self-Awareness. What practice behaviors do you observe the social worker using to engage with the client and gain awareness of the client's culture? Consider your own cultural experiences and explore your own handling of this interview—would you utilize a different approach or questions?

PRACTICE TEST
The following questions will test your knowledge of the content found within this chapter. For additional assessment, including licensing-exam type questions on applying chapter content to practice, visit **MySocialWorkLab.**

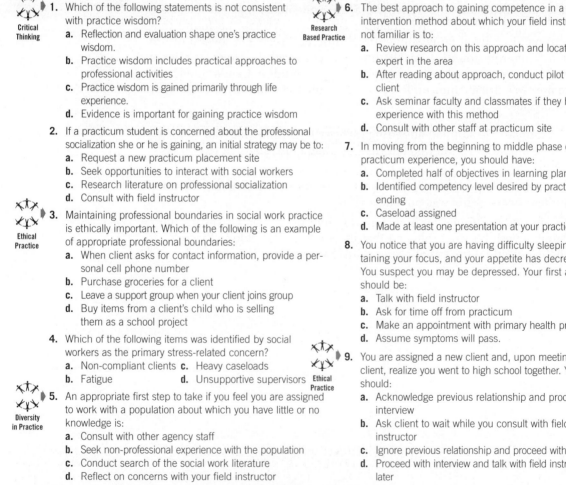

Critical Thinking

1. Which of the following statements is not consistent with practice wisdom?
   a. Reflection and evaluation shape one's practice wisdom.
   b. Practice wisdom includes practical approaches to professional activities
   c. Practice wisdom is gained primarily through life experience.
   d. Evidence is important for gaining practice wisdom

2. If a practicum student is concerned about the professional socialization she or he is gaining, an initial strategy may be to:
   a. Request a new practicum placement site
   b. Seek opportunities to interact with social workers
   c. Research literature on professional socialization
   d. Consult with field instructor

Ethical Practice

3. Maintaining professional boundaries in social work practice is ethically important. Which of the following is an example of appropriate professional boundaries:
   a. When client asks for contact information, provide a personal cell phone number
   b. Purchase groceries for a client
   c. Leave a support group when your client joins group
   d. Buy items from a client's child who is selling them as a school project

4. Which of the following items was identified by social workers as the primary stress-related concern?
   a. Non-compliant clients   c. Heavy caseloads
   b. Fatigue   d. Unsupportive supervisors

Diversity in Practice

5. An appropriate first step to take if you feel you are assigned to work with a population about which you have little or no knowledge is:
   a. Consult with other agency staff
   b. Seek non-professional experience with the population
   c. Conduct search of the social work literature
   d. Reflect on concerns with your field instructor

Research Based Practice

6. The best approach to gaining competence in a specific intervention method about which your field instructor is not familiar is to:
   a. Review research on this approach and locate an expert in the area
   b. After reading about approach, conduct pilot with client
   c. Ask seminar faculty and classmates if they have experience with this method
   d. Consult with other staff at practicum site

7. In moving from the beginning to middle phase of the practicum experience, you should have:
   a. Completed half of objectives in learning plan
   b. Identified competency level desired by practicum ending
   c. Caseload assigned
   d. Made at least one presentation at your practicum site

8. You notice that you are having difficulty sleeping, maintaining your focus, and your appetite has decreased. You suspect you may be depressed. Your first action should be:
   a. Talk with field instructor
   b. Ask for time off from practicum
   c. Make an appointment with primary health provider
   d. Assume symptoms will pass.

Ethical Practice

9. You are assigned a new client and, upon meeting the client, realize you went to high school together. You should:
   a. Acknowledge previous relationship and proceed with interview
   b. Ask client to wait while you consult with field instructor
   c. Ignore previous relationship and proceed with interview
   d. Proceed with interview and talk with field instructor later

Log onto **MySocialWorkLab** once you have completed the Practice Test above, to access additional study tools and assessment.

Answers:

Key: 1) c 2) d 3) c 4) b 5) d 6) a 7) b 8) c 9) b

3

Safety in Social Work Settings

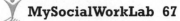
Core Competencies in this Chapter (Check marks indicate which competencies are covered in depth)				
✔ Professional Identity	✔ Ethical Practice	☐ Critical Thinking	☐ Diversity in Practice	☐ Human Rights and Justice
☐ Research Based Practice	☐ Human Behavior	☐ Policy Practice	☐ Practice Contexts	✔ Engage, Assess, Intervene, Evaluate

*Life is either a daring
adventure or nothing.
Security does not exist
in nature, nor do the
children of men as a
whole experience it.
Avoiding danger is no
safer in the long run
than exposure.*

—Adapted from
Helen Keller

Have you wondered about your physical safety at your practicum site? Does the thought of home visits create feelings of anxiety? Have family members worried about your choice of profession because of safety issues? Have you heard other students and faculty discuss agency safety issues?

Many students, especially beginning students, have concerns about safety and security and struggle with the decision to voice their concerns to their professors, other students, and their field instructors. Students may be reluctant to discuss safety fears and concerns with others for fear of being viewed as uncommitted to the profession or to clients. Other students may assume that the role of the social worker is viewed as strictly one of helper and enabler and cannot fathom being viewed as a threat. However, the practice of social work typically does involve some degree of risk. If not addressed, concerns about personal safety can significantly affect learning opportunities in the field placement. This chapter will address safety concerns associated with social work and provide guidelines that can assist you in minimizing the risk of harm.

THE SCOPE OF PERSONAL SAFETY RISKS IN SOCIAL WORK

> *On her first day of practicum, Corina was given a tour of the detention facility, introduced to all of the staff, oriented to the various systems, and provided with agency manuals and policy guidelines. She began shadowing other social workers and sat in on their group therapy sessions. On the third day, she remembered to ask about the unusual name of the unit in which she would be completing her practicum. She was told it was named after a staff member who had been shot to death by a client in the office a year ago. She was shocked. She had no idea that this practicum could pose a threat to her well-being. Are her fears real? What would you do on learning this information?*

Faced with this kind of information, most students would be concerned about working at the agency. Some might even contemplate requesting a transfer to another agency. Other students might consider the likelihood of this kind of incident occurring twice to be very small and so disregard safety as a serious matter.

Should safety be a concern for students in practicum? Research findings suggest that concern over personal safety issues in social work is warranted. Estimates of the number of social workers who report experience with work-related violence range from 50 to 88 percent (Weinger, 2001). The National Institute for Occupational Safety and Health defines workplace violence as "violent acts (including physical assaults and threats of assaults) directed toward persons at work or on duty" (National Institute for Occupational Safety and Health, 2002). Almost half of all nonfatal injuries in the United States from work-related assaults and violent acts occurred in health care and social services (U.S. Department of Labor, 2004). More than half of all mental health professionals, including social workers, will be physically or psychologically assaulted at least once in their professional careers (Arthur, Brende, & Quiroz,

2003) with social workers being nearly six times more likely than other workers to experience workplace violence (Respass & Payne, 2008). Social workers are the target of violence for a wide variety of reasons, including (Newhill, 2008; Weinger, 2001):

- Social problems (e.g., unemployment, poverty, and racism) create an environment conducive to violence.
- Budget cuts cause rising caseloads, resulting in less time with clients to assess for violence.
- The paradox of the professional role as a helper and as an agent of social control.
- Inadequate mental health services for the potentially violent client.

Safety in the Practicum Setting

Social work practitioners and students are increasingly subject to threats in the workplace. Students are well advised to consider safety and liability issues when considering practicum sites and learning activities. The anxiety felt by many students regarding safety is justified by the experience of previous students. Although most students never experience any personal risk in practicum (Knight, 1996), approximately one-fourth of MSW and BSW practicum students experience some form of violence in the field placement, the majority of cases occurring within the practicum agency (Tully, Kropf, & Price, 1993). Violence, mostly in the form of verbal abuse, occurs frequently in field education sites (Mama, 2001). More than half of students in one study were verbally or physically threatened by a client at least once during their practica (Knight, 1996). The most common form of threat to a practicum student is a verbal threat from clients, paraprofessionals, or other professionals (Reeser & Wertkin, 2001). While the 2008 Council on Social Work Education (CSWE)

educational policy standards do not address physical safety, assessment of potentially dangerous clients, or strategies for ensuring safety in the workplace, social work programs vary widely in their knowledge of and approach to safety concerns. Only 12 percent of social work schools have a formal written policy on student safety (Reeser & Wertkin, 2001). While safety is a concern for students, the topic is often not directly addressed in field sites (Barlow & Hall, 2007).

Reasonable Concerns and Caution

Although being careful is important, strive to separate stereotypes and myths by having a realistic portrayal of risks in order to be an effective practitioner

Social workers often work in neighborhoods, communities, and with groups and clients that others may deem unsafe. Although being careful is important, strive to separate stereotypes and myths from reality by having a realistic portrayal of risks in order to be an effective practitioner. If not addressed, the beginning anxiety you may feel can impede a willingness to draft ambitious and valuable learning plans. Talking with other students in practicum at your site, other current and former practicum students at the agency, and your field instructor can help you determine the level of risk involved in conducting specific tasks and your comfort level in completing those tasks. You must ensure your safety and avoid allowing unfounded fears or inexperience to become impediments to the delivery of effective services.

The agency setting can significantly influence the level of perceived risk to the staff. If you are working in a residential setting (e.g., a children's residential facility, hospital, substance abuse treatment facility, domestic violence facility, or a correctional facility), you will likely encounter a highly structured setting with specific procedures regarding some or all of the following:

- Locks
- Metal detectors
- The need to receive permission from security guards for movement within the site
- Confidentiality regarding location
- Client restraints
- Moving to and from your car in the agency parking lot
- Situations in which staff must work in teams to ensure safety
- Standard precautions (e.g., universal precautions) for avoiding exposure to illnesses such as HIV/AIDS, hepatitis, and tuberculosis
- The completion of safety and violence response workshops in which you are trained to respond to violent aggression by clients and are expected to intervene physically with clients

If you are working in a community-based agency, you may find fewer (if any) protocols and safety guidelines. Situations posing physical threats to social workers can occur in any setting, and students should exercise due caution regardless of the perceived risk.

Your field instructor may discuss safety matters with you during your interview to provide a realistic view of risk prior to your commitment to the agency. The field instructor will likely discuss policies and procedures regarding safety as you begin your practicum, as well as the agency process for reporting safety policy and procedure violations. Completing the following practice applications can help you gain a realistic perception of the safety risks in your setting and implement agency safety policies.

Practice Application 3.1 Gathering Information

Completing this exercise will enable you to gather pertinent, current, and accurate information about the safety risks, resources, and protocols associated with social work practice in your practicum site as well as the safety resources and protocols of your social work program.

At Your Practicum Site

▸ Inquire about the number of recent incidents of physical or verbal abuse, harassment, and other violence that staff has experienced inside or outside the agency.

▸ If not included in the orientation, inquire about agency safety protocols (e.g., telephone number for emergency assistance, location of the first aid kit, emergency exit procedures for the building, and locations of fire extinguishers), as well as the process for reporting protocol violations.

▸ Request a tour of the surrounding neighborhood, particularly if you will be conducting home visits.

▸ Ask whether certain neighborhoods or areas should be avoided or approached with more caution than usual by staff members for safety reasons, and be prepared to follow suit when working independently.

▸ Observe safety protocols implemented by staff members conducting similar duties to those you have planned for the practicum both inside and outside the agency (to include cellular phone usage).

▸ Inquire about the availability of safety training.

Within Your Social Work Program

▸ Ask how many students have experienced problems related to safety in practicum in recent years.

▸ Research the safety protocols of your social work program.

▸ Take advantage of safety resources available from your social work program, or ask the faculty for assistance in obtaining resources such as safety training, seminars, videos, handouts, and discussions.

After you have gathered all the information noted, demonstrate the knowledge you have gained through a discussion with your field instructor, a reflection paper for your integrative seminar class, or a journal entry.

Practice Application 3.2 Gaining Skills

Ask to be observed by a staff member as you are making the transition to independent work with clients, and ask for feedback regarding safety risks and the implementation of safety guidelines. Journal about these early experiences related to safety issues as well as safety precautions utilized and not utilized by you or by staff.

Practice Application 3.3 Assessment and Reflection

Discuss and critique the following with a member of your practicum team:

▸ Information gathered regarding safety issues in the practicum site

▸ Skills you are developing related to the implementation of safety guidelines

▸ The safety training and/or protocols of both the agency and your social work program (Were the protocols sufficient? Was the training helpful?)

▸ Your apprehensions or fears concerning your safety while conducting practicum activities (Are your apprehensions based on reality and experience? How much of a factor could myths, stereotypes, inexperience, or bias be playing in your fears?)

BOX 3.1 Factors That Increase the Risk of Harm

History is often the best prediction of risk. Increased caution should be exercised when working with clients who have these characteristics (Newhill, 2008; Weinger, 2001):

1. Severely violent behavior
2. History of remorseless parental brutality
3. History of fighting and school problems
4. Difficulty getting along with others and authority figures
5. History of overt parental seductiveness
6. Familiarity with weapons
7. Currently under the influence of drugs or alcohol
8. Currently under severe stress and are feeling overwhelmed or hopeless
9. Currently verbalize being upset and angry or will not communicate with you
10. Currently threatening to you either verbally or physically
11. Currently involved in illegal activities
12. Erupted verbally or physically in the last 30 to 40 minutes
13. Unable to sit still or are pacing
14. Currently suicidal

Engage, Assess, Intervene, Evaluate

Assessment includes client strengths and limitations. How could you focus on client strengths, while also assessing for potential violence?

ASSESSMENT OF POTENTIALLY VIOLENT CLIENTS

Due to the increased safety risks faced by social workers in many settings, it is critical that you be able to assess potential risk accurately. While human behavior is unpredictable and you will not be able to determine risk accurately in advance of an actual threat to your safety, be aware that certain factors may increase the risk of harm (see Box 3.1). Caution should be exercised when working with certain client groups under the following circumstances (Scalera, 1995; Weinger, 2001):

- Young male clients with criminal records or histories of substance abuse, weapons possession, or violence
- Clients with a mental illness with specific risk factors and acute symptoms (i.e., paranoid delusions, command hallucinations, and syndromes such as mania, paranoid schizophrenia, and panic)
- History of weapons possession
- History of child or adult violence, substance abuse, or ritualistic or cult practices
- Pending or actual removal of a family member
- Geographic location that may pose danger (e.g., rural, isolated, or high-crime area)
- Working during the evening or nighttime hours
- Presence of animals that may pose a threat

SPECIFIC GUIDELINES FOR SAFETY WITHIN THE OFFICE

Many students will meet with their clients in an office setting and encounter few problems. However, even the most structured setting cannot guarantee complete safety. The following suggestions can reduce the chances of experiencing physical harm in the office (Newhill, 2009; Weinger, 2001):

- Follow agency safety policies to the letter. Take advantage of any agency safety training opportunities.

▶ Study the files of all clients before interacting with them to ascertain the risk involved in working with them.

▶ Learn how to do a risk assessment, to include consideration of a client's history of violence, involvement with correctional systems, client's appearance, degree to which client is compliant with requests, client's demeanor, client's intent to harm self or others, and psychiatric or medical risk factors including substance abuse.

▶ Ask a staff member to accompany you when working with a client with a history of violence or one who exhibits behaviors that may pose a threat.

▶ Remove all objects from your desk (pens, staplers, and paper weights) that could be used as weapons.

▶ Leave a client who is becoming belligerent or threatening, and seek help from a colleague.

▶ If there is not one in place, develop a system whereby you can discreetly signal another staff member for assistance (e.g., call another staff member, state the client name, and say that you need "the progress folder").

▶ Leave office doors open and arrange the furniture so that you and the client both could make a quick exit.

▶ When possible, develop relationships with those who are charged with ensuring your safety. Let them know when you will be working late, and ask the guards/safety patrol officers to escort you to your car when needed.

▶ Maintain a confidential, locked location for your valuables at the agency.

▶ If clients have access to the office in which you are working, lock it whenever you leave.

While all violence cannot be prevented, these steps represent the efforts that you can make to help ensure your safety in the office setting. If safety is an issue within the practicum office and some of the aforementioned suggestions are not being utilized, consider suggesting some of the procedures. It is important to take safety issues seriously within an office setting.

INTERACTING WITH CLIENTS WITHIN THE HOME AND THE COMMUNITY

Ben was unsure about the contents of the long case in the client's hand. The client walked quickly, put the case in the backseat, and joined Ben in the front seat. As Ben greeted him and reiterated the need for the trip to the office, the client began to ramble incoherently. However, Ben was able to understand that the client wished to go first to a different location to pick up a check. When Ben objected, the client referred to the shotgun he had placed in the backseat. The client made disparaging remarks about Ben's Asian heritage. Frightened and unclear about what he should do, Ben drove to the office the client requested and then drove him home. As Ben debriefed later with his field instructor, he found himself shaking and short of breath. Did he do the right thing in this situation? How did diversity issues impact the interaction?

As Ben discovered, stepping into the community to serve clients entails leaving the structured environment of the office setting. Working with clients outside an office setting can also, as in Ben's case, leave a practitioner wondering which course of action is best as an interaction with a client unfolds in the real world. Making home visits and encountering clients in the community can offer the opportunity to gather a rich array of information about them that is not available from a meeting in the office. The home visit enhances the delivery of services to clients in their natural setting. While interacting with clients outside of the agency can be intimidating for a new professional, the delivery of professional services on the "home turf" of the client can be essential to the success of the intervention. Although not every home visit poses a safety risk, consider the following suggestions to decrease the potential for harm.

Preparation
Preparing for work with clients outside of the agency can minimize your risk of physical harm and liability.

Transportation
If you will be transporting clients in a vehicle, check the following:

- The ages of any children you may be transporting. Make arrangements for carseats for young children.
- The number and condition of seatbelts.
- The travel location resources available in your car. Have access to a current street map (either hard copy or electronic) or GPS device, and practice using the map/device prior to independent home/community visits.
- Whether your car is equipped for emergencies, including a spare tire (and the necessary changing equipment), ample fuel, and battery cables. If your work will involve extensive travel, consider obtaining emergency roadside assistance coverage.
- Ensure insurance coverage for clients transported in your personal vehicle. Before using an agency vehicle, verify that students and volunteers are covered by the agency policy.
- Keep only necessary keys on your key ring. Consider obtaining a two-part key ring that allows you to detach a portion that contains your car keys.

Other
The following precautions may minimize your risk in the community (Burry, 2003; Respass & Payne, 2008; Spencer & Munch, 2003; Weinger, 2001):

- Before leaving for a home visit, gather information from colleagues, administrators, and the case file at the agency to assess any known risks, including acute symptomatology, noticeable behavior changes, alterations or discontinuance of medication, known or suspected use of drugs or alcohol, mandated treatment, previous threats, and known history of violence.
- Determine whether the visit could occur in a public location and/or with another worker, supervisor, or law enforcement personnel.
- Inform agency staff of the addresses you plan to visit, and your expected route and expected return time. If you suspect a potential for danger, arrange for someone to call you during your visit, or take another staff member.
- Take only materials necessary for the home visit, and leave valuables (e.g., extra cash, unneeded credit cards, and jewelry) at the agency or at home.
- Schedule home visits in the morning when possible. Neighborhoods and homes tend to be calmer during the morning hours than at any other time of day.

- If cellular phones or beepers are standard for other staff in the field, consider asking for a loan of this equipment during your practicum. Leave these numbers with agency staff. Also know that these items can be tempting for thieves. If not available from the agency, consider taking your own (charged) cellular phone. Plan to keep it concealed but turned on during your visits (possibly with the vibration function activated) so that you can use it at a moment's notice.
- Prominently display forms of identification to the client (e.g., agency name badge, business card, or logo on the agency vehicle).
- Pattern your dress after the other field staff. Some agencies prefer a professional look in the field, while others promote a casual dress style. Limit jewelry.
- Have clear written directions to the home location. Allow extra time if you are unfamiliar with the area. If you get lost, retrace your route. If you must ask for directions, do so at a public place. Do not ask directions from persons on the street, and *never* allow anyone to get into your car to show you the way to your destination.
- Listen to and trust your instincts. If the situation seems uncomfortable and you sense the possibility for trouble, reschedule the appointment or make alternative arrangements.

During the Visit

Adhering to the following suggestions can ensure safety during home visits (Burry, 2003; Weinger, 2001):

- Use confident nonverbal behavior. Avoid acting timid.
- Park your car as close to the client's home as possible in a location that allows for a quick departure, and store unnecessary belongings in the trunk (e.g., large bags, backpacks, coats, a purse.)
- Lock all car doors, and keep your keys in a place in which you have quick, easy access to them (e.g., pocket, on your clipboard).

Professional Identity

Developing a professional identity includes considering the risks of practice. How can you develop a professional demeanor while addressing practice risks?

Practice Application 3.4 Role-Play: Offsite Safety Rules

Review and role-play the physical safety protocols practiced by your agency for offsite work with your field instructor. Situations to role-play include (1) leaving the agency, (2) arriving at the home, (3) interacting within a home, (4) leaving a home, and (5) returning to the agency. In the role-plays, include such details as the following:

1. Making an appointment with a client
2. Obtaining directions to the home
3. Gathering information about the client from agency sources (as mentioned earlier)
4. Ensuring that the vehicle is in optimum working order
5. Appropriate personal and professional items to take and safe methods of transporting and carrying them

6. Appropriate attire
7. Appropriate locations to stand/sit in the home
8. Greeting the client with a review of the purpose of the meeting
9. Ending the visit and leaving
10. Documentation and follow-up with the field instructor
11. Appropriate responses for various situations that warrant caution (e.g., walking past a crowd on the front porch, presence of a dog, presence of unknown individuals, a loud argument occurring in the house, or vague reference to weapons nearby by the client)

Developed by Ellen Burkemper, PhD, LCSW

- Note the presence of any animals on the property, and ask the client for assistance with any unleashed animals.
- Avoid walking through a group of unknown individuals when attempting to enter the house. (You may wish to leave and call to reschedule.)
- Avoid entering any elevators with anyone who appears threatening.
- Take note of individuals present in the home, and ask the client about strangers. If you are uncomfortable in the presence of others in the home, ask if you can meet with the client alone or somewhere quiet. Encourage the client to keep confidential the information you will be discussing by asking others to leave the home.
- If possible, sit with your back to a wall on a hard chair so that you can leave quickly if necessary.
- Take note of all exits as you enter the house.
- Avoid talking with a client in the bedroom or in the kitchen, as weapons are frequently stored in these rooms.
- Leave the home immediately if weapons or drugs are visible or anyone appears to be under the influence.
- After the visit, move your car to another location to complete the paperwork. Avoid sitting in a car in front of a client's home after a home visit. Document any risks associated with your visit.

WORKING WITH ANGRY, RESISTANT, OR AGGRESSIVE CLIENTS

Despite the best planning, preparation, and adherence to protocol, you may find yourself in a situation with an angry, resistant, or aggressive client. Ideally, you would be able to leave a situation or attempt to get help. If this is not an option, consider the following strategies (Burry, 2003; Respass & Payne, 2008; Weinger, 2001):

- Maintain a quiet, calm, and firm demeanor. Avoid exhibiting any alarm, hostility, distress, or defensiveness.
- Talk to the client with simple, direct sentences. Facilitate the expression of feelings and thoughts through empathy and paraphrasing, encourage problem solving and attempt to redirect the client.
- Offer positive choices to the client (e.g., "Would you like to move over to my desk so that we can sit and discuss this?").
- Attempt to slow down the pace of the interaction so that the client has time to ventilate, calm down, and think.
- Avoid any physical contact with the client.
- Attempt to engage verbally with a client at the first outward signs of agitation to allow for ventilation at the earliest possible point.
- Allow ample room between the two of you (more than one arm's length) to give the client plenty of personal space. Approach the client at an angle rather than from the back or directly from the front.
- Make every effort to seat the client. If it is not feasible to sit, allow ample room between the two of you and stand off center to the client to give yourself plenty of room to maneuver.
- Use minimal force if attacked. Apply only the amount of force needed to restrain the person or to free yourself and move to another location for assistance.

Working with agitated clients requires a calm, professional demeanor and preparation. If you are presented with a risky situation in the office or in the field, these suggestions can serve to defuse a potentially dangerous interaction.

FOLLOW-UP TO CRISES

Even with the best preparation and planning, crises still occur. If you are involved in an incident, report the incident to your field instructor in a manner that is in accordance with the agency policy. Your field instructor should communicate with agency administration and provide you with the support and guidance you need. Agencies should thoroughly review an incident and support those who are involved in and those who are affected by a serious incident. Such efforts might include filing a police report, holding debriefing sessions, making changes to staff schedules and suggested routes, and identifying resources and protocols to ensure staff safety in the future (Spencer & Munch, 2003; Weinger, 2001).

Regardless of the response of your field instructor and agency, take advantage of the peer-support networks available at your agency and within your social work program as well as your personal support system. If the incident involved a high degree of risk or you are finding that you have been deeply affected by the situation, you may wish to consider contacting a mental health practitioner to process and work through the incident.

ETHICAL DILEMMAS INVOLVING SAFETY ISSUES

Ethical Practice

How can you reconcile your need for safety in practice while ensuring that client needs are primary in your service delivery?

- What should I do if my agency physically restrains clients and I hold a personal philosophy against this?
- How do I decide whether to carry out activities in my practicum that my family or friends have asked me not to do?
- What should I do if I observe another staff member not following agency safety procedures?
- What should I do if I am required to conduct a home visit even after I discuss my uneasiness about the arrangements with my field instructor?
- What should I do if I am required to work at night even though I feel uncomfortable doing so?

These questions are evidence that even under the best circumstances with clear guidelines, students sometimes encounter situations that demand difficult decisions.

At times, difficult situations emerge that involve conflict between your personal beliefs, agency protocols, and client interests. At the practicum site, you may be asked to carry out activities to which you are personally opposed or about which you feel uneasy. Although the NASW *Code of Ethics* (2008a) is silent on the matter of safety, the primacy of client interests is clear (Section 1.01: "In general, clients' interests are primary"). The *Code of Ethics* discusses the obligation social workers have to carry out the work of their employers in good faith (Section 3.09: "Social workers generally should adhere to commitments made to employers and employing organizations"); however, the *Code* does not explicitly require social workers to follow agency policies and procedures. You may be left in a quandary when determining the best course of action in a situation that involves conflict between your beliefs and comfort level, agency procedures, and client interests.

Ideally, you were informed of the need for the activities in question prior to your commitment to the agency and you either made a decision to allow the interests of the agency and the clients to supersede your feelings or negotiated different arrangements prior to your commitment. If expectations or arrangements related to safety emerge after your commitment, you may decide to do one of the following:

1. Negotiate your involvement with activities about which you feel strongly with your field instructor/agency after you begin the practicum.
2. Make a decision to engage in the activities in question, regardless of your feelings.
3. Process and explore your feelings with your field instructor to determine whether your fears are founded.
4. Discuss your experiences and feelings in integrative seminar in order to determine a course of action.
5. Discuss the situation with your faculty liaison.
6. Attempt to switch to another practicum site if you are unable to resolve the conflict.

Although the guidelines outlined in this unit are suggestions, situations are rarely clear cut, and students are often left to their own best judgments to discern a course of action. Indeed, students often struggle with the same dilemmas faced by seasoned social workers. As social workers strive to deliver quality services under increasingly volatile circumstances, the struggle to integrate personal feelings with professional demands and to resolve safety dilemmas becomes more difficult and more common.

HARASSMENT

An openly homosexual female staff member has asked Lauren out several times for drinks after work. Despite Lauren's repeated refusals, she continues to ask. She seems to create reasons for contact with Lauren and brings her small gifts of food. Lauren surmises that the staff member perceives that she is also lesbian. The field instructor and staff member are good friends. In discussions with her family about the situation, Lauren has been pressured to end the problem by involving administrators or outside agencies. Is she being harassed? What should she do?

Situations such as this call for careful thought, tact, and a judgment call. It may be very difficult to distinguish between friendliness and harassment. It is important to note that an additional safety issue that occurs is *harassment,* defined as "any intentional unwelcomed, unsolicited, and offensive conduct that tends to injure, degrade, disgrace, or show hostility toward a person based on one of more dimensions of diversity, such as sex, race, color, religion, national origin, ancestry, disability, age, sexual orientation, marital status, military status, pregnancy, or any other characteristic protected by law" (Saint Louis University, 2007). Armed with good intentions, the NASW *Code of Ethics* (2008a), and professional work experience, many students conclude that harassment will not be an issue.

Given the value base and humanist orientation of the profession, you might think that the social work workplace would be free of harassment. However, social workers encounter harassment in their workplaces, with one of the most common forms being sexual harassment (Macdonald & Sirotich, 2005). Sexual harassment is the third most common type of abuse encountered by social workers in practice (Macdonald & Sirotich, 2005). Social work practicum students can expect to encounter sexual harassment as frequently as do social work practitioners. Although the majority of those experiencing sexual harassment are female and young, male workers experience sexual harassment as well (Fogel, 2008). Most sexual harassment crosses gender lines, but same sex sexual harassment is also a problem (Equal Employment Opportunity Commission (EEOC), 2009).

Defining Features of Harassment

Harassment occurs in many forms, ranging from jokes to sexual intercourse. *Sexual harassment* is currently defined as verbal (pressure for sexual activity, comments about the female or male body, sexual boasting, and sexist and homophobic comments); nonverbal (looking up dresses or down shirts, obscene gestures, and suggestive sounds); physical contact (touching, patting, pinching, and kissing); or environmental (sexually offensive literature, pictures, or music). Agencies are compelled by law to address the issue of sexual harassment according to Title VII of the 1964 Civil Rights Act and under guidelines issued by EEOC's 1980 guidelines regarding policy statements and grievance procedures (Gould, 2000). The NASW *Code of Ethics* (2008a) requires social workers to reject sexual activities with clients under all circumstances, renounce all forms of discrimination, avoid relationships that pose a conflict of interest, maintain a clear interest in social justice, and to preserve human dignity. Both your field instructor and your agency have a clear interest in maintaining an atmosphere that is free of harassment.

Harassment occurs in many forms, ranging from jokes to sexual intercourse

Intervention

What should you do if you encounter harassment of any type at the practicum? The circumstances of the harassment will determine the response. Consider the following steps (EEOC, 2009):

- ▶ Document the circumstances of the harassment, including dates, times, quotations, other details of the interaction/situation, and verification from any witnesses.
- ▶ Document your work accomplishments and maintain copies of evaluations. This documentation may be critical if your work performance becomes an issue when you take action against the harassment.
- ▶ Seek other victims of harassment and consider taking action as a group.
- ▶ Confront the harasser in person or in written form. Include the facts, your feelings, and a clear directive to stop the harassment.
- ▶ If appropriate, report the experience(s) to your field instructor and your faculty liaison.
- ▶ Explore the complaint process available at the agency, as well as within your social work program and affiliated institution, and consider filing a formal complaint.
- ▶ Consult with other social work students. Take advantage of field seminars or other mechanisms to consult with and receive support from other students.

Practice Application 3.5 Safety: Your Comfort Zone

To increase your comfort zone, role-play the following situation with your field instructor:

▶ During a routine office visit, one of your clients begins to share her despondency over her life situation. She has just broken up with her abusive boyfriend and discusses her suicidal thoughts with you. She mentions that she has a gun and is tempted to "do it" now and "get it over with." In her rambling, she talks about how no one, not even you, has been able to help her, and she is angry. As she talks about killing herself, she mentions "taking you with her." Should you take the threat seriously? What should you do?

Practice Application 3.6 Role-Play: Harassment

Read the two vignettes presented here and select one for role-playing with your field instructor, colleague, or classmate:

1. You are a female social worker. You are preparing to take clients of the day treatment center for the chronically mentally ill on an outing. A male client of a different ethnicity has approached you as you climb into the agency vehicle. This client has made several remarks to you in the past that have been of a sexual nature. He has commented that he thinks you will not date him because he is of a different ethnicity. When you discussed the situation with your field supervisor, she suggested that you confront the client. While obviously leering at you, he comments, "Boy, you have a great set of wheels there! Will you take me for a ride?"

2. You are a male social worker. You have been uncomfortable working around an older, recently divorced, female staff member at work. She has dropped by your desk several times without reason, asked many questions about your personal life, and exhibited flirting behavior in several encounters. Other staff members are beginning to tease you about this staff member. She is in the administration of the agency and a friend of your field instructor and you interact with her often. You are uncomfortable with her behavior and are contemplating how to approach a discussion with your field instructor about this issue. Several other issues also are involved in the situation: (1) you would like a job at this agency when you graduate and wish to maintain good relationships with the staff; (2) you question whether her behaviors constitute sexual harassment; (3) you are contemplating whether to use the agency grievance procedure; and (4) you wonder whether your field instructor will take the situation seriously. As you engage in a dialogue with your field instructor about this, you would like to role-play a confrontation with the staff member.

▶ If an agency complaint process does not exist, consider advocating for one.
▶ Consider contacting outside resources. You may wish to contact an attorney or a local, state, or federal agency charged with addressing complaints of harassment (e.g., the EEOC), a nonprofit organization (e.g., NAACP), or another resource.

Regardless of the order in which you take the actions suggested, it is important to take action if confronted with this problem. Victims of harassment must take action to advocate for themselves, use the resources that are available, and seek support from others.

Ethical Dilemma: Confidential Medical Information

Rosa facilitates a group of Hispanic mothers in a weekly parenting support group. She has recently learned information with which she is struggling. One of the mothers in the group shared privately with

Rosa that she was recently diagnosed as HIV positive. Rosa has observed infants being passed around during the group meeting and mothers and children in the group having close physical contact. She is uncertain whether this client's HIV status should change any of the practices of the group. She is also unclear whether she should ask the women to stop this practice or to use universal precautions during the group. Finally, she does not want to violate HIPAA or agency confidentiality practices.

What are the appropriate steps for Rosa?

HELPING TO ENSURE CLIENT SAFETY

As a practicum student, you have a responsibility to implement agency policies designed to ensure clients' safety. For example, as a student, you must follow agency policies and procedures to avoid falls and other injuries. The NASW *Code of Ethics* (2008a) requires social workers (and you as a practicum student) to provide appropriate professional services during "public emergencies," such as public disasters, when a client needs immediate medical attention (e.g., CPR), or during and after terrorist activities. Depending on your setting, you may also need to use *universal precautions* to protect yourself and your clients, such as the use of materials that serve as protective barriers (e.g., gloves, masks, and protective eyewear).

SUMMARY

This chapter addressed the issue of safety in the social work setting, including the scope of personal safety risks in social work, safety in the practicum setting, reasonable concerns and caution, assessment of potentially violent clients, specific guidelines for safety within the office and the community, safety suggestions for home/community visits, working with angry, resistant, or aggressive clients, follow-up to crises, dilemmas involving safety issues, harassment, and client safety. In your capacity as a social work student, you are well advised to explore the topics of safety risks and safety procedures with your field supervisor. Know the risks, implement safety procedures, use the resources at hand, and serve your clients well.

Raising the issue of safety with faculty, other students, and your field instructor is an important facet of your practicum experience as it enables you to take the appropriate precautions when working with clients. After all, many dangerous situations can be avoided if the practitioner requests assistance from a colleague (Weinger, 2001). Practitioners and students are well advised to trust their instincts about their safety and to seek support whenever needed. Indeed, you cannot adequately serve your clients in a state of significant mental or physical impairment. Your safety is imperative to the effectiveness of your work and, ultimately, to the benefit of your clients.

Corina's fear after hearing of a homicide of a worker at the site immobilized her for the remainder of the day. She realized that she could not function without addressing her concerns. In her supervision session with her field instructor the next day, she inquired about the incident. Although she had been informed about security procedures during orientation, she raised questions regarding these issues:

- Security procedures that had been in place at the time of the incident
- Changes in security procedures that had been implemented since this incident
- Prevalence of dangerous encounters with clients in the office

To increase her comfort level, she also role-played a dangerous situation with her field instructor. Are there any other reasonable steps that she could take to ensure her safety?

Ben shared with his field instructor that he responded to the client's rambling about the shotgun in the backseat only out of fear and that he never considered the safety of the client while in the interaction. In their discussion, the field instructor allowed him to vent his feelings and began to problem solve with him. Other options for a response they discussed included the following:

- Confronting the client while in the car, thereby risking agitating the client (and harm)
- Getting out of the car immediately and fleeing the scene
- Driving to the office over the objections of the client
- Driving to the location the client preferred, following the client inside the office, and calling the police

Can you think of other alternatives? What response would you have made? Why?

Lauren decided that she must confront the situation with the staff member who made uncomfortable overtures to her. The next time she asked Lauren to have drinks after work, Lauren began by thanking the staff member for the invitation and commented on the friendliness of the staff at the shelter. She informed her that due to a demanding work, practicum, school, and family schedule, she had decided to eliminate most of her social life for the semester and was turning down all invitations. Therefore, she was unable to join the staff at any social occasions but appreciated the offer. Did she confront the situation? How would you handle the situation?

Succeed with PEARSON mysocialworklab

Log onto **MySocialWorkLab** to access a wealth of case studies, videos, and assessment. (*If you did not receive an access code to* **MySocialWorkLab** *with this text and wish to purchase access online, please visit* www.mysocialworklab.com.)

1. Watch video one of the assessment (under engagement, assessment, intervention, evaluation video). The woman begins to get agitated when the limits of confidentiality are discussed. What would you do if the client became so agitated during this conversation that you began to get worried about your safety?

2. On page 9 of the Child Welfare module, the social work begins to take a history of the client's substance use. What would you ask to elicit information about factors that increase the risk of harm to you, as well as to the client's child?

PRACTICE TEST The following questions will test your knowledge of the content found within this chapter. For additional assessment, including licensing-exam type questions on applying chapter content to practice, visit **MySocialWorkLab**.

1. The degree of safety risk by social workers can <u>best</u> be described as:
   a. Overwhelming
   b. Significant
   c. Troubling
   d. A mild concern

2. The most common form of violence encountered by social workers is:
   a. Being threatened with a weapon
   b. Being hit or punched
   c. Being verbally threatened
   d. Verbal abuse

3. Most practicum-related violence occurs:
   a. Within the agency
   b. In the field
   c. In client homes
   d. In dangerous neighborhoods

4. All of the following factors increase the risk of harm except:
   a. Someone recently ended a significant relationship with the client
   b. The client is currently suicidal
   c. The client is currently involved in illegal activities
   d. The client is unable to sit still

Engage Assess Intervene Evaluate

5. The best course of action when a client is belligerent or threatening you in your office is to:
   a. Leave the client and seek help
   b. Do not leave the client until the client is calm
   c. Negotiate your leaving the office with the client
   d. Ask your client to leave the office with you

6. Social worker students should determine their style of dress for field work by:
   a. Preference of the client
   b. Their personal preference
   c. The dress style of other field staff
   d. Community customs

7. If a social work student encounters drugs or alcohol on a home visit, the best course of action is to:
   a. Leave immediately
   b. Ask the client about the drugs or alcohol
   c. Assess the client for substance abuse
   d. Take note of the drugs and alcohol, say nothing at the time, and follow-up later with the client.

8. Developing a professional identity that best reflects safety concerns while offsite does not include:
   a. Appropriate attire
   b. Greeting the client with a review of the purpose of the meeting
   c. Developing appropriate responses for situations that warrant caution
   d. Sitting in the location indicated by the client

Professional Identity

9. If you encounter agency expectations related to safety that you think may render you vulnerable to violence, using the NASW *Code of Ethics*, you must:
   a. Follow agency policy
   b. Consider your alternatives and determine your course of action. The Code of Ethics is silent on matters of safety
   c. Inform your supervisor
   d. Consider foremost the primacy of the client's best interest

Ethical Practice

10. The best <u>first</u> action when confronted with harassment, is to:
    a. Inform your field instructor
    b. Confront the harasser
    c. Consult with other social work students
    d. Document the harassment

Log onto **MySocialWorkLab** once you have completed the Practice Test above, to access additional study tools and assessment.

Answers

Key: 1) b 2) d 3) a 4) d 5) a 6) c 7) d 8) d 9) b 10) d

4

Making the Most of Your Practicum Supervision

Core Competencies in this Chapter (Check marks indicate which competencies are covered in depth)				
✓ Professional Identity	✓ Ethical Practice	☐ Critical Thinking	✓ Diversity in Practice	☐ Human Rights and Justice
☐ Research Based Practice	☐ Human Behavior	☐ Policy Practice	☐ Practice Contexts	☐ Engage, Assess, Intervene, Evaluate

What is *practicum supervision*, and why is it important? Social work educators and practitioners place considerable emphasis on the provision and receipt of supervision, in general, and on the field training experience, in particular. The Council on Social Work Education (CSWE) requires social work programs to "specify the credentials and practice experience of its field instructors necessary to design appropriate student learning opportunities to demonstrate program competencies" (2008, p. 10). CSWE also requires programs to provide "orientation, field instructor training and ongoing dialogue with field education settings and field instructors" (2008, p. 10).

A major component of the social work curriculum is delivered through a real-life, experiential field practicum in which you work directly with clients, client systems, community resources, and governmental bodies. For this reason, access to a seasoned social work practitioner who can serve as a teacher and guide to challenge and support you through the social work learning and socialization process is essential to your satisfaction in practicum. Your practicum/field supervisor or field instructor will play an important role in your social work education.

Supervision within the social work field experience is defined as the guiding and development of a person by a professional with more knowledge, skills, and experience (Shulman, 2008). The field instructor–student relationship is typically implemented through an individualized, one-on-one teaching arrangement based in a community agency (Bogo, 2005). Along with supervising practicum tasks and activities, the field instructor can (but may not always) become a mentor. The mentoring relationship is an interpersonal helping relationship between two individuals who are at different stages in their professional development that involves advice, consultation regarding professional development, and care about a person's career (Johnson, 2007). The mentoring relationship can continue beyond your practicum experience and maintain a prominent place in your professional growth and development. Even if the mentoring relationship dissipates over time, the experience may still hold a significant place in your development as a social work professional.

The mediocre teacher tells.
The good teacher explains.
The superior teacher demonstrates.
The best teacher inspires.
—William Arthur Ward

WHAT IS PRACTICUM SUPERVISION?

Operating within CSWE policies, each social work program establishes individualized criteria and policies for the specific implementation of field instruction by the agency and the field instructor. Thus, individual agencies and field instructors determine the teaching approach to be used.

An important distinction to make when describing practicum supervision is to note what is *not* included in the definition. First, practicum supervision should be distinguishable from employment supervision. The focus of *practicum supervision* is on the teacher–learner relationship, in which the learner grows and develops personally and professionally. *Employment supervision* emphasizes the supervision of the employee in the implementation of the duties for which he or she has been hired by the organization. Often, the employee learns and grows and the supervisor may become a mentor, but the primary mission is the delivery of social services by the employee. Second, supervision is not comparable to professional consultation. Consultation is considered as input/feedback that is intended to be suggestive or in recommendation form toward a work-related objective (Harkness, 2008). Consultation may be provided by a supervisor or colleagues and may be provided individually or in a group setting, such as a staff meeting.

Who Provides Practicum Supervision?

". . . being socialized into the profession by a social worker is considered the ideal learning environment"

Social work programs have the discretion to approve supervisory arrangements that meet the educational interests of the practicum student. Supervision can thus be provided by a graduate-level social worker, a baccalaureate-level social worker, or a non–social worker. Social work educators recognize that valuable learning can be facilitated by professionals from a variety of disciplines. Under specific circumstances, many social work programs will approve a field instructor who does not possess a social work degree. In fact, practicum students placed in agencies that do not employ social workers may have the opportunity to gain a nontraditional social work experience and learn interdisciplinary collaboration skills. However, most social work educators agree that non–social work supervision is not the optimal educational situation. Although a professional of a different discipline can enrich the student's learning, being socialized into the profession by a social worker is considered the ideal learning environment. Specific attention should be given to matching the learning needs, learning style, and personality of the student with the site and the field instructor, as well as taking the student's developmental level and the agency culture into consideration (Abram, Hartung, & Wernet, 2000).

Professional Identity

Supervision includes socialization into the social work profession. If you have a non-social work supervisor, how can your field instructor assist in your socialization into the social work profession?

In the case of a student being supervised by a non–social work supervisor, the social work program is, nonetheless, obligated to ensure that the student is provided with the social work perspective (CSWE, 2008). Each social work program has a policy for monitoring the provision of this perspective. The social work perspective may be provided by a degreed social worker employed elsewhere within the practicum agency, a volunteer with the organization, or a social work program faculty member. To ensure optimal learning, you should have a clear understanding of the parameters of a nontraditional supervisory arrangement and adhere to them.

Students may also have the opportunity to complete their practica at the sites in which they are employed (CSWE, 2008). A place-of-employment practicum can create opportunities for flexibility, providing service to your agency, learning different aspects of your agency, preparing for a new position, financial benefits, and expanded supervision. You should exercise caution if you are completing or considering this practicum arrangement because potential pitfalls include a diminished quality of learning, inadequate monitoring, confusion of your dual roles and relationships, and conflicting agency demands (Barlow, Pelech, & Badry, 2005). Additional requirements may be in place should you opt to complete a place-of-employment experience. Although a place-of-employment placement can be rewarding and can reduce the stress of balancing school, work, and practicum, you must call on your adult learner skills to ensure that you have a high-quality learning experience.

The Practicum Supervision Approach

The supervisor–supervisee relationship is an extremely important aspect of the social work student's educational experience (Bogo, 2005). You may come to admire and respect your field instructor for his or her knowledge, abilities, competence as a practitioner, and willingness to serve as a mentor. However, the field instructor–student relationship can also be emotionally charged, have elements of ambivalence and resistance, and elements of the parent–child relationship (Kadushin & Harkness, 2002). It is essential that both you and your field instructor are committed, knowledgeable, and clear regarding the parameters and expectations of the supervisory relationship. Attaining the optimal teacher–learner fit can be a goal for the student and field instructor as well as a part of the learning experience. Achieving an effective and meaningful relationship with your field instructor will enable you to take advantage of his or her knowledge and skills and to apply that experience to your current learning situation. Learning to negotiate and function effectively in a supervisory relationship can provide you with a foundation for future supervisory relationships in which you may be either a supervisee or a supervisor.

As an adult learner, you are responsible for identifying your learning style along with the teaching style of your field instructor. Routinely engaging in discussion about each other's style will enable you and your supervisor to continue to understand how the other processes and utilizes information. The insights gained from identifying your field instructor's supervision style will serve as a guide for your field instructor in assigning tasks and activities, teaching knowledge and skills, and evaluating your performance and progress.

Supervision style can be defined as the way your field instructor shares his or her theoretical orientation and practice and supervisory philosophies (Munson, 2002). The field instructor style may be generally categorized as (1) *active,* which is problem oriented, directive, and interpretive, or (2) *reactive,* which is process oriented, indirect, and noninterpretive (Munson, 2002). Which style of supervision does your field instructor use? How does this fit with your previously identified learning style?

Gaining awareness of teacher–learner styles does not guarantee a match of styles. An examination of the two individual styles may reveal that your field instructor's style is dissimilar to your learning style. Learning of such a mismatch need not predict supervisory relationship outcome. In fact, a teacher–learner style difference can serve as an opportunity for new learning for both the teacher and the student. Each of you can use the situation to explore different methods of interacting with someone who perceives the practicum experience with a different method of information processing. You can apply this experience to work with your clients, co-workers, agencies, and the community, who frequently perceive situations in a different light.

Regardless of field instructor–student style congruence, you may be initially unsure of and uncomfortable with this new relationship. Unless you have completed previous practica, your relationship with the field instructor will be unfamiliar. Initially, you may feel anxiety about your lack of skills (Gelman, 2004) and a greater sense of dependence on your field instructor, thus creating a desire for increased structure and more directive supervision. You are cautioned to resist the temptation to allow your learning style to be folded into the teaching style of your field instructor (Munson, 2002). Supervisees, often eager to learn and please the field instructor, may subjugate individuality to enhance the supervisory relationship. To normalize and allay such concerns, you should pay particular attention to preparing for your new role as a supervisee and consumer of social work supervision.

WHAT CAN I EXPECT FROM PRACTICUM SUPERVISION?

After reflecting on his concerns about boundary issues in his practicum site (delineating his social work role from his role as a recovering person and an Alcoholics Anonymous sponsor), Cameron discussed the issues with his field instructor. The field instructor validated Cameron's concerns and shared that other students and staff struggle with similar challenges. The field instructor suggested that both of them make a concerted effort to proactively address boundary issues and Cameron's concerns on an ongoing basis. What would you suggest to Cameron if his field instructor (1) had not been so supportive or (2) does not follow through with this commitment?

Cameron's situation is not uncommon. Students often have concerns about personal or professional issues that they need and want to raise with their field instructors but feel uncomfortable because they are unsure of what to expect from the supervisory relationship. When you begin your practicum, engage in exploration and self-reflection to gain clarity regarding your expectations of your field instructor, the supervisory relationship, and yourself. The field instructor–student relationship may be unlike any relationship you have previously experienced because your field instructor is responsible for monitoring the completion of tangible duties as well as for mentoring, teaching, and socializing you as a member of the social work profession and for evaluating and awarding or recommending a grade for the practicum. A legal obligation for your work is assumed by your field instructor (Lynch & Versen, 2003). Your supervisor can be sued by a client for work that you perform because your supervisor is legally responsible for your work (Lynch & Versen, 2003). You should enter the supervisory relationship with a clear understanding of the expectations of your field instructor and yourself, including the need to carefully and professionally document your work, share your documentation with your field instructor, and communicate important and professional aspects of your work in a clear and timely manner with your field instructor.

You may want to begin preparation for supervision by considering the reasons that a practitioner is motivated to serve as a field instructor. Gaining insight into your field instructor's motivations for supervising you may enable you to understand how your supervisor approaches and carries out the task. This role is voluntary, in most cases, and is sometimes completed above and beyond the field instructor's normal workload. Field instructors are intrinsically motivated to seek out the opportunity to mentor a new social work professional, but they may be unable to continue in this role on a long-term basis due to organizational or personal conflicts. Some social workers may also view serving as a field instructor as a way to return the gift of supervision and mentoring received earlier in their social work careers, and/or may view teaching through field instruction as a mechanism for further personal and professional growth (Globerman & Bogo, 2003). Unfortunately, some field instructors may be fulfilling an employment obligation and may perceive the student primarily as an additional staff resource. Regardless of the motivation, your field instructor makes a significant investment in your professional training by his or her willingness to serve as your field instructor.

Your expectations of practicum supervision might also be linked to the type of supervision that you receive. You might receive one or more different types of supervision:

- ▶ *Individual supervision* involves regularly scheduled, one-on-one meetings between your field instructor and you.
- ▶ *Small-group supervision,* a meeting that includes an instructor and two or more students, may augment individual supervision but should not be the sole source of supervision.
- ▶ *Peer supervision* involves meetings between social workers and students (and may or may not include your field instructor) in which feedback about work activities is sought.
- ▶ *Formal case presentations* are meetings in which you describe your work with a specific case and seek guidance from staff and other students.
- ▶ *As needed supervision* may also occur to provide guidance between formal meetings in addition to formal individual or small-group supervision.
- ▶ *Ad hoc supervision* can occur when you work side by side with your field instructor.

Ethical Dilemma: Addressing Your Field Instructor

The first few days of Rosa's practicum had not gone well. She had eagerly looked forward to starting her practicum. She arrived a few minutes early for the first day but then waited for 30 minutes in the agency parking lot until another worker arrived. Her field instructor arrived an hour later, had nothing for her to do the first day, and sent her home five hours early. On the second day, Rosa read files and shadowed her field instructor on home visits during the morning, but she was again sent home hours early because she was given nothing to do. While the clients seemed interesting, Rosa was very discouraged and did not know what to do. Her program faculty encouraged her to talk to her field instructor, but Rosa did not know how to professionally address her, particularly since she did not know her well. What should Rosa do? If you were Rosa and chose to have a conversation with the field instructor, what would you say?

Expectations of Your Field Instructor

Each member of your practicum team—the social work program, the agency, your field instructor, and you—will have similar but possibly differing perspectives on the implementation of the practicum and the structure and format of the student–field instructor relationship. Depending on the experience of all parties, the perspectives may range from the rigidly defined to the seemingly undefined. Although you are responsible for understanding the expectations placed on you, the social work program is responsible for conveying expectations and information to the agency, your field instructor, and you that is relevant for your placement and functioning within your practicum.

Practitioners assume special ethical obligations when agreeing to the task of field instruction. In addition to assuming the legal risks for your work, the NASW *Code of Ethics* (2008a) states that social workers who provide supervision have these responsibilities:

- ⟩ Possess necessary knowledge and skills to supervise or consult appropriately and should do so only within their areas of knowledge and competence.
- ⟩ Responsible for setting clear, appropriate, and culturally sensitive boundaries.
- ⟩ Avoid dual or multiple relationships when a risk of exploitation or potential harm to supervisees exists.
- ⟩ Evaluate performance in a fair and respectful manner.
- ⟩ Ensure that clients are routinely informed when services are provided by students.

The supervisory relationship is often a balancing act for your supervisor. The field instructor must balance his or her role as a worker, supervisor, or administrator with the added role as a field supervisor/teacher/mentor. If student supervision is a new role for your field instructor, he or she may be unsure of the expectations and responsibilities required of the role. Social work programs routinely provide a general orientation for new field instructors; however, some nuances and aspects of field instruction evolve as the practicum develops and are unique to the specific agency setting.

Regardless of the field instructor's longevity as a practicum supervisor, you and the field instructor must develop your own relationship. Initially, you may have only your past experiences as a supervisee (or supervisor) on which to rely, while the field instructor may have a wide repertoire of experiences on which to draw. The field instructor is responsible for initiating the relationship and setting the stage for the future of supervision. Box 4.1 provides general expectations for field instructor responsibilities:

Throughout the course of the practicum, you should receive feedback from your field instructor that focuses on areas in which you need to improve. While feedback ideally involves identifying strengths and specific suggestions for areas of improvement, you may experience anxiety about hearing balanced, constructive feedback from your field instructor. To grow professionally, remember that you need to hear both positive and challenging feedback. If your field instructor has not provided constructive feedback in the first few weeks, you might consider asking him or her to talk about needed changes and assure him or her that the feedback will help you become a more effective social worker.

Ethical Practice

The *Code of Ethics* clearly specifies that supervisors ensure that clients are informed when students deliver services. What would you do if your field instructor asked you not to reveal that you were a student to your clients?

"To grow professionally, remember that you need to hear both positive and challenging feedback"

BOX 4.1 Field Instructor Responsibilities

▶ Demonstrate commitment to your learning by creating a safe and trusting environment and culture that are conducive to optimizing your professional growth and development

▶ Transmit knowledge that integrates theory and practice activity and apply research knowledge and methodology to practice

▶ Provide a clear structure and format for the supervisory relationship, in general, and the supervisory sessions, in particular, that includes the following:

  ▶ Boundary limitations

  ▶ Expectations and goals of supervision

  ▶ Times and location of supervision sessions

  ▶ Format for supervision, including opportunities for alternative forms of supervision (group, interdisciplinary, peer, or off-site)

  ▶ Mutual preparation expected for supervision sessions (e.g., written agendas, case/project presentations, or topics identified for discussion)

▶ Serve as a professional role model by engaging in ethical, competent social work practice

▶ Demonstrate critical thinking by utilizing a variety of supervisory models, techniques and strategies that may be implemented through individual, group, or interdisciplinary supervision formats

▶ Possess a supervisory style that is flexible and responsive to your needs and stage(s) of development

▶ Commit to the supervisory arrangement by ensuring regular and consistent time for supervision, location, privacy, and absence of interruptions and by taking the initiative to make alternative arrangements if needed.

▶ Adhere to the social work program–agency training agreement regarding provision of supervision, learning opportunities, information, liability coverage, and safety precautions

▶ Commit to the creation and maintenance of an effective supervisory style that enhances student learning

▶ Assign appropriate tasks and activities based on practice behaviors that you must demonstrate, your level of experience, training, interests, and goals; these assignments should be clearly stated and include your participation in their development

▶ Communicate clear expectations about your performance of assigned tasks

▶ Establish and maintain an appropriate professional supervisor–supervisee relationship, including boundary setting (understanding behavior appropriate to a professional relationship) and avoiding the development of mutual/dual relationships with you (dual relationships, in this instance, refers to those relationships that are social, therapeutic, or financial/business in nature)

▶ Be sensitive to your feelings and appropriately ask you about your feelings and discuss your concerns

▶ Provide frequent, ongoing, and balanced feedback regarding your performance and progress toward practicum and personal goals

▶ Embrace the role of teacher and display a positive attitude when answering questions and providing explanations

▶ Assist you in being reflective about your performance

▶ Assist you in integrating classroom learning and field work

(Bogo, 2005; Bogo, et. al, 2004; Dettlaff & Wallace, 2002; Dill, 2007; Gourdine & Baffour, 2004; Itzhaky & Eliahou, 2001; Kadushin & Harkness, 2002; Knight, 2001; Lynch & Versen, 2003; Maidment, 2003; Munson, 2002; Reamer, 2006; Shulman, 2008).

Your attitude about hearing feedback will determine its usefulness. For example, expecting to learn something important, actively listening and accepting the validity of the message (if appropriate) are important to your potential for growth from feedback. You may wish to take notes to review later. Depending on the scope of the feedback, you may not be able to absorb the entire message at the time. If the feedback is particularly difficult to hear because it is not as positive as you had hoped, respond professionally in the moment by acknowledging the content of the message and its possible validity. Remember to ask questions to clarify your understanding of the behavioral changes needed, and refrain from getting defensive and argumentative. After the meeting, refrain from wholly accepting or rejecting the feedback containing needed changes.

Practice Application 4.1   Forewarned Is Forearmed

Within the first two weeks of your practicum (and before any differences of opinion have to be negotiated), ask your field instructor the following questions:

1. How would you like me to address any concerns or differences of opinion that may arise during my practicum?
2. How have you handled differences in the past?

Should a difference of opinion occur during your practicum, be mindful of keeping the discussion at the cognitive level. Strategies to employ include using "I" statements and avoiding references to feeling words (i.e., "I think . . ." versus "I feel . . .").

_____

Developed by Ellen Burkemper, PhD, LCSW, MFT

Consider the feedback carefully, and if needed, process the feedback with a friend. Reframe the feedback that may seem negative and critical into opportunities for future growth and development. Even if you decide to reject the feedback as inaccurate, consider the actions that led to the problematic perception and consider making changes. Finally, pay attention to feedback that is consistently similar. If you receive the same message from a variety of sources, the message is likely to be valid (Birkenmaier & Timm, 2003).

What Should I Expect from Myself in Supervision?

The supervisory relationship is a mutual and interactive process. Your field instructor is responsible for facilitating your application of theories and knowledge, learning agency policies and procedures, and professional socialization. While you are considering the contributions that your field instructor will make to your learning, you should also contemplate the responsibility that you will assume for the learning experience. Your expectations of yourself should be similar to those that you have of your field instructor and should include the following rules (CSWE, 2008; Ligon & Ward, 1998; Reamer, 2006):

Critical Thinking

Critical Thinking

Field instructors help students apply and integrate knowledge, including theory. How can you contribute to the process of identifying, analyzing and selecting multiple sources of knowledge for practice?

- Demonstrate a commitment to your own learning by being open to new learning and experiences, motivated to learn, flexible in your personal, theoretical, and practice ideas, interpersonally curious, committed to critical thinking, minimally defensive, and introspective about yourself.
- Clearly communicate your expectations of learning to your field instructor, including the practice behaviors, tasks, and activities that you wish to undertake and client populations and issues that you wish to experience.
- Develop your knowledge of the social work program's practicum policies and procedures.
- Commit to your supervisory arrangement by ensuring preparation, regularity, and consistency of time of supervision, location, privacy, and absence of interruptions.
- Adhere to the social work program's rules and expectations.
- Commit to the creation and maintenance of an effective supervisory arrangement that enhances your learning.
- Actively participate in the development of your educational/learning plan and utilize the plan as a working document to monitor your progress through the field experience.

- Clearly understand the evaluative criteria and ensure that the learning agreement matches the evaluation, and tasks and activities are moving you toward the goal of demonstrating practice behaviors and competence.
- Maintain an appropriate professional supervisor–supervisee relationship, which, in most cases, precludes development of dual relationships with your field instructor.
- Be willing to take risks and discuss your fears and anxieties regarding your practicum as well as controversial, uncomfortable issues with which you are confronted during your practicum experience.
- Be willing to provide feedback to your field instructor regarding his or her supervisory style.
- Commit to communicating with your social work program faculty for consultation and feedback throughout your practicum.

Personal disclosure is an issue that may arise for you as you work with your field instructor. There may be issues or experiences that you bring to the practicum experience that are relevant to share with your field instructor. For example, if you received services from a social worker earlier in your life and that experience influenced your decision to become a social worker, you may choose to share that experience. However, you may not feel comfortable sharing the issues that brought you into contact with a social worker, unless they have direct relevance to your practicum responsibilities. Sharing personal information and experiences is usually voluntary and done to enhance the supervisory experience. If you have personal information or experiences that are pertinent to your ability to deliver services, inform your field instructor of that part of your history. You may be required to share information with the agency if a criminal record, child abuse/neglect, or physical health check is required. If you are unsure about the appropriateness of sharing historical or current information about yourself (e.g., mental/physical illness, addiction, sexual assault/molestation, or criminal record), discuss this issue with your faculty liaison. As a general rule, sharing the information is preferred, as it can often enhance the quality of your learning experience.

In particular, self-disclosure about diversity in the supervisory relationship provides an opportunity to learn about the application of culturally competent

Practice Application 4.2 Supervision from the Other Side of the Desk

This practice application will help you gain insight into the field instructor's experience. It will enable you to assume the posture of a supervisory social worker. Read the following case and, using the list of questions provided, develop a plan of intervention from the field instructor's perspective. Following your completion of the questions, consider discussing or role-playing this case with your field instructor, with your fellow students, or in integrative practice field seminar.

The Case

Your practicum student has come to you in a very agitated and emotional state. She has just learned from another staff member that a support staff member who lives in the student's community has begun telling the agency's staff that she (the student) is a lesbian. The support staff person is in your department but does not report to you. While the information is, in fact, accurate, the student had purposefully not yet shared her sexual orientation with her family, other students, faculty, or practicum agency staff because she had not yet felt comfortable presenting herself as lesbian. As the field instructor, what should you do? What should you say to the student? How should you support the student? Is it appropriate for the support staff person to reveal this information without first approaching the student? What is your responsibility regarding the handling of the support staff person's behavior?

practice. Subjects relating to diversity often create discomfort and self-doubt, and can easily be avoided in supervision (and practice!). The supervisory relationship provides a venue for dialoging and learning about your ability to provide culturally competent practice to clients. Your field instructor may help you to normalize your feelings of discomfort about discussing diversity and oppression, facilitate candid discussion about dimensions of diversity that you are experiencing in the agency, including any differences between the two of you, and discuss the struggle of the agency to become more culturally competent. Your ability to discuss differences between the two of you, as well as implications of those differences, will strengthen your ability to have discussions about diversity with clients (Armour, Bain, & Rubio, 2004). You are encouraged to broach the topic with your field instructor, ask for assistance and feedback to grow in your cultural competence, take risks in these discussions, and remain open to growth as you learn about your strengths and areas for growth.

ETHICAL AND INTERPERSONAL ISSUES IN SUPERVISION

Lauren identifies equally with both of her racial and ethnic backgrounds (European and African). However, her new field instructor is extremely Afrocentric and feels adamant that anyone of African heritage should identify primarily with that heritage. Lauren is concerned that this issue may interfere with her practicum experience and could even affect her grade. What do you think she should or could do in this situation?

Although not every student will share Lauren's experience, some may encounter areas in which they and their field instructor differ. These differences may be related to personal (as in Lauren's case), philosophical, political, or work style issues. Having differences does not necessitate a negative experience and can create a powerful learning opportunity.

Despite the fact that most practica are relatively free of problems, occasional problems can occur. The nature of these problems can range from administrative to interpersonal to ethical. Such situations can create personal and professional dilemmas for you, your agency, and the social work program. If the problem is addressed appropriately, valuable learning can result for all involved. With effective communication, problems can be avoided. For example, if you are asked to share information about clients in class, gain permission first to share details about a case from your field instructor to make sure that no ethical violations occur inadvertently.

Some dilemmas can result from a lack of clear communication or understanding of philosophy, policy, or requirements. The NASW *Code of Ethics* (2008a) should be integrated into your supervisory sessions as a tool for interpreting and applying the profession's ethical standards. The *Code of Ethics* (2008a) is an essential facet of contemporary social work practice because it serves as a guide for practice and a resource when an ethical dilemma arises (and more than common sense is needed) (Reamer, 2006).

Regardless of your awareness of and sensitivity to ethical practice issues, situations may arise in which a problem becomes insurmountable and the practicum experience or site must be terminated. This situation should not continue without the prior involvement of the social work program faculty, whose responsibility it is to provide consultation, to intervene, and to mediate, if necessary.

Dilemmas that may arise for you may be categorized as problems with the field instructor–student relationship, with the agency, or with professional behavior/practice. Field instructor–student problems may include (Giddings, Vodde, & Cleveland, 2003):

▶ Student perception that field instructor is not assigning an appropriate number or type of assignments; not being clear regarding expectations, boundaries, or procedures; or not fulfilling the expectations set out in the learning plan regarding type and location of learning experiences

▶ A field instruction style that is either too rigid or authoritarian, or over- or lack of supervision

Agency problems may include the following:

▶ Your perception that you are not accepted by:

   ▶ Staff, possibly due to lack of clarity regarding the student role, or a perception of competition from the student

   ▶ Client system(s) or community, due to your status as a student

▶ Lack of adequate resources, space, or equipment available for your use

▶ Lack of availability of assignments for you due to decreased client census, inadequate funding, or inadequate administrative support for student involvement

Professional behavior/practice problems may include the following:

▶ Your perception that your field instructor or staff are behaving in an unprofessional or unethical manner in the areas of client–worker interactions, dual relationships, resource management, or field instructor–student relationship (e.g., sexual harassment, dual relationship, misuse of authority or power, and incompetent supervision).

Of particular relevance to the field instructor–student relationship is the issue of a sexual relationship developing. Not only can a sexual relationship be detrimental to a student's learning experience and self-esteem, but such a relationship also can be an abuse of power by the field instructor and creates considerable role conflict (Kadushin & Harkness, 2002).

Students are often fearful of raising potential issues with their field instructors, particularly when the problem is sensitive or controversial and when the field instructor is involved. To maintain your silence about a problem heightens the problem, and can result in missed learning opportunities. It is critical that you, your field instructor, and the social work program faculty be able and willing to raise and intervene in potential or actual problems at the point at which they first arise.

Proactive strategies may serve to prevent a conflict from occurring. For example, your ability to provide constructive feedback to those in positions of authority may significantly impact the quality of your practicum experience. Providing balanced feedback, or sharing information about your positive and negative perceptions and providing specific suggestions for areas that can be improved, is an important professional skill that can be developed in a practicum setting. While delivering positive feedback is easier than delivering feedback about areas for growth, the latter is vitally important. Providing an atmosphere of trust and a non-judgmental supervisory relationship can help students provide feedback about desired changes.

Some suggestions for providing negative feedback include the following (Birkenmaier & Timm, 2003):

1. Before meeting, prepare by structuring your message with careful wording. You might even consider writing key words down to help you deliver the message (particularly if you are nervous).

2. Consider framing your feedback in a sequence of positive feedback— needed changes—positive feedback. This sequence can convey a spirit of caring and sensitivity to the field instructor.

3. Focus on describing problematic behaviors, rather than your feelings or beliefs. Behaviors can be the focus of positive change efforts.

4. Discuss the problem behaviorally, accurately, and completely, and with assertiveness.

5. Use "I" language when describing the problem.

6. Check for your field instructor's understanding of the issues.

7. Depending on the problem, acknowledge that the feedback may be difficult to hear. Doing so can convey empathy and positive regard to the recipient.

8. Engage your field instructor in a dialogue, and problem solve about the feedback. Focus on the specific behavioral changes that you would like, and then link those changes to your learning goals ("These changes would help me have a better learning experience because . . .").

9. If needed, consider developing a behavioral contract that outlines a plan of action in which both you and your field instructor participate.

On the other hand, you are encouraged to be open to hearing constructive feedback about your performance. Munson (2002) offers these suggestions for receiving evaluative information:

1. Make an effort to hear the details provided without becoming immediately defensive about your performance.

2. Be open to the possibility that the information is, in fact, valid, and consider ways in which you can incorporate the information in a change of behavior.

3. Ask questions to clarify your understanding of the feedback provided. If specific behavioral information is not provided after repeated requests, the feedback may not be valid.

4. Keep the encounter professional. Do not assume that your field instructor is being critical of you as a person.

5. Resist the temptation (no matter how emotional you may become) to display anger, personalize (internally or externally) responsibility, refuse to listen to criticisms, deflect the attention to another issue, justify your behavior, blame the field instructor, trivialize the situation by using humor, or bargain for a revised evaluation.

6. Acknowledge that you have heard the information provided to you by your field instructor.

7. Initiate discussion regarding strategies for changing or improving your performance.

8. Reframe feedback that seems negative and critical into opportunities for future growth.

Practice Application 4.3 What Are You Saying and What Are You *Really* Saying to Your Field Instructor?

Monitoring your interactions with your field instructor is a helpful way to gain insight into your interpersonal skills and behaviors. For each of the following statements, consider the response that you would offer to address (1) the content (i.e., the substance or factual information) of the statement being presented to you and (2) the process (i.e., the dynamics between you and the field instructor) of the interpersonal interaction.

Field Instructor to Student

1. "I am quite concerned about whether I should have you see this particular client."

2. "The manual asks you to do it this way, but I'm thinking it might be better to approach it this other way."
3. "I am having a little bit of difficulty understanding how you are dealing with this client."
4. "I am concerned that you are taking on too much responsibility."

After you have developed responses from both the content and the process perspectives to these statements, discuss them with your field instructor and fellow students to gain additional perspectives.

_____

Developed by Ellen Burkemper, PhD, LCSW, MFT

In sum, your ability to provide and receive constructive feedback is an essential element of your professional development. If one or both is difficult for you initially, you are encouraged to purposefully work on these skills during your practicum experience.

STRATEGIES FOR MAXIMIZING THE EFFECTIVENESS OF YOUR PRACTICUM SUPERVISION

The practicum experience is intended to be a challenging and rewarding experience that can be enhanced by developing a repertoire of techniques and strategies designed to allow you to take full advantage of the learning opportunities. Although not exhaustive, the following list suggests areas in which you can take further responsibility for your learning:

- Prepare for supervisory sessions by developing a written agenda and sharing it with your field instructor prior to the meeting so that he or she can be prepared with the appropriate information or materials.
- Develop and maintain reasonable and realistic expectations of your supervisor regarding his or her time, availability, knowledge, and patience.
- Engage in professional behavior by being on time and fully engaged for all activities and supervisory sessions.
- Reflect on your attitudes, feelings and behavior when engaging in practicum activities, with the goal of increasing your self-awareness toward a professional use of self (Kadushin & Harkness, 2002).
- Document the supervision sessions (issues discussed, assignments, recommendations, and responsibilities), and share the notes with your field instructor (Floyd, 1995).
- Suggest a variety of supervision techniques, including reviewing process recordings and journals, reviews of audio/videotapes, role-playing, live supervision, and case presentation (Kadushin & Harkness, 2002).

▶ Utilize the learning agreement regularly as a tool for monitoring your learning and progress made toward your practicum, personal, and professional goals. Renegotiate the agreement as needed.

▶ Conduct meetings with your field instructor and any other staff members with whom you have worked during the practicum to discuss your performance evaluation (Kadushin & Harkness, 2002).

▶ Assert yourself in communicating with your field instructor regarding training needs and supervision issues or assignment of tasks and activities, particularly if you feel the assignment is inappropriate for your level of training, experience, and goals (Kadushin & Harkness, 2002).

▶ In the case of a problem or conflict with the field instructor or practicum setting, utilize any and all available resources provided by the social work program, university, agency, and professional social work organizations as soon as possible. If all perceived possibilities have been exhausted, request consultative or interventive support from social work practicum faculty.

Implicit in these suggestions is the need for you to be assertive when needed. Although we naturally desire to avoid difficult discussions or disagreements and are often encouraged to avoid such situations, your professional learning experience may be enhanced through assertive communication with your field instructor. Learning assertiveness skills can also strengthen your ability to implement your ethical mandate to advocate on behalf of your clients (NASW, 2008a).

Practice Application 4.4 Supervision: Expectations and Assessment

Both you and your field instructor should develop a list of your expectations and assessment criteria for the supervisory relationship. Specifically, you should develop a list of expectations for yourself and your field instructor, and the field instructor should develop a list of expectations for him- or herself as well as for you. Compare and contrast the completed lists and develop a mutually agreed-upon set of expectations of each other regarding supervision. Examples of areas to consider in developing your lists include the following:

Expectations of Self *(List specific expectations of yourself)*	Assessment Criteria *(List measurable outcomes used to determine whether expectations are achieved)*
Use of supervision	
Preparedness for supervision	
Follow-up to supervisory recommendations	
Demonstration of adult learning	
Demonstration of assertiveness	
Demonstration of appropriate professional feedback	
(Add your own)	

Expectations of Field Instructor *(List specific expectations you have for your field instructor)*	Assessment Criteria *(List measurable outcomes used to determine whether expectations are achieved)*
Preparedness for supervision	
Facilitation/stimulation of appropriate student learning opportunities	
Follow-up to student requests	
Constructive use of student feedback	
(Add your own)	

Practice Application 4.5 Use of Self: Finding Trends in Interactions?

To help you optimize your use of your practicum supervision, this practice application will help you explore your ongoing interactions with your field instructor. Develop a journal (or journal within your practicum journal) that specifically addresses your supervisory interactions. Spend approximately five minutes following each supervision session documenting your reactions to the session and your field instructor, paying special attention to your (1) cognitive reactions (i.e., what you are *thinking*), (2) affective reactions (i.e., what you are *feeling*), and (3) behavioral reactions (i.e., what you *do* as a result of what you were thinking and feeling). Identify the trends in each category.

_____

Developed by Ellen Burkemper, PhD, LCSW, MFT

Practice Application 4.6 Questions to Consider

This practice application is designed to help you explore your perceptions of practicum supervision. Develop responses to the following questions, and include discussion of your responses in an upcoming supervisory session.

1. What is practicum supervision, and how does it differ from other types of supervision?
2. For each of the following, identify four characteristics and explain the reasoning behind them:
   a. A practicum supervisor who would fit your learning style.
   b. A difficult practicum supervision relationship.

3. What emotions do you think you will (or did) experience at the beginning of your practicum related to supervision? Why? How have you reacted in the past to any other type of supervisory experiences, and how may these reactions and experiences influence your current/future supervisory experiences?
4. Identify four learning experiences that you would like to receive from a practicum. What kinds of supervisory activities would facilitate the accomplishment of these goals?

_____

Developed by Doris Westfall, LCSW

Practice Application 4.7 A Student's Worst Fear

In this practice application, you have the opportunity to examine a challenging situation from a dual perspective—your own and your field instructor's. Read the following scenario, and respond to the questions that follow. Share this exercise with your field instructor, and ask him or her to share his or her reactions to the scenario.

(*continued*)

Practice Application 4.7 A Student's Worst Fear   (*continued*)

The Scenario

During a group therapy session, a student strongly confronts a client regarding the client's interpersonal behaviors with other family members. As a result, the client writes an unflattering evaluation of the program and the student.

Discussion Questions

1. If you were this student, how would you feel and how might you respond to this situation, particularly as you discuss the evaluation in supervision?

2. If you were the student's practicum instructor, how would you respond to the situation, and what might you say to the student during supervision?

_____

Developed by Doris Westfall, LCSW

SUMMARY

The field instructor–practicum student relationship is a unique and powerful part of your professional development as a social worker. As discussed in this chapter, an important facet of a successful supervisor–supervisee association lies with the negotiation and communication that occurs throughout the learning process. The primary factor that predicts your perception of your field instructor is the field instructor's skill and the quality of the experience created by the field instructor (Bogo, 2005). As you move through your practicum, you have the opportunity to be mentored by an experienced social work professional, to learn skills necessary for social work practice, and to gain insights into your thoughts, feelings, and values, toward the development of your professional self.

Cameron demonstrated the skills of an adult learner by sharing his concerns with his field instructor regarding his worries about his potentially conflicting roles. He took a risk that his field instructor would suggest that a substance abuse treatment facility is not an appropriate practicum for someone who clearly has not resolved his own addiction issues. Fortunately, the field instructor validated Cameron's concerns and shared that other students and staff struggle with similar challenges. Cameron's field instructor suggests that both of them make a concerted effort to address proactively boundary issues and Cameron's concerns on an ongoing basis. Had the field instructor not been supportive of Cameron's concerns, he would be faced with two choices.

1. He could have stated his case to his field instructor and asked for the opportunity to forge on with his practicum. He may have experienced difficulty, however, as he would be both struggling with his own recovery issues and working in an environment in which he may now not feel comfortable.
2. He could have opted to leave his practicum.

Fortunately, Cameron continued in his practicum and in his journey toward his own recovery.

Had Cameron's field instructor initially conveyed support and then not provided it, Cameron would be faced with choices similar to those just described. Cameron is an adult learner who assumes responsibility for his own learning, and could therefore confront his field instructor regarding the lack of follow-up.

Lauren has identified an issue (racial and ethnic identification) that may significantly impact her practicum experience, particularly if she does not feel that she can adequately address her concerns. After considerable reflection and discussions with her fellow students and a trusted faculty member, Lauren elected to raise the issue with her field instructor in a supervisory session. Initially, the field instructor exhibited a defensive posture and inquired whether Lauren was accusing her of being discriminatory. Her field instructor's response was the worst-case scenario that Lauren had anticipated but had hoped would not occur. She wanted to run out of the room. But, with professionalism, Lauren stated that she was not suggesting this but was concerned that the field instructor might have negative feelings toward Lauren because she does identify equally with both her European and African heritages. Because Lauren was calm and mature, the field instructor was eventually able to hear Lauren's concerns and engage in dialogue that was ultimately helpful for Lauren (who had little experience with an extreme Afrocentric perspective). As a result of this discussion, Lauren gained insight into the contribution that an Afrocentric perspective can offer in empowerment work with clients. In addition, Lauren and her field instructor were able to discuss issues of diversity openly in a meaningful way.

Log onto **MySocialWorkLab** to access a wealth of case studies, videos, and assessment. (*If you did not receive an access code to* **MySocialWorkLab** *with this text and wish to purchase access online, please visit* www.mysocialworklab.com.)

1. Under the competency videos, choose Ethical Practice, then watch Recognizing Personal Values. In the video, the client shares personal decisions about which a social worker may not agree. How might a field instructor assist a student to prepare for this type of situation? How would a supervisor best assist a student who did not ethically handle a situation?

2. Under the competency videos, choose critical thinking, then watch Applying Critical Thinking. In this video, the social worker begins to take a history of the client's experience with domestic violence. How could a field instructor help you apply critical thinking in this situation? Watch the vignette with your field instructor, and discuss the practice behaviors that demonstrate critical thinking that are demonstrated.

PRACTICE TEST The following questions will test your knowledge of the content found within this chapter. For additional assessment, including licensing-exam type questions on applying chapter content to practice, visit **MySocialWorkLab.**

1. The following aspects about a supervisory relationship are true, except:
   a. The relationship is typically implemented through a one-on-one arrangement
   b. The field instructor can additionally become a mentor
   c. The mentoring relationship must cease at the end of the practicum
   d. If the relationship is not satisfactory, the student is advised to take some action

   Diversity in Practice

2. Supervision cannot be provided by:
   a. A graduate-level social worker
   b. A non-social worker
   c. A baccalaureate-level social worker
   d. A staff member without a degree

3. If the student has a learning style that differs from the teaching style of the field instructor, the student should not:
   a. Bring the difference to the attention of the field instructor
   b. Accommodate his/her learning style to the teaching style of the field instructor
   c. Seek consultation from other students
   d. Seek consultation from the Faculty Liaison

4. Types of practicum supervision does not include:
   a. Individual   c. Web-based
   b. Peer   d. Ad hoc

   Ethical Practice

5. Social workers who provide supervision have specific responsibilities, including:
   a. Evaluating performance in a fair and respectful manner
   b. Suggesting that students to inform clients that they are a student
   c. Sharing responsibility with students to maintain clear, appropriate, and culturally sensitive boundaries
   d. Gaining necessary knowledge, skills and values to supervise

6. The following are all ways to increase the potential for growth from feedback except:
   a. Expecting to learn something important
   b. Actively listening
   c. Overlooking feedback that is incorrect and acting on feedback that is correct
   d. Accepting the validity of the message

7. The following is true about diversity in the supervisory relationship except:
   a. The supervisory relationship provides a venue for dialogue about diversity within the supervisory relationship
   b. The supervisory relationship should be well developed prior to a discussion about diversity within the supervisory relationship
   c. The field instructor can promote a discussion about diversity in the supervisory relationship by normalizing student feelings of discomfort
   d. Discussion about diversity within the supervisory relationship will strengthen student ability to have discussions about diversity with clients

8. Some suggestions for delivering negative feedback to those in positions of authority does not include:
   a. Checking first with the person's supervisor
   b. Framing your feedback in a sequence of positive feedback – needed changes –positive feedback
   c. Using "I" language when describing the problem
   d. Engaging your field instructor in a dialogue

9. Suggestions for receiving evaluative information does not include:
   a. Asking questions to clarify your understanding of the feedback provided
   b. Being open to the possibility that the information is valid
   c. Professionally communicating your need to end the encounter if the feedback is unfairly critical
   d. Acknowledging that you have heard the information provided to you

Log onto **MySocialWorkLab** once you have completed the Practice Test above, to access additional study tools and assessment.

Answers:

Key: 1) c 2) d 3) b 4) c 5) a 6) c 7) b 8) a 9) c

5

Organizational Context

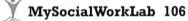
Core Competencies in this Chapter (Check marks indicate which competencies are covered in depth)				
✓ Professional Identity	☐ Ethical Practice	☐ Critical Thinking	✓ Diversity in Practice	✓ Human Rights and Justice
☐ Research Based Practice	☐ Human Behavior	☐ Policy Practice	☐ Practice Contexts	☐ Engage, Assess, Intervene, Evaluate

Organizations are like a puzzle
Little pieces everywhere
Every piece is symbolic
Pieces of fate and pieces of care
Each puts his piece together and when they are set
A single effort is what we get
Together all the pieces make one whole
United in one goal
—Adapted from "The Missing Piece" (Jason Garay)

The feedback from Ben's supervisor about his first few weeks of practicum at the community-based outreach program was mixed. He was told that although he was performing adequately with clients, he needed to be more independent and to take more initiative to do things on his own. Co-workers had complained that he was too hesitant to carry out his work autonomously and he constantly asked others for guidance and permission to conduct activities with which he should have been comfortable. Ben agrees with the assessment. He is confused about which staff member to turn to with questions and the limits of his autonomy to carry out work on his own. Ben feels that his previous work experience in a publicly funded research institution has not prepared him for work in this setting. How can Ben gain the knowledge he needs to succeed in this organization? What does he need to know? What are some of the differences between public and nonprofit agencies?

Many social work students are enthralled with the idea that they are finally going to be able to work with individuals and families in their practica. However, like Ben, you may find that your previous work experience has not prepared you to work in your practicum setting. Expectations differ widely from setting to setting—a work style that works well at one organization may not fit another organization. You may be puzzled in the early weeks about your inability to serve clients to the extent needed. You may be so busy learning about the logistics of service delivery in the first few weeks of practicum that you may not have the time to gather information about the organization.

Accredited social work programs must establish standards for approving field practicum settings within the guidelines of the Council on Social Work Education's (CSWE) accreditation standards (CSWE, 2008). Programs are required to provide students with the opportunities to develop competencies and corresponding practice behaviors, including the ability to analyze social and agency policy that impacts practice, the ability to respond to contexts that impact practice, and the ability to engage in professional practice within organizations (CSWE, 2008). Your analysis of your agency context is a critical element of your field learning experience.

Ben has come to realize that understanding the context in which services are delivered in his agency is important to his performance and to the quality of his services. He is struggling with both his knowledge of the context of the services delivered and his socialization into the agency. As you begin to work with client systems, you will begin to discover the importance of the agency context. The image you create within the organization—your behaviors, relationships, and methods of interacting with others—can be critical to your practicum success and satisfaction. The professional working style you develop in the early part of your practicum may have ramifications for you throughout the duration of your practicum and your future career. Based on your performance of duties early in the practicum, your supervisor and other staff may make decisions about your practicum activities and level of responsibility. Striving to exceed minimum requirements to learn about and become a part of the agency may enable you to be viewed as a desirable future employee. Being perceived as a student who is willing to go above and beyond requirements can be positively noted in job references made by your field instructor and other staff.

. . . The image you create within the organization – your behaviors, relationship, and methods of interacting with others – can be critical to your practicum success and satisfaction."

This chapter will focus on the importance of understanding the organization within which you will complete your practicum, the essential elements of an organization, strategies to uncover needed information about the agency, and the process of becoming socialized into an organization. Nonprofit, for-profit, and public organizations are defined; differences between them are explained; and the positive and challenging factors of working within each type of organization are debated. Faith-based organizations are discussed. Finally, the impact of various leadership theories on organizations is discussed and the role of social work within organizations is defined.

Ethical Dilemma: Staff Interactions

Rosa was experiencing difficulty acclimating to her practicum agency. She was troubled by her interaction with two staff members. She was told by her field instructor that staff members would help with any typing or filing needed. However, they both seemed very impatient with her when she asked them about doing things. She tried to be unassuming in asking for their help by assuring them that the tasks were not urgent and thanking them profusely when they completed the tasks. However, her greetings to them in the hallway were not returned, and they both appeared frustrated and were rude when she made requests. The turnaround time on work that she gave them was unreasonably long. Her field instructor insisted that she should continue to give work to the staff, but she wished that she could avoid working with them. What should she do? Is this an ethical dilemma?

THE IMPORTANCE OF ORGANIZATIONAL KNOWLEDGE

Many students find the early weeks of practicum to be a series of emotional highs and lows. Beginning a professional role in an agency and serving clients can be exhilarating. More complex, however, can be gaining insight into the culture and function of your practicum agency. Organizations can be very complicated; mastering an understanding of the agency can take time and the persistence needed to work through early challenges.

Most social work practice takes place within the parameters of an agency's mission, philosophy, values, communication structure, and resources. Just as the environment of your clients is pivotal to their social functioning, the framework of your sponsoring organization is a defining influence on your social work practice.

You may find your role as a practicum student in your practicum agency to be clearly defined, your role well understood by agency staff and administrators, and mechanisms established to enable you to glean the important information about the agency. However, some students find their positions within agencies to be nebulous, misunderstood by others, and unclear even to them. Are you a staff member? Volunteer? Is your role as practicum student clearly delineated? Where can students get information about the agency administrative context?

For many students, accessing information about the agency's structure and administration and the students' role is akin to a scavenger hunt. If you find yourself in the latter situation, be persistent and willing to work through the unknown. As a social worker, your understanding of agency functioning becomes the backdrop and basis for your work. Agency structures, procedures, culture, and relationships with external systems directly affect the work you can do with clients (Cameron et al., 2009).

As a student, you can make a difference in the lives of your clients by possessing thorough knowledge of your organization. You will possibly engage in work at all system levels within your practicum organization. For example, within agencies that stress practice with individuals, families, and groups, you can observe staff and management meetings, gather data utilized for evaluation of services, and attend interagency meetings. In agencies that emphasize practice at the community and/or organizational levels, you may engage in direct practice by utilizing effective communication skills with staff members of your practicum site and facilitating task meetings. Later in this chapter, suggestions for uncovering administrative information and becoming involved in administrative functions are provided.

INTERNAL ELEMENTS OF AN ORGANIZATION

Organizations are defined as "collectives of individuals gathered together to serve a particular purpose" (Netting, Kettner, & McMurtry, 2008, p. 213). Whether you are completing your practicum in a for-profit, nonprofit, or public agency or within a large, medium, or small agency, your practicum organization was established to serve a purpose that would be impossible to accomplish well by one individual. Your practicum site is an entity that has many features that make it distinct from any other agency, including a history, culture, goals and objectives, structured administrative and service delivery system(s), communication patterns and practices (Netting et al., 2008). As a type of organization, social service agencies have problems that differ from those of other organizations in which you may have worked (see Box 5.1). As you begin to examine your practicum organization and observe its characteristics and administrative style, a brief discussion of types of organizations may assist you.

BOX 5.1 Common Challenges of Social Service Organizations

The following are several categories of challenges common to social service agencies. Many problems stem from the complexity of working with human beings (Kirst-Ashman & Hull, 2009). These include:

1. *Unstable environment:* Funding sources, social policy, accreditation standards, and affiliated organizations are in constant flux.
2. *Oversight difficulties:* The nonstandardization of human services makes oversight inherently difficult.
3. *Lack of clear, measurable organizational goals of service delivery:* Evaluating the effectiveness of services is difficult without quantifiable performance goals.
4. *Goal displacement:* The shift from an original goal of the agency to meet an identified human need to the goal of organizational survival can alter service delivery.
5. *Impersonal behavior:* Individuals both inside (i.e., employees) and outside organizations sometimes experience difficulty understanding that organizational actions are not a personal response to them; using policies and procedures, organizations demonstrate impersonal behavior (i.e., the motive behind an organizational action is not a personal response to an individual).
6. *Lack of rewards and recognition:* Social service organizations often lack a system of positive, public feedback to employees.

GOVERNMENTAL (PUBLIC) ORGANIZATIONS

Public organizations are federal, state, regional, county and city government entities. Like in any type of organization, there are positive and challenging aspects of working within public organizations. For example, depending on the source of funding, public organizations may have to comply with mandates, rules, regulations and procedures, and be highly responsive to elected officials (Netting et al., 2008). Other challenging characteristics of a public agency can include large quantities of paperwork, complex rules and procedures, a relatively rigid bureaucratic structure, lack of staff training, poor quality supervision, and a conservative administrative philosophy. Government agencies often have less flexibility, due to a higher degree of control within the top layers of administration (General Accounting Office, 2003) and social stigma is often attached to those receiving services from a public agency (Johnson & Schwartz, 1997).

Several advantages exist for those working within public agencies. Compared to working within the private (i.e., nonprofit and for-profit) sector, needed services in some public agencies can be offered to clients with less consideration given to cost effectiveness. Furthermore, social workers in public agencies tend to enjoy relative predictability and job security, due to a fairly stable funding source (McInnis-Dittrich, 1994), and they enjoy higher salaries than in the nonprofit and for-profit sectors, depending on the position (O'Neill, 2002; Whitaker, Weismiller, & Clark, 2006). Clients served are typically those without many alternatives; therefore, they tend to be those with few resources. Social workers in these agencies carry out social work's historical preference for working on behalf of those in most need.

The future for public agencies may force significant changes. Since the 1980s, services traditionally delivered by government agencies are increasingly being delivered by the private sector under the presumption that the private sector can deliver services in a more efficient and effective manner than can large government bureaucracies. Predictions are that this trend will continue and that the role of government will continue to shift from service provider to supervisor of services delivered by private agencies (Patti, 2008). Examples of government agencies commonly used as practicum sites include public child welfare agencies, aging services, veteran health systems, and corrections institutions. A practicum in a public setting can offer the opportunity to gain knowledge about the public social service system that can prove invaluable whether you stay within a public setting or move to a private setting after graduation. Students in these settings work with a wide range of client issues and with clients presenting complex problems because governmental agencies tend to be the resource of last resort for clients. Providing services to clients with complicated or chronic problems can challenge your social work abilities and provide you with excellent experience.

FOR-PROFIT ORGANIZATIONS

The number of for-profit social service agencies has grown, and social work programs are increasingly utilizing these agencies as practicum sites (Green, Baskind, Mustian, Reed, & Taylor, 2007). In contrast to *nonprofit* organizations, the driving goal of *for-profit* (or *proprietary*) agencies is to produce a profit for their owners or shareholders. A for-profit agency may be a small, one-agency business (such as a private practice) or part of large, centralized, diversified national corporations (such as a health maintenance organization). The capitalistic, free-enterprise economic system in the United States and the process of privatization of services have catalyzed the growth of for-profit social service agencies, as under this system, business has looked to new, expanding markets for growth (Holden, 2005). For-profit agencies have expanded into many areas of social services, particularly employee assistance programs, addictions treatment, residential care facilities, medical and psychiatric hospitals, home health services, health maintenance organizations, and child welfare services (Netting et al., 2008; Patti, 2008). Common for-profit practicum sites are hospitals, residential care facilities, and outpatient health care agencies. One-fourth to one-third of social work programs use private practice settings for practica (Green et al., 2007).

There can be obvious advantages to completing a practicum in a for-profit setting. Many social workers ultimately expect to practice in for-profit agencies or private practice settings; therefore, completing a practicum in a for-profit setting can help prepare you for the real world of practice within the type of setting in which you might hope to find employment (Green et al., 2007). Students in a proprietary setting can also help the agency carry out the goals of client-centered human services and help to ensure the fulfillment of for-profits' moral and legal obligations to serve the community. Because the mission is earning a profit in for-profit settings, social workers in these settings may find it necessary to advocate for client-centered services such that the provision of needed services to individual clients and the community is the primary concern of service delivery (Kong, 2007).

Social work field faculty may be apprehensive about placing students in for-profit agencies (Green et al., 2007). Prior to 1950, professional social work was practiced almost exclusively in public and nonprofit organizations (Green et al., 2007). Unique barriers to the successful achievement of learning competencies and practice behaviors can exist in the for-profit setting, where profit motive is the driving factor behind service delivery and there is a high degree of control over types of clients served and eligibility criteria (Lohmann & Lohmann, 2008). For-profit settings may not serve poor and oppressed populations, which could pose a challenge to the socialization aspect of the practicum. For-profit settings may also stress the need to provide services to clients fairly quickly, which may be challenging for the student learning process that requires time for a thorough decision-making process, reflection, and supervision.

NONPROFIT ORGANIZATIONS

Most social services are offered through a wide range of nonprofit organizations (Holland, 2008). Private nonprofit organizations can be *sectarian* (affiliated with an organized faith tradition) or *nondenominational* (freestanding, without ties to the government or to an organized faith tradition) (Boddie, 2008). Unlike for-profit organizations, many nonprofit social service organizations have historical commitments to serve the poor (Netting et al., 2008). Nonprofit social service organizations also vary considerably in size, from advocacy organizations with single staff members to hospitals with thousands of staff members, although most are generally small (O'Neill, 2002).

Nonprofit organizations tend to have diverse funding bases. Possible sources include government funding (e.g., contracts, grants, fee-for-service agreements, and matching funds); direct client payments; fundraising appeals and events; grants from private foundations; donations from individuals; a

Human Rights and Justice

For-profit organizations strive to produce a profit for their owners or shareholders. Yet, each person has basic human rights. Can for-profit organizations engage in practices that advance social and economic justice, if the primary motive of the organization is to produce a profit?

religious denominational sponsor; endowments; investments; third-party payers (i.e., insurance companies); indirect contributions (e.g., United Way); memberships; and a for-profit unit of the agency. Nonprofit organizations also benefit from in-kind sources of revenue such as volunteer time and tax benefits. Nonprofit agencies classified as 501c(3) organizations by the Internal Revenue Service (IRS) are exempt from paying most federal taxes, and most contributions to them are tax deductible to the contributor (Wing, Pollak, & Blackwood, 2008). Nonprofits tend to aspire to a very diverse funding base to ensure autonomy and flexibility. With a diverse funding base, the loss of one source would not risk the existence of an organization. On a national scale, nonprofit organizations rely on government sources for approximately half of their funding (O'Neill, 2002), therefore, governmental policy changes can dramatically affect the work of most nonprofit organizations. Due to declining government resources for social services and a changing economic climate, many nonprofits have utilized multiple strategies to maintain their mission, to include increased fundraising activities (Golensky & Mulder, 2006), and may resemble the corporate sector (Kong, 2007). Still, social workers employed within nonprofit organizations tend to be paid less than their counterparts in the public and for-profit sectors (Jayaratne & Faller, 2009).

Nonprofit organizations rely on the use of volunteers for a variety of purposes. Most of these agencies have all-volunteer boards of directors, while others involve volunteers directly in the operations of the agency through fundraising, public relations efforts, and even service delivery. Due to the range of size of agencies and the scope of services delivered, practicum experiences within nonprofit social service organizations vary considerably. Although resources may be more constrained in a nonprofit than in a for-profit organization, you will likely find that the agency readily serves vulnerable and disenfranchised populations. Both nonprofit organizations and staff within nonprofits tend to have the ability to respond with more creativity and flexibility to client needs and can offer more flexibility than can those in public agencies. If you find that flexibility, creativity, and innovation are important to you, you may find that a nonprofit agency is well suited to your style.

One type of nonprofit organization commonly found in social services is the *faith-based organization,* which is directly associated with a religious group or a denomination of a faith. Such an organization pursues a dual mission for its clients and spiritual growth for those involved in its operation. This mix of service provision and spirituality makes faith-based organizations unique and challenging (Boddie, 2008). Faith-based organizations may have a complex governance structure, possibly including a board of directors as well as a religious entity, overseeing all aspects of operations. Directions for services may come through many layers of decision making, and service delivery may be structured around particular religious beliefs. Staff and volunteers may be members of a particular religious faith and feel a particular religious calling for their work. Social workers in faith-based organizations often have the option (or requirement) of addressing certain issues, such as spirituality and reproduction issues, with their clients (Birkenmaier, Rubio, & Berg-Weger, 2002).

Of course, no agency exists in a vacuum; each affects and is affected by its environment. Of current concern to nonprofits is the turbulent environment many nonprofits are facing. Recent economic developments and social policy changes—such as the devolution of human services from the federal to state governments, increased privatization of human services, and increased accountability requirements—have impacted nonprofit organizations and changed services. Such changes have impacted agencies, and, in turn, those that work within them. As a result of these changes, students in nonprofits often function as staff members and fill service gaps within these agencies.

AGENCY SIZE

In addition to the type of agency, the size of an organization can also affect the practice of social work. In particular, very large and very small agencies can offer unique opportunities and challenges.

Large Agencies

Large agencies are considered "centralized" and have formal structures with organizational charts, formal channels of communication, and lines of authority specified in writing (Kirst-Ashman & Hull, 2009). Public, private, and nonprofit organizations can be large, bureaucratic agencies (see Box 5.2). Although some believe large organizations have more ability to deliver efficient and effective

---

BOX 5.2 How to Survive in a Bureaucracy

In addition to the tips outlined in chapter 2 and chapter 4, the following tips may help you thrive in a practicum within a large, bureaucratic organization (Knopf, 1979):

1. Treat administrators with the same respect with which you would treat clients. Administrators are human beings with feelings. Resolve conflict without resorting to dehumanizing the opposing party.

2. Avoid extreme adversarial situations with bureaucracies. Organizations will often find a way to weed out individuals who are extremely adversarial in their dealings with the bureaucratic structure.

3. As a practicum student, you are in the role of learner. This role may limit your ability to affect change within the organization.

4. If your needs or those of your clients are not being met, talk with your field instructor. Seek permission to use the problem-solving approach to attempt to address the need (i.e., [a] identify the unmet needs within the bureaucracy or service delivery; [b] generate a wide range of options for meeting the needs; [c] evaluate the positive and negative merits of each option; [d] select a solution; [e] implement the solution; and [f] evaluate the solution).

5. If you do not receive permission to make any changes, realize that you are a short-term guest in the environment. You may not fully understand the context, history, or current efforts being made to address unmet needs. Recommit to your

learner role and strive to learn all you can about the difficulties in the system as well as efforts that have already been made and those currently being made to address problems.

6. Develop and maintain a support system with your colleagues at the practicum. Use the informal system of the agency as much as possible.

7. If you receive permission to work toward a change, focus on an area(s) over which you have some control. Dismiss the illusion that you can change everything, and spend your energies on those areas that you have a reasonable chance of influencing. Start small and build to larger problems.

8. Interact with the bureaucracy with neutral emotions. Control counterproductive emotions (i.e., angry outbursts), and learn to channel and deal with stress in appropriate ways.

9. Seek opportunities to interact with the administrators in informal settings. Sit with your supervisor and other administrators at lunch, or attend occasional weekend social gatherings. Work-related socializing prevents isolation and can provide you with a glimpse of administrative issues at the agency.

10. Seek self-actualization and meaning in life through other pursuits, to maintain a balanced life.

11. Periodically assess if your career goals can be achieved in the bureaucracy of your practicum site. If they cannot, consider seeking employment in a different bureaucracy or a smaller agency after graduation.

services, others believe that the highly specialized units, close supervision, and minimal independent functioning that characterize large agencies offer little discretion to the work and may impede their efficiency and effectiveness (Kirst-Ashman & Hull, 2009). As a practicum student, you may find that working within a large organization requires considerable knowledge of forms, procedures, and the lines of authority. However, large organizations can offer opportunities to learn competencies and practice behaviors within a variety of programs and services.

Large systems can pose formidable challenges for the delivery of human services. For example, while the primary interest of helping professionals is the interests of the clients, large agencies typically consider agency survival and growth as the primary concerns. This tension between the social worker's and the employing organization's primary concerns can cause value conflicts. Although large organizations typically resist innovation and change, social workers within them can advocate to tailor services to meet needs of clients within the policies and guidelines of the organization.

Small Agencies

Small for-profit and nonprofit agencies are usually more decentralized than public, larger organizations, and offer workers discretion and a wide variety of possible experiences (Kirst-Ashman & Hull, 2009). These agencies also typically have a less formal structure than larger agencies. Students in these settings are often required to exercise more autonomy, independence, and initiative than in large agencies because smaller agencies often have less structure in place for employees and students. If you are completing a practicum within a small agency setting, you may find that you are quickly able to assume a great deal of responsibility. Job responsibilities for the staff are often fluid. Students in these settings are often required to become autonomous quickly, to be able to work in informal settings, and to assist others in collective tasks.

Management in Agencies

As a result of recent changes in social service delivery, including the increase of privatization of services, all types of agencies are experiencing an increased emphasis on more economic, efficient, and effective services. In general, agencies

Practice Application 5.1 Reflections on Practice Context

To gain a clearer perspective on the type of agency in which you are completing your practicum, follow this list:

1. Define your practicum site as a nonprofit, for-profit, or public entity.
2. Categorize it as a small, medium, or large agency.
3. With a member of your practicum team, discuss the characteristics of your agency relative to the following:
   a. The source and amount of funding
   b. The number and type of clients served
   c. Community perception of the agency
   d. Personnel issues (e.g., turnover, job security, salaries, morale)
   e. The amount and type of bureaucracy

Compare and contrast your practicum setting and experience within the setting with those of other students.

are experiencing increased competition for funding, and in some cases, clients, the effects of increased contracting of services from public to private agencies, increased scrutiny and accountability regarding outcomes of services, increased expectation of productivity with fewer resources, and increased attention to consumerism (Aldgate et al., 2007). In your practicum experience, you may notice these forces and trends as they impact agency functioning. For example, you may be asked to achieve measurable and/or preset outcomes in your services with clients. You may also participate in staff meetings where managers ask staff for increased flexibility, creativity, and accountability in their service provision. The greater complexity of management tasks in agencies may mean that you may notice these trends in service delivery and work with managers under increased pressure to respond to these contemporary forces.

THE ROLE OF SOCIAL WORK WITHIN THE ORGANIZATION

Social work settings can be classified as primary and secondary. *Primary settings* are those in which social work is the primary profession represented within the organization. The advantage of this type of setting for the employees is shared values and perspectives emanating from similar education and training. The roles, responsibilities, and abilities of social workers are understood throughout the organization (Kirst-Ashman & Hull, 2009). Examples of primary settings are child welfare agencies, domestic violence shelters and counseling, and mental health and family service agencies. If your practicum is in a primary social work setting, you may notice a high level of camaraderie among the staff. There may be a shared vision and agreement among the staff regarding the services needed by clients. Due to the lack of professional diversity

within the setting, staff may experience greater difficulty with interdisciplinary collaborative projects, which require skill in working and negotiating across various disciplines.

Secondary (or *host*) *settings* are those settings in which there is a variety of professional staff, such as health care organizations, correctional facilities, and schools. Secondary settings can be challenging for social workers because they must learn the language of other disciplines. Social work values and perspectives can clash with those of other professionals (Kirst-Ashman & Hull, 2009). In these settings, social workers may find themselves possessing little power to make or carry out decisions that involve other professionals. If you are in a secondary setting, you may find the field instructor providing detailed instructions regarding collaborative work with a group of professionals or describing the history of relationships between social workers and other staff. Working in such a setting usually requires increased assertiveness, tact, and awareness of the role of power within relationships. Take the opportunity to notice the topics and activities around which perspectives diverge between members of the professional staff and the method by which such conflicts are resolved. You may notice that after working within a secondary setting, you are easily able to articulate the role of professional social work as related to other disciplines, have gained assertiveness skills, and possess a higher level of negotiation skills.

"Working in [a secondary setting] usually requires increased assertiveness, tact, and awareness of the role of power within relationships"

Social Worker as Manager

Approximately 25 percent of social workers are primarily involved in management roles in human service agencies, and many more are involved in management activities second to their direct practice responsibilities (Patti, 2008). Social work managers are primarily involved with the business aspects of the organization, including risk management, facilities management, human resources, supervision of staff, financial management and budgeting, legal matters, board development, and related matters. Managers are currently working in an environment that is increasingly competitive, privatized, and outcomes-oriented. The need to stay competitive often requires new, creative strategies, a highly competent agency workforce, and increased use of technology and measurement of outcomes (Patti, 2008).

Developing the cultural competence of the organization is another aspect whose importance is growing. Persons of color are underrepresented in the social work workforce relative to clients serviced. Currently, 86 percent of licensed social workers in the United States are non-Hispanic Whites; Blacks represent 7 percent and Hispanics are only 4 percent (Whitaker et al., 2006). The challenge for managers is to recruit more persons of color as employees, support their professional development as employees, and to develop inclusive agency cultures that value diversity (Patti, 2008).

Evaluation of practice is a key management activity in which you may be involved. Evaluation of practice may involve gathering data about client outcomes, service quality, service coordination, degree of goal attainment, service comprehensiveness, service coverage, worker and client satisfaction, and other areas (Jaskyte, 2008). Your practicum site may have formalized internal systems to gather data needed for evaluation of their practice, and you can participate in these systems as a student. Even if the system of the organization is unstructured, you may wish to become involved in the process to gain first-hand experience of the process of practice evaluation.

Diversity in Practice

Cultural competence of the organization is an important aspect of service delivery. How might you, as a student, help the organization to assess the extent to which the organization's structure may oppress, marginalize, alienate or create or enhance privilege and power?

If your field instructor is a manager, you may want to take advantage of the opportunity to learn more about the agency management role. As a student, you can discuss the activities of your field instructor to learn about the experiences of responding to the current challenges to managers. You may find yourself in a management role in your social work career, and would benefit from learning about these challenges and opportunities as a student.

Practice Application 5.2 Gathering Information

To explore your practicum site's organizational characteristics, gather the following specific information and discuss it with a member of your practicum team or in integrative practice field seminar:

- Agency mission, goals, and objectives (What is the purpose and intention of the agency?)
- Agency history (Why was the agency started? What need did it intend to meet?)
- Agency philosophy and value system (What is important to the administration? On what basis does the agency make resource and procedural decisions?)
- Programs and services provided (What does the agency do?)
- Types of clients served and eligibility requirements (Whom does the agency intend to serve? Who is served?)
- Funding base of the agency (What entities supply monetary resources for the agency? Any changes in funding planned? Any sources in danger of being lost? New possible sources?)
- Organizational structure and context (What are the hierarchy of and qualifications for staff positions? What diversity is represented among the staff and administration? What are the compensation ranges for the various staff and administration positions? What are the procedures for filling vacant positions?)
- Important organizations in the environment of the agency (What agencies serve as referral sources to the agency? To whom does the agency refer clients? Is the agency accredited and by whom? With what agency[ies] does the organization collaborate to deliver services? With which organizations does the agency network? What conditions or task forces has the organization joined?)
- The current issues for the agency (With what is the agency most struggling?)
- What are the strengths of the agency?
- The future directions of the agency (Where is the agency headed?)

- Characteristics of oversight entity (What body or person[s] oversees the work of the agency? How does the person/group make decisions? What diversity is represented by the oversight entity? What are the professional and other affiliations of the board of directors/supervisors?)
- Policy advocacy (In what sort of policy advocacy does the agency engage?)
  - With what business aspects of the organization is your field instructor involved? What are the challenges and opportunities associated with working with these aspects?
  - What is the diversity of the organization's workforce? What diversity goals does the organization have? In what ways does the organization work to develop inclusive cultures?

As a student, you may have access to public and confidential documents and sources to learn about the agency. If you have access to confidential materials, be sure to observe any confidentiality agreements about the information.

Sources of this information for your practicum agency may include the following materials (Netting et al., 2008).

- Recent annual reports
- Policies and procedures manual
- Articles of incorporation (for-profit or nonprofit) or executive order or statute (public)
- By-laws
- Minutes of recent board of directors meetings as well as of various committees of the board
- Agency brochures/marketing materials
- Lists of members of the board and various committees, which may ascertain professional affiliations and background
- Agency mission statement
- Lists and descriptions of programs and services provided
- Programs' goals and objectives

- Copies of recent program evaluation reports
- Organizational chart
- Personnel guidelines and job descriptions for staff and administrators
- Interviews with administrators and other representatives of various disciplines within the organization (e.g., chief executive officer, executive director, teachers, physical therapists, counselors, other program staff, accountants)
- Interviews with members of the board of directors or entity to which staff and administration are accountable
- Recent newspaper and magazine clippings or publicity videos
- Recent budget information (agency budget, governmental appropriations, and grant proposals/reports)

- Copies of recent (funded and unfunded) private and government grants and purchase of service contracts
- Notes of recent meetings regarding agency collaborative projects, community task forces, and other interagency efforts
- Needs assessment surveys
- Case records
- Human resources plan, including affirmative action/equal employment opportunity plans
- Personnel recruitment and selection procedures
- Performance evaluation forms
- Statistics on absenteeism, turnover, and usage of sick leave
- Grievances and complaints filed with the human resources department
- Financial audit reports

THE INFORMAL ORGANIZATION

During her fifth week of practicum, Lauren discovered that her car would not start. She dutifully left a message on her field instructor's voicemail that she was unable to come in that day due to car problems, but she was confident that she would be in Friday, her next regularly scheduled day for practicum. On Friday, she was pulled aside by Cathy, the program director, and reminded that she needed to call in when she was unable to come to practicum. When she explained that she had called her field instructor, she was told that "everyone" knows that when unable to come in, staff should call Cathy, as she is the one who makes the staff schedule. Cathy chastised Lauren, stating that the shelter had been short staffed on Wednesday and that she should have made more efforts to make personal contact with someone or should have called Cathy directly. Lauren feels terrible about the confusion and the hardship she created for the other staff. Should she have known about the correct procedure? Was Cathy right to admonish Lauren for the effects of her behavior?

Professional Identity

Using professional demeanor, how might you handle a situation where you are held responsible for understandings and unwritten rules about which you have not been informed?

Equally important as learning the formal structure of an organization is learning the informal structure or the processes unique to an organization that may not appear in its official documents. Lauren is learning the hard way about the informal structure and rules of her practicum agency. Informal structures and rules of organizations are often uncovered by talking to more experienced workers or by unintentionally violating an unwritten rule.

Assume responsibility for learning the informal organization that exists in every agency. The *informal,* or *shadow, organization* is the result of groups of people who work together. It consists of "understandings and unwritten rules that produce an influence flow and a control system" (Russo, 1993) (see Box 5.3).

BOX 5.3 Examples of Explicit and Implicit Organization Rules

Explicit Rules	Implicit Rules
Do what is best for the clients.	Do what is best for the agency.
Take all concerns to the administrator.	The administrator's door is always closed.
Treat clients with respect and individualized attention.	See as many clients as possible so that we'll look good for funders.
Everyone's voice should be heard in decision making.	Voicing dissenting opinions runs the risk of hurting someone's feelings.
Multiple opportunities exist for student participation and projects.	Students should handle low-level work so that staff can do "real" work.
Feel comfortable about approaching staff and discussing your needs.	Staff have better things to do than bother with students' petty concerns.

Based on Um and Brown-Standridge (1993).

Practice Application 5.3 Reflection on Explicit and Implicit Rules

Review the information in Box 5.3 and reflect on your experiences at your practicum site. Journal on your reflections. In your entry, discuss the following questions:

1. Which (if any) of the explicit and implicit rules listed match those at your practicum site?

2. What other conflicting explicit and implicit rules are implemented at your practicum site?

3. How does the implementation of implicit rules affect the work of the agency? The staff?

Share your reflections with your field instructor or in integrative practice field seminar.

These relationships, understandings, and unwritten rules can profoundly affect the day-to-day work of an organization (Russo, 1993). They can be considered the "grease" that allows tasks to be completed. Knowledge of this system can be acquired through observation: Who gives information to whom? Who supervises others? Who helps whom? Who is really in charge of decisions? What priorities does the agency emphasize to staff versus the kinds of activities that are actually rewarded? Although this system does not appear on the organizational hierarchical chart, informal processes and implicit rules have a powerful influence on decision making within an organization. More important, learning the formal and informal rules can help you recognize the constraints under which you are operating and make you less likely to operate under misunderstandings in the practicum site, which may reduce the stress you might otherwise feel as a new worker within the agency.

SOCIALIZATION INTO THE SOCIAL SERVICE ORGANIZATION

The process of socialization into the social service organization depends on many factors, including your prior socialization to both the profession of social work and a work environment. If you arrived at the organization with values and work behaviors that are congruent with those of the organization,

---

BOX 5.4 Laying the Groundwork for a Positive Experience within an Organization

In the first few weeks of your practicum, try to do the following:

- Adopt the attitude that you are in practicum to learn and obtain skills and knowledge.
- Adjust your expectations. The experience will have its ups and downs and strengths and weaknesses.
- Master "breaking-in" skills. Seek to start out with energy, patience, and initiative.
- Manage the impressions you make. Attempt to leave a positive impression on each staff member by displaying an attitude of openness and eagerness to learn.
- Build effective relationships. Develop professional relationships with as many people as you can, and offer assistance when appropriate. Avoid workplace gossip.
- Become a good follower. Observe others in their work, and ask questions.
- Understand your organization's culture. Learn its formal and informal rules.
- Understand your new-hire role. In the first few weeks, adopt an attitude of humility and seek to fit within the structure of the agency.
- Develop work savvy. Learn to maximize your efforts by working efficiently.
- Master the tasks associated with practice behaviors and competencies. Focus on learning the skills needed to succeed in your practicum.
- Acquire needed knowledge, skills, and abilities. While succeeding in your day-to-day tasks, maintain the long-term perspective of acquiring transferable practice behaviors and competencies.

---

the socialization process may be smoother than if this is your first experience in such an organization. If, however, your personal values and norms are not consistent with or affirmed by the organization as you anticipated, a successful socialization process must first involve a detachment of your former values and norms before a new definition of your professional self can occur (Kolb, Rubin, & McIntrye, 1971). This process can be unpleasant and involve a great deal of time and commitment.

As you become grounded in your practicum, you may develop ideas about ways in which programs and services might be operated more smoothly or better serve clients. Unless you are asked for new ideas and feedback, resist the temptation to make major contributions or to share ideas until you have earned acceptance from others at the agency and have a clear understanding of the organization. Approaching the organization and being assigned tasks as a learner and being willing to share your lack of knowledge and experience may be the optimal strategy for learning. (For some tips, see Box 5.4.) Agency staff often enjoy sharing their expertise, knowledge, and experience. Seize opportunities to learn the agency's culture and politics. Investigate the expectations staff have of you as a student, discover the work ethic and social norms, and find ways to blend in with others in the organization. Although you may not always be comfortable as a new employee, the learner approach will lay the groundwork for gaining an understanding of the procedures of the organization and being accepted by others. Once you have gained the respect and acceptance of your peers, you will likely be more productive because you will be "in the know," valued, and connected. Additionally, you will then also be in a position to assert yourself and to share your suggestions.

Last, realize that socialization into an organization can take considerable effort. A supportive work group can be pivotal to your socialization effort. A peer group of other students or staff members is often a buffer between you and the more challenging aspects of working within an organization. Use a peer group to provide additional feedback regarding your performance and the

Practice Application 5.4 Reflections on Your Organizational Socialization

Discuss your socialization into your practicum site with a member of your practicum team. Include these topics:

- Personal values and norms of which you have become more aware since beginning the practicum and any conflicts of these with those of the organization
- The work behaviors/ethics that you expected of staff within the organization and any differences of which you have become aware since beginning the practicum

- Your observations of the culture and politics of the agency
- Your perception of the expectations others (staff and administration) have of you as a student
- Your feelings about being a newcomer in the organization
- Your field instructor's perception of your socialization process
- Your overall perception of your socialization process

subtleties of agency functioning. Although the values of a peer group can be partially out of sync with the organization as a whole (Kolb et al., 1971), a supportive group can offer an appropriate mechanism for releasing tension. Without a thorough socialization, the prospects for a successful practicum experience are slim.

UNCOVERING STAFF VIOLATIONS

Through hands-on work in an agency, you may discover staff violations of policy, procedure, or even law. Violations can range from taking small items home from the agency without approval to fraud and extorting funds. You may wonder whether to report a violation that you witness. A decision to report a violation can be difficult and complicated. Should you find yourself in such a situation, consider these factors:

1. Your length of service to the agency
2. Your reputation and relationship with the administration
3. The nature, seriousness, and effects of the violation
4. The length of service to the agency of the staff member in question and his or her reputation
5. Your relationship with the staff member
6. The possibility that you have misinterpreted an action due to lack of knowledge or experience

Depending on the severity of the infraction, reporting a staff infraction could damage your reputation and relationships with others. Before taking any official action, consult with your field instructor and possibly other staff members. Consider the following questions:

- Does the infraction seriously affect clients or the viability of the agency?
- Is there a pattern of infractions?
- Are you willing to risk the potential consequences of reporting an infraction?

Answering yes to one or more of these questions may provide you with the basis needed to make the decision to report. Otherwise, reporting an infraction could result in more harm than good.

Practice Application 5.5 Reflections on the Organization

The following activities will help you acquire knowledge about your practicum site and critique various aspects (e.g., mission, diversity, and effect of change) of the organization:

▶ Read the agency mission statement and review the agency organizational chart. Are the staff positions well suited to carrying out the mission statement of the agency?

▶ Review the diversity (i.e., racial, ethnic, sexual orientation, and gender) of the agency's staff members. Talk with your field instructor about the diversity represented by the staff. How well does the staff reflect the diversity of the local community? What efforts are being made to recruit and maintain a diverse staff?

▶ Ask your field instructor about any recent changes (personnel, administrative, structural, or funding source) that the agency has undergone. What was the impetus for the change(s)? What effects has the change(s) had on client services? The mission of the agency? Staff? The community?

Discuss your findings with a member of your practicum team or in integrative practice field seminar.

———

Developed by Jan McGillick, MA

Practice Application 5.6 Reflection through Illustration

This exercise will assist you in the process of learning about external entities with which your practicum site has relationships and the types of relationships that exist.

Create an agency eco-map and include the following:

1. All entities external to the organization with which the organization interfaces (e.g., governmental entities, other social agencies, businesses, community organizations, and religious institutions)

2. A graphic description of the relationships between the organization and these entities using different types of connections (e.g., broken lines, thin lines, thick lines, and curving lines)

3. A legend/key that explains the types of connections

Explain and discuss your eco-map with a member of your practicum team or in integrative practice field seminar.

Practice Application 5.7 Learning about Agency Structure through the Lens of Service Area/Client Issue

An important aspect of learning about your practicum site is comparing and contrasting the organizational structure with agencies that provide similar services. The process of making career choices within social work also entails determining your organizational fit with agencies that provide the type of services in which you are interested. This exercise will help you learn about another agency that provides services in which you are interested.

Select a service area/client issue about which you would like to learn more (e.g., play or art therapy, attention-deficit disorder [ADD], or school social work). This may be a client issue addressed by or a service provided by your practicum site. Working with three to four students, select at least one agency to visit (other than your practicum site) that provides the service or works with the client issue of interest. Request approval from the agency and coordinate a group visit. Develop a list of questions to ask during the visit, including questions about the funding, philosophy, staffing, service delivery, and agency responses to current social policy changes as well as the past, present, and future role of social work within the agency. If possible, try to contact a social worker at the site. After the visit, discuss your experiences in your integrative practice field seminar. Compare and contrast agencies relative to client issues and service area(s).

Practice Application 5.8 Tying Together the Agency and Social Work Values and Principles

Social workers implement the social work *Code of Ethics* (NASW, 2008a) in their work within a wide variety of contexts. An important aspect of your learning is linking your work to the profession. This exercise will contribute toward explicating the goodness of fit between the service delivery of the agency and social work values and principles.

Obtain a copy of the agency mission statement and policy and procedures manual. Using these documents and drawing on your experiences thus far in the practicum, engage your field instructor in a dialogue concerning the service delivery of the agency relative to the social work values and principles articulated in the *Code of Ethics*. Discuss whether the agency does/does not operationalize the following values and principles (NASW, 2008a):

- Service—"Social workers' primary goal is to help people in need and to address social problems."

- Social justice—"Social workers challenge social injustice."

- Dignity and worth of the person—"Social workers respect the inherent dignity and worth of the person."

- Importance of human relationships—"Social workers recognize the central importance of human relationships."

- Integrity—"Social workers behave in a trustworthy manner."

- Competence—"Social workers practice within their areas of competence and develop and enhance their professional expertise."

Developed by Ellen Burkemper, PhD, LCSW

SUMMARY

This chapter focused on the importance of understanding the organization within which you will complete your practicum, the essential elements of an organization, strategies to use to uncover the needed information about the agency, and the process of becoming socialized into an organization. Nonprofit, for-profit, and public organizations were defined, as were faith-based organizations. The differences among them were explained, and the positive and negative factors of working within each type of organization were debated. Finally, the impacts of various leadership theories on organizations were discussed, the role of social work within organizations was examined, and tips for gathering needed organizational information were provided.

Knowledge of organizations is crucial to the success of your practicum. Just as knowledge of clients' environments is central to understanding the issues clients present, knowledge of organizational matters is essential to understanding the parameters of service delivery in an organization. Learning the methods by which to serve clients within your organization and the organizational framework for those services should occur simultaneously.

Ben shared with his field instructor his insights regarding his hesitance to be more independent and to take more initiative in his work at the practicum. He discussed his experiences working at large publicly funded institutions, explained that he had been rewarded for work behaviors that included taking little initiative in work assignments, and that he had become accustomed to a high degree of structure and bureaucracy. His field instructor explained that he was now in a loosely structured organization with an expectation that staff would take a great deal of initiative and exercise flexibility in their work environments. He was encouraged to "jump in and make mistakes," rather than to wait until someone gave specific instructions. As the semester went on, Ben became more comfortable with the structure, yet he realized that he felt more comfortable with a higher level of structure and would probably seek employment in a large nonprofit or a public agency after graduation.

Lauren called her field instructor immediately after she finished talking with Cathy. She explained to her field instructor that although she had called the agency to report her absence in a timely manner, she had not known that she was to call Cathy and she felt terrible that the shelter had been short staffed because of her lack of knowledge. Lauren's field instructor apologized, stating that she should have told Lauren about the informal rules of the shelter, and said that she would talk with Cathy and take the responsibility. Lauren then asked her field instructor to tell her explicitly about other informal rules so that she could avoid duplicating the mistake. Although Lauren felt that Cathy could have handled the situation better, she chalked it up as a lesson learned about the informal rules of organizations—a lesson learned the hard way.

Succeed with PEARSON **mysocialworklab**

Log onto **MySocialWorkLab** to access a wealth of case studies, videos, and assessment. (*If you did not receive an access code to* **MySocialWorkLab** *with this text and wish to purchase access online, please visit* www.mysocialworklab.com.)

1. Under the Interactive Cases, choose the Child Welfare case, and go to page 19 of 26. Watch the "Clarification of Role of Agency" video. What other aspects of the agency might be important to share with this client?

2. Under the Interactive Cases, choose the Domestic Violence case. Go to page 4 of 28, and watch the "Engagement" video. The social worker introduces herself as the Director of the Women's Shelter. What organizational aspects about the women's shelter might impact the experience of this client while in shelter? Why?

PRACTICE TEST The following questions will test your knowledge of the content found within this chapter. For additional assessment, including licensing-exam type questions on applying chapter content to practice, visit **MySocialWorkLab.**

Practice
Contexts

1. Programs are required to provide students with the opportunities to develop competencies and practice behaviors. Those that directly relate to organizational practice include all of the following, except:
   a. The ability to analyze social and agency policy that impacts practice
   b. The ability to respond to context that impact practice
   c. The ability to engage in professional practice within organizations
   d. The ability to analyze human behavior across the life course

2. Most social work practice takes place within the parameters of an agency's:
   a. Mission and values
   b. Mission, values, and philosophy
   c. Mission, values, philosophy and communication structure
   d. Mission, values, philosophy, communication structure and resources

3. _____ directly affects the work you can do with clients
   a. Agency structures and procedures
   b. Agency structures, procedures and culture
   c. Agency structures, procedures, culture, relationship with external systems and Board of Directors
   d. Agency structures, procedures, culture, and relationship with external systems

Practice
Contexts

4. _____ organizations are federal, state, regional, county and city government entities.
   a. Public
   b. Private
   c. Inter-agency
   d. Nonprofit

5. The driving goal of for-profit agencies is to:
   a. Serve their clients
   b. Produce a profit for their owners or shareholders
   c. Grow to be a national corporation
   d. Provide client-centered services

6. Non-profit organizations rely on government sources for approximately _____ of their funding:
   a. One-half   c. Three-quarters
   b. One-fourth   d. Seven-eighths

7. Approximately _____ percent of social workers are primarily involved in management roles in human service agencies.
   a. 10   c. 20
   b. 10   d. 25

8. Hispanics are currently _____ percent of the licensed social work workforce.
   a. 4   c. 7
   b. 5   d. 8

9. The informal organization can best be described as:
   a. Understandings
   b. Understandings and unwritten rules
   c. The organization prior to formal incorporation
   d. The volunteers for the organization

10. If you uncover a staff infraction of policy, procedure or law, the best course of action includes:
    a. Reporting to authorities immediately, then consulting with your field instructor
    b. Consulting with your field instructor
    c. Consulting with your field instructor and considering questions about the violation
    d. Consulting with your field instructor, considering questions about the violation and reporting to authorities

Log onto **MySocialWorkLab** once you have completed the Practice Test above, to access additional study tools and assessment.

Answers:

Key: 1) d 2) d 3) d 4) a 5) b 6) b 7) a 8) d 9) b 10) c

6

Social Work Practice in the Field

Working with Individuals and Families

Core Competencies in this Chapter (Check marks indicate which competencies are covered in depth)									
	Professional Identity	✔	Ethical Practice		Critical Thinking		Diversity in Practice		Human Rights and Justice
	Research Based Practice	✔	Human Behavior		Policy Practice		Practice Contexts	✔	Engage, Assess, Intervene, Evaluate

The opportunity to work one on one in direct practice with adults and children is the impetus for many students and practitioners to pursue social work as a career. While social work practice with individuals and families may be the motivation for entering the profession, you have learned by now through coursework that an effective generalist social work practitioner develops competence at all three levels of social work practice—micro, mezzo, and macro. In fact, the National Association of Social Workers (NASW) *Code of Ethics* (2008a) mandates that all social workers develop and practice a range of social work skills to ensure effective delivery of social work services.

Although each social work program has the autonomy to define and operationalize the teaching of generalist social work practice consistent with the program's mission and philosophy (CSWE, 2008), a general definition is practice with "individuals, families, groups, communities and organizations in a variety of social work and host settings. Generalist practitioners view clients and client systems from a strengths perspective in order to recognize, support, and build upon the innate capabilities of all human beings. They use a professional problem solving process to engage, assess, broker services, advocate, counsel, educate, and organize with and on behalf of client and client systems. In addition, generalist practitioners engage in community and organizational development. Finally, generalist practitioners evaluate service outcomes in order to continually improve the provision and quality of services most appropriate to client needs" (Association of Baccalaureate Program Directors, 2006, Para. 1).

The focus of this chapter, social work practice with individuals and families, is but one facet of the generalist practice perspective. Also known as *micro practice*, working with individuals and families is generally considered to be those "professional activities that are designed to help solve the problems faced primarily by individuals, families and small groups" (Barker, 2003, p. 272). Micro social work practice places a strong emphasis on the development of assessment and intervention skills. However, the practice of micro-focused interventions can be far ranging.

EXPECTATIONS FOR STUDENT LEARNING IN PRACTICE WITH INDIVIDUALS AND FAMILIES

Working at the individual and family level focuses the scope of practice on the interactions of individuals and families and their environments (Sheafor & Horejsi, 2008). The range of tasks and activities is broad and can include operating a food pantry in a community-based center, conducting intake assessments for a mental health center, providing family preservation services for a faith-based family service agency, and providing discharge planning services in an acute care medical setting.

Recent work has advanced the profession's perception and knowledge of those areas deemed essential for social work practice with individuals and families. In general, social work programs and field instructors expect that students engaged in practice with individuals and families will develop competencies in engagement, assessment, intervention, and termination/evaluation. More specifically, in working with individuals and families, social work students will learn to (1) use critical thinking to assess client situations, (2) develop therapeutic relationships, (3) understand and utilize contracts with clients, (4) understand

the process of incorporating empathy, understanding, and explaining into the client–worker relationships, (5) use of self, and (6) develop listening skills (Simpson, Williams, & Segall, 2007).

These skill areas are intentionally broad and may seem vague. You have the opportunity to work closely with your field instructor to identify specific tasks and activities that will enable you to develop and refine your skills in these areas for your present experience. Although you may identify areas specific to your current practicum setting, the value of micro-practice competence is that each of the skills identified and developed can be transferred to almost any other setting and population. Your social work program will establish practice behaviors that relate to working with individuals and families that can be linked to the learning activities that you incorporate into your learning plan.

As you have learned through your prepracticum coursework and experiences, practice with individuals and families is based on a model of planned change and includes such skills as relationship building, empathy, cultural competence, assessment, intervention, termination, and evaluation. You are now well schooled in the philosophy that these skills are essential at *all* levels of social work practice. The aim of this chapter is not to review content on practice with individuals and families that you have covered in your social work practice courses but rather to aid you in integrating theory and practice, to understand the parameters of evidence-based practice with individuals and families, and to establish a foundation for chapters 7 and 8, which address learning practice in the field with groups, organizations, and communities. This chapter will specifically address two primary areas on which your practicum team can focus to direct your learning of social work practice with individuals and families: (1) the "business" of practice—administrative, agency-related, and caseload-related issues; and (2) the "process" practice—client-related issues.

LEARNING THE "BUSINESS" OF PRACTICE WITH INDIVIDUALS AND FAMILIES

Direct social work practice intervention skills are central to the overall delivery of social work services, regardless of the type and level of practice or the setting in which social workers work. Practicum settings and field instructors therefore place considerable emphasis on the development of these skills. Applying knowledge and gaining the skills needed to interact effectively with clients are the major, but not the only, aspects of learning necessary for competent practice with individuals and families. Learning to function within the social service setting and the community are essential achievements to be made during your practicum experience. This discussion will focus on the areas to be covered in your practice learning, including orientation, caseload assignment, identifying yourself as a student, role transition, charging for services, confidentiality, documentation, seeking answers, coverage, collaborative practice, ongoing evaluation, and administrative issues. Although many of these issues apply across all levels of social work practice, this discussion focuses on the relationship of each area to practice with individuals and families.

Orientation

You may be in the midst of the formal orientation to your practicum, or you may have completed the formal orientation process. There are additional facets of the practicum learning experience that will continue throughout the entirety of your time in this setting. Regarding your practice learning, you will continually be oriented to agency rules, policies, cultures, traditions, and even clients well known to the agency.

A concern often voiced by students in the early phases of the practicum experience is the issue of the *orientation.* Some students find the orientation process to be too long, while others fear that the orientation is not long enough to prepare them adequately for actual social work practice. Out of a fear of making mistakes and appearing incompetent, students have wished for or actually prolonged the orientation process. Your own reaction is probably dependent on several factors: learning style, previous social work-related experiences, and comfort level within the practicum setting. Are you eager to jump in and get started with learning, or do you prefer to absorb all you possibly can about the situation before launching into the experience? Take a few moments and recall your insights regarding your learning style (refer to Practice Application 1.1) and think also about the related issues of experience and comfort. This exercise may help you evaluate your feelings regarding the orientation process.

Caseload Assignment

Regardless of the fears and anxieties related to practicum, students are usually eager to receive their case assignments. A number of questions arise, however, regarding case assignments:

- What is an appropriate, manageable number of cases for the beginning, middle, and end phases of my practicum?
- Am I going to "shadow" my field instructor (or other worker) before I am assigned my own caseload? If I am shadowing another worker, when will I be able to assume responsibility?

‣ Will I have sole responsibility for my cases?

‣ What types of cases will I be assigned—clients new to the agency, clients who have been with the agency previously, or clients who are typically assigned to the practicum students?

‣ Are there only certain categories of clients to whom I can be assigned because of restrictions regarding third-party reimbursement or legal issues?

‣ Will I have a balance in my caseload (e.g., will the cases be easy or hard, or a balance of both types)?

‣ What is my role with my clients? Do I have the authority to make decisions with the clients, or does that have to be approved by my field instructor?

‣ Will I have a lighter caseload than workers, and will I be taken seriously by other workers if I am not carrying a full caseload?

‣ Will I be able to work with clients from the intake through the termination process, or will I enter the helping relationship after another worker has established a relationship? If I am receiving a transfer case, what were the circumstances of the previous worker's termination with the case, and will the client be able and willing to accept me?

Have these questions arisen for you? What other questions do you anticipate as you receive your case assignments? Be assured that most practicum students contemplate these questions at some point. You are encouraged to raise and discuss any and all questions regarding case assignment with your field instructor. Despite the fact that your field instructor may not unassign a case because you verbalize anxiety, you are obligated to raise your concerns and welcome the opportunity to process your feelings and develop a plan for handling the situation.

Identifying Yourself as a Student

Lauren has been shadowing and observing her field instructor and other social work staff for the first several weeks of her practicum at the shelter for women survivors of intimate partner violence. She has now been assigned her first client—a woman who has been sheltered at this site a number of times. Lauren has read the client's file, discussed the case with her field instructor, and feels anxious but ready to get involved. Upon meeting the client the day after her arrival at the shelter, Lauren introduces herself to the woman. Due to her "first-client encounter jitters," Lauren forgets to identify herself as a student. The client does not recognize Lauren from her previous stays at the shelter and asks her about her qualifications, experience in domestic violence, and success rate with working with women who have been battered. The client tells Lauren that she has been to every agency in town (and this shelter eight times) but no one can help her. The client states that she sure hopes Lauren can help her because no one else has. Lauren now remembers to inform the client that she is a student. The client becomes upset, stating that if the others could not help her, how could a student? The client then declares that she does not want to work with Lauren. What are the practice issues that arise for Lauren? How might Lauren have handled this situation differently? How might she handle the situation at this point?

The issue of your role as a practicum student may have been addressed during the social work program or agency practicum orientation. You may wish to clarify with your field instructor the manner in which the agency and your field instructor would like you to introduce and identify yourself to clients. Although some students may be issued nametags or badges that identify them as students or volunteers, others are not so readily identified as nonemployees.

Despite the fact that you may be acutely aware of your "rookie" status, most clients, in all likelihood, will not be. Students may feel uncomfortable or inadequate informing clients of their status, feeling that the client will feel shortchanged by being assigned to "just a student." In actuality, being assigned to a practicum student provides the client with not only your expertise but also that of your field instructor, agency staff, and possibly faculty at your social work program. As a practicum student, you will likely be able to spend more time with clients, unlike your colleagues, who probably have more extensive and demanding responsibilities. If you are unsure about the way in which you will approach this issue, you may want to rehearse with your field instructor or fellow students alternatives for introducing yourself to your clients (as required by the NASW *Code of Ethics* (2008a)). When the opportunity presents itself, you will feel comfortable and confident in your role.

In the preceding scenario, the student experienced a negative client reaction to her student status. You have considered the issues and Lauren's potential responses to the client's comments. Foremost, Lauren should not become defensive or apologetic regarding her status as a student. She can inform the client that while she is a learner, she has developed knowledge and skills regarding domestic violence and, with the help of her field instructor and other staff, she believes that she can competently serve the client. Lauren can acknowledge to the client that she does not have the experience of domestic violence and ask the client to share that experience with her. Not only does this potentially defuse the client's anger and frustration, but can serve as the entry into the relationship-building and intervention process. Should the client still be unwilling to work with Lauren, Lauren has the opportunity to discuss with the client the client's feelings regarding being assigned to a student. Lauren and her field instructor may determine that being assigned to work with this client may not be in Lauren's best educational interests or in the best interests of the client.

Role Transition

Most field instructors and students believe that the optimal approach to learning individual and family practice skills is for the student first to observe seasoned professionals modeling appropriate skills. As with the orientation process, the length of time for which you function in the observer role can be determined through a negotiation between you and your field instructor. The process for this negotiation should occur at the onset of your practicum and center on the question of whether your field instructor expects that you will let him or her know when you are ready for the transition or if your field instructor will determine when you are ready to make the transition. Do you have the option of assuming partial responsibility for a case and gradually moving toward assuming more or full responsibility? Being clear about your mutual thoughts regarding this shift can prevent the possibility of unmet expectations in the future. While assuming responsibility for cases and projects is certain to evoke anxiety and fear of failure, practicum provides a safe and supportive opportunity to seek out experiences and responsibilities that exceed your expectations.

You may find yourself in an agency in which practicum students are not allowed to assume sole responsibility for cases. Should this happen, how can you maximize your learning, despite not being able to have the experience of handling a case on your own? Again, negotiating with your field instructor can shed light on this issue. Clarifying the extent of the role you can assume, ensuring that you have access to as much information as possible about the progress of each case, and being assigned responsibility for a portion of the case are three strategies for optimizing your learning.

Charging for Services

Engage, Assess, Intervene, Evaluate

Client engagement is focused on rapport-building and connecting; how might charging for services impact the engagement and assessment process?

Student-generated revenue can present a dilemma for students, agencies, and social work programs. As a result of funding challenges and the need for agencies to generate revenue, increasing numbers of students may find practicum agencies exploring or expanding client-generated fees. The important task for you, as a practicum student, is to obtain clarity regarding both agency and social work program policies regarding student-generated revenue. Should a conflict occur (e.g., your agency wants to charge, but your social work program prohibits charging for student-provided services), involve your faculty liaison immediately. If you are completing a practicum in which the agency will receive income from services provided by you, you will need clarification regarding the liability issues related to charging for services.

The task of informing clients about fees and, in some cases, actually collecting the money can be awkward for students. You may wonder if charging for services (particularly a student charging for services) is ethical social work practice (i.e., does charging for services conflict with the social work/agency mission to serve underserved and oppressed groups?). This activity may have implications for your future practice and can be a valued learning experience.

An issue related to charging for student-provided services is the practicum that is completed in a managed care setting. Some practicum sites have been eliminated because of the student's inability to charge for services or the practitioner's need to spend all his or her time in billable activities (which would not include field instruction). Social work programs regularly explore strategies to collaborate with community agencies to create opportunities for student learning that will better prepare graduates for real-world practice in which such issues as managed care, economic challenges, and legal issues will confront them (Lager & Robbins, 2004). Your feedback and input regarding your experience becomes critical for shaping an effective practicum experience.

Confidentiality

You have heard, learned, and discussed much about the issue of confidentiality throughout your social work education. The NASW *Code of Ethics* (2008a) clearly directs social work practitioners on the issue of confidentiality by stating that "social workers should protect the confidentiality of all information obtained in the course of professional service, except for compelling professional reasons." The *Code* prohibits the sharing of any client-related information without assurance of complete privacy; therefore, discussing client information in public areas (e.g., agency public spaces, restaurants, parties, etc.) is prohibited (Grobman, 2003). As you know at this point, client confidentiality is considered sacred and is fiercely protected by social work professionals. Despite the strong emphasis on the preservation of client confidentiality, practicum students are often unsure how the concept is defined and practiced in their field settings. You will want to have a clear understanding of these issues before you experience your first client encounter.

The issue of confidentiality has been so strongly emphasized during social work coursework that students are often concerned about violating confidential information regarding a client. As a practicum student, you are responsible for ensuring that you understand the parameters of confidentiality and strategies for preventing the violation of clients' confidential information along with knowing circumstances that are appropriate for disclosing client information. Such situations may include client threats of harm to self or others; possible child or adult abuse, neglect, or exploitation; and legal proceedings (Reamer, 2009).

Questions to pose to your field instructor to ensure your understanding of confidentiality might include the following:

- What information is appropriate to know about the client prior to the first contact?
- What questions can I ask and of whom can I ask them prior to the first client contact?
- What information is recorded in the client's chart/file?
- How do I treat information received unsolicited about the client from another person?
- What client information can I share with others? What steps do I take to share that information?
- Can I talk freely about the client with agency staff?
- Under what circumstances can I discuss the client in my classes?
- Where is it appropriate to discuss the client (e.g., lunch/break room, hallway, or behind closed doors only)?
- How do I approach discussions with the client's family members? What information can I share?
- What information can I share with professionals to whom I might be referring the client?
- What can I share with the person(s) who referred this client to this agency?
- Are any of the following a violation of confidentiality?
  - Leaving a detailed message on a client's voice mail?
  - Using my school, agency, or personal e-mail or cell phone (to include text messaging) to communicate with a client, field instructor, faculty member, or fellow student about client-related information?
  - Giving my cell phone or e-mail address to a client?
  - Talking with a client, co-worker, or field instructor who has called my cell phone when I am in the presence of others (e.g., home, school, or a public place)?
  - Storing client-related information on my cell phone or personal data assistant device (PDA) or computer?
  - Sending client-related information via an e-mail or text message to myself for future use in a paper or presentation or to catch up on documentation at home?
  - Photographing clients with my cell phone, digital, still, or video camera without written consent? If I have written consent, can I transmit photographs electronically?
  - Sharing information about my clients on an online bulletin board or chatroom monitored by a faculty member?

> ◗ If my agency provides services to clients electronically, what precautions should I take to ensure confidentiality?
>
> > ◗ Am I using a secure, password-protected computer located in a private area?
> > ◗ Can I use an unsecured wireless connection, real-time communication, or video conferencing?
> > ◗ If the information is saved, what is the appropriate method of storage?

Although other legal issues related to confidentiality will be further discussed in chapter 9, the questions presented here are important to consider as you begin to build relationships with your clients and to engage in practice with individuals and families.

Documentation

Why do you need specific writing skills for working with individuals and families? Social work practitioners, by necessity, are required to demonstrate professional writing skills for several reasons. The ability to provide social work services is a result of agency funding, and program funding is often linked to providers' documentation of services provided and needed (Munson, 2002). In fact, approximately 30 percent of a social service practitioner's time is spent documenting the way in which he or she delivers services (Munson, 2002).

In general, social work record keeping serves a range of purposes, including: accountability, supporting, monitoring, and improving practice interventions (Kagle, 2009). The Council on Social Work Education (CSWE) requires that students have the opportunity in the field experience to demonstrate program competencies derived from evidence-informed practice, while connecting theoretical and conceptual content learned in the classroom with a practice setting (CSWE, 2008). Effective documentation skills are an example of a practice behavior that demonstrates mastery of practice competencies.

Documentation is critical to agency survival. On the aggregate level, client information is used for compiling data on services delivered and not delivered, identifying gaps in the service delivery system, justifying funding needs, and supporting or rejecting legislative actions related to the passage of laws. On the individual level, client records are critical documents for treatment planning, case management, court actions, referrals to intra- and interagency services, and internal and external utilization reviews (particularly for program accreditation).

Documentation skills are not fully learned in the coursework that precedes the practicum experience. The actual writing skills required for documentation of social work activities are unlike any writing that you have produced to date. Social work practice writing includes facets similar to general academic writing (e.g., conciseness, clarity, and appropriate presentation of information [grammar, spelling, and punctuation]). Additional characteristics of "good" practice documentation include being accurate, objective, current, well documented, compliant with agency and legal guidelines, and comprehensive (Kagle, 2009). An equally important practice behavior is to learn the characteristics of ineffective documentation, including being incomplete, inaccessible, unorganized, out-of-date, or biased and not inclusive of client preference, assessment, culture, or input (Kagle, 2009).

Each agency/organization that provides direct services to clients has specialized documentation policies, practices, and requirements. Your field instructor or other agency staff will instruct you regarding the concrete documentation requirements—that is the easy part. The challenge is condensing and organizing the wealth of client information you will possess into a useful, efficient, and easily readable document. Your field instructor may ask you to review records written by other workers. You will want to review client files compiled by several different workers so that you can learn various styles and approaches to documentation.

Regardless of the particular documentation style, format, or system that your practicum site utilizes, there is consensus within the social work community regarding the general content appropriate for service-centered client record keeping. In order to achieve accountability, such a record should include: a description of client-need situation and service delivery (i.e., goals, decisions, plans, actions, progress, and outcomes); evidence of social work knowledge, values, and ethics; content in the context of the agency mission, standards, and best practices; only the information necessary for the client situation; client characteristics and perspectives that can impact the client–worker relationship and outcomes (e.g., cultural issues, resources, goals, etc.); content that can be accessible to an array of relevant persons or groups (Kagle & Kopels, 2008).

Kagle and Kopels (2008) provide the following general guidelines for the content to be included in service-centered client records, while we offer examples of appropriate and inappropriate documentation:

Area of documentation	The Wrong Way	The Right Way
Client demographics	Ms. Jones, a 53-year-old overweight, never-married female requests energy assistance because she cannot pay her bill this month	Ms. Jones requests energy assistance
Means and reasons for initiating service	Ms. Jones cannot pay her utility bill because she took a trip to see her sister and her car broke down on the way home and then she went to her church, which could not help her but sent her here.	Ms. Jones was referred to the energy assistance program by her minister.
Description of client-need-situation	Ms. Jones goes to visit her sister in Florida every Christmas and then cannot pay her electric bill because she lets her grandchildren stay in the house while she's gone and they party round-the-clock and run the electricity bills up so that she can't pay them in January.	Ms. Jones has applied for energy assistance each January for the past three years.
Resources, barriers, and unmet needs	Ms. Jones's family should be a resource for her, but I think they're actually a barrier because they seem to abuse her.	Ms. Jones agrees to talk with her grandchildren about two issues: (1) contributing to the utility bills and (2) limiting their use of electricity during her absence. The client also believes that she could ask other family members to check on the grandchildren while she is away in Florida and possibly to lend her money to pay the utility bills.

Area of documentation	The Wrong Way	The Right Way
Assessment (including strengths and cultural factors impacting service)	Ms. Jones's grandchildren are taking advantage of her generosity and she shouldn't let them get away with this.	Ms. Jones appears to have established a pattern of need. Each January, she applies for energy assistance because, by her report, she cannot pay her December electric bill. The cause appears to be linked to Ms. Jones's grandchildren excess electricity use during her two-week absence from the house.
Purpose of service	Keep client from asking for help every winter.	Assist client in identifying reason for her need and develop a plan with client to address the present need and prevent future need in this area.
Goals and plans of service	Told client to get level payment plan and demand that her family help her.	In collaboration with client, developed a plan to prevent future energy assistance needs: (1) Enroll in the electric company's level payment plan to create a fixed bill amount per month. (2) Ask grandchildren to decrease electricity usage during her absence and to contribute financial support for household bills. (3) Ask three adult children (particularly the parents of the two teenage grandchildren who live with client) if they would ever be able or willing to contribute financial support in an emergency situation. (4) Worker will follow up with client in two to three months.
Service reviews	Called client—no answer.	Telephone call to client on 3/1—no answer. Telephone call to client on 3/3—she has not yet applied for level payment plan or talked with her family. Discussed with client her questions regarding the level payment plan application and strategies for approaching her family about these difficult issues.
Reasons for terminating service	Maxed out.	The client has received maximum financial assistance from the program and guidance to develop plan to prevent future need.
Review of client-need situation from opening to closing (including: review of service purpose, process, goals, and activities; evaluation of outcomes and impact of services; and referral or other planned activities)	Level plan, talk with others.	During the two visits with Ms. Jones, a plan was developed and implemented: (1) Contact electric company to enroll in level payment plan. (2) Talk with grandchildren about decreased electricity usage and contributions to household bills. (3) Talk with three adult children about their willingness and ability to provide occasional financial support.

(Continued)

Area of documentation	The Wrong Way	The Right Way
Follow-up	(No entry made).	3/16—Telephone call to client who reports she followed through with the plan, has enrolled in level payment plan; talked with grand-children about electricity use and contributing financially to the bill and three adult children, who agreed to provide financial support.

As you begin to document your own service activities, you are encouraged to discuss with your field instructor his or her expectations for content *and* process for documentation. First, ask your field instructor to clarify for you the format, language, and information to be included in the client's record. In cases in which the agency maintains client records and communications in an electronic system, be certain that you know how to access the system and enter and save information and who else will have access. If client information is electronically transmitted, ensure that you are aware of the process and rules of privacy related to such transmissions. Second, consider these three questions related to the completion of the client record:

1. What is the agency timeframe for completion of records?

2. Does your practicum agency require that student documentation be approved and co-signed by a field instructor or other staff member? (This may impact the deadlines for submitting documentation.)

3. What are your field instructor's expectations regarding your initial and later recording responsibilities (e.g., you complete a draft, he or she reviews the draft, and you edit the draft before formally entering the information into the client record)?

Do you have other questions regarding the documentation process? If so, be sure to include them on your supervision session agenda.

If your practicum site's policy regarding official documentation precludes you from having sole responsibility for recording client encounters in the file, you can record your thoughts and impressions simultaneously with the official record keeper. You can then use this "mirrored" record as a mechanism for identifying your strengths and areas for growth in record keeping. Overall, an important skill to have regarding your social work writing skills is to be willing to ask for *feedback*.

Seeking Answers

In the early weeks of your practicum, you are highly motivated to provide efficient and effective client services, but you may be unsure of your ability to do so autonomously. You are striving to attain independence as a competent social work professional and do not want to appear dependent on your field instructor. Students often struggle with the tension between feeling that they want and need to ask questions but not wanting to appear unsure, incompetent, or overly needy (or to jeopardize their practicum grade).

This issue is best addressed by viewing your field instructor as a mentor or consultant and openly raising your concerns with him or her. As you and your field instructor approach your journey to independence, it may be helpful to

Practice Application 6.1 Documentation: Your Turn

There are numerous formats for documenting client encounters. One such format is the SOAP format. This acronym describes four components of the documentation process: S—subjective information (e.g., client feelings, thoughts, perception of needs, etc.); O—objective information (e.g., factual and verifiable data); A—assessment (e.g., your conclusions based on the subjective and objective information); and P—plan (e.g., contracted tasks and activities to meet the client's goals) (Sheafor & Horejsi, 2008).

After reading the following scenario, use a SOAP format and rewrite the entry. Discuss your documentation with a member of your practicum team.

Ms. Jones is a 32-year-old, African American woman. Although she is not certain whether she would like to adopt a boy or girl, Ms. Jones has said that she would like the child to be under the age of 5. Ms. Jones would not want a child who has severe emotional or behavior challenges because she is a single parent. She recently moved into a three-bedroom, two-bathroom home with her 8-year-old daughter, Jackie, from a previous relationship. Currently, Ms. Jones has worked for the state department of corrections as a parole officer for two years, where she makes a little over $42,690 a year. She became interested in adopting a child after seeing a profile of a little girl available for adoption, "Kimberly," in the local newspaper two years ago. At that time, Ms. Jones had just begun her new job and wanted to wait until she was settled.

Developed by Janelle George, MSW

(Note: For our suggested revisions, see the Practice Application 6.1 Follow-Up at the end of this chapter.)

consider the type of learner you are and the type of teacher that your field instructor is. Discuss with your field instructor his or her preferences for the following:

- The types of questions that are appropriate
- The questions to be directed to him or her and the questions appropriate for other staff
- How and when questions should be presented (any time, any place, or saved for weekly supervision sessions) and the format to be used (voice mail, e-mail, note, text, instant messaging, or in person)
- Person(s) to consult in his or her absence
- When or at what developmental phase you should be functioning with some level of autonomy
- How to define *autonomy* (This concept may be defined and operationalized differently, depending on the field instructor or agency.)

Coverage

Students often have the opportunity to provide coverage for a field instructor or other workers who are away from the agency. Although this situation can result in valuable learning, you should consider several related issues. First, does providing coverage for another worker meet your educational needs and goals or just fill a personnel need for the agency? Second, are you qualified to provide coverage for others whose cases may be different from those with which you have become familiar? Third, will covering for another worker create excessive work for you? Last, if you provide coverage for a worker other than your field instructor, will your field instructor have the authority to supervise your work or does that need to be negotiated with agency administration?

Should the opportunity present itself for you to take responsibility for another worker's cases, clarification of these issues is important: (1) duration of coverage; (2) expectations for involvement (i.e., monitoring, actual intervention, or responding to requests on an as-needed basis); (3) process for transition from the other worker to you—Will you be able to review client information, ensure that the client(s) is told that you are available and told the extent of your role, verify your contact information, and meet the client prior to the transition; and (4) process for transition from you back to the original worker.

You should also consider how your own caseload will be covered when you must be absent by having a clear understanding with your field instructor regarding planned absences (e.g., does a university holiday excuse you from practicum, and do official agency holidays count toward practicum hours?). Practicum students are not typically in the agency on a full-time basis, therefore determining the way in which your clients can and will be served on those days you are not available is essential. Your field instructor or other worker may be available to respond to client needs, but your clients must know when you are not available and the person(s) to contact should a need arise. You will want to discuss with your field instructor the plan for coverage when you are away from your practicum for longer periods of time (e.g., semester breaks, university holidays, and vacations).

Collaborative Practice

Working with other professionals is a part of every social worker's responsibility, regardless of the type of social work practice or the setting. With our foundation in ecological and empowerment perspectives, social workers are poised to engage in partnered practice that is dependent on developing and connecting networks and resources (Aronoff, 2008). The ever-changing world of social service delivery has created both opportunities and challenges for social workers engaging in intra- and interprofessional collaboration. Practice with individuals and families routinely involves collaborating with other social workers, other professions, and community groups on such issues as individual client treatment and management planning, client advocacy, resource development, program planning, and coalition building.

Practitioners who receive training on collaboration early in their careers tend to feel more positive and open about incorporating collaboration in their practice (Arndt et al., 2009). Becoming an effective interprofessional collaborator involves learning about and respecting other disciplines while also mastering the ability to work together toward a common goal *and* maintaining one's professional identity (Moxley, 2008). The more opportunities you can seek out to gain familiarity and comfort with and knowledge of effective collaboration, the better able you will be to represent your clients and your profession.

How does intra- and interprofessional collaboration fit into your practicum experience, in general, and becoming competent to work with individuals and families, specifically? You can begin to answer this question by asking your field instructor about his or her collaborative experiences with co-workers and other professions and organizations, your practicum agency's philosophy about and attitude toward collaborations, and opportunities to observe and engage in collaborative relationships. Examples of ways in which you may be able to collaborate with other agency staff on individual client issues include one-on-one consultations, case presentations/staffings, referrals, and group supervision sessions.

Agency collaboration or "partnerships" may provide the opportunity for both intra- and interdisciplinary collaborative practices, depending on the staff composition of your practicum agency. Interagency collaborations can also present the opportunity for both intra- and interdisciplinary partnered practices, but they provide a different experience. Working with other organizations enables you to observe the blending of policies, practices, cultures, and leadership approaches (Lawson, 2008).

Ongoing Evaluation

A discussion of evaluation is typically considered an ending activity, whether at the end of a course, workshop, book, or practicum. However, evaluation of your growth and development as a practitioner should be integrated into your practicum experience from the outset. As you develop your learning plan and outcomes, identify ways in which your performance will be evaluated. You can use these checks and balances as a mechanism for assessing learning and outcomes and monitoring your progress in completing the learning objectives and becoming a competent practitioner.

Your field instructor may have established a routine for ongoing evaluation. For instance, your field instructor or other staff member(s) may regularly observe your encounters with your clients. Although observation is possibly the most convenient evaluative technique, either live or through web-based services such as Skype, other strategies include audio- or videotaping and process recording. Videorecording of client sessions is not always possible or feasible, particularly if equipment is not available or if the nature of the agency's work does not lend itself to recording. Although video is an excellent tool for assessing and monitoring the development of practice skills, other techniques can be just as effective. Audiorecording is a useful way to listen to yourself as you engage with clients. You do not have the opportunity to observe your nonverbal communication, but having only the audio portion of the encounter available eliminates the potential distraction created by the picture and allows you to listen critically to the exchange. Process recording can be valuable for processing and analyzing your client encounters and discussing your observations during supervision. This technique involves the recording of session purpose, observations, and content and specifically includes the student's recollections of the interview content, personal "gut level" feelings, client's feelings and affect, and identified interventions and major themes (California State University San Bernardino School of Social Work, n.d.)

Employing a variety of evaluative strategies and evaluators is beneficial for your learning experience. The key is to structure the process for ongoing evaluation formally and to incorporate the structure into your daily practicum activities and regular supervisory meetings. Evaluation, although often perceived as a burdensome task, need not be a negative experience. Creatively approaching the evaluation process can provide you and your field instructor with data helpful to assessing your strengths, competencies, and practice behaviors and guiding areas for growth and development during the remainder of your practicum experience. What other evaluative methods does your field instructor, agency, or fellow students use? You may want to broach this issue with others to share ideas.

Administration of Practice with Individuals and Families

As a student, your exposure to the practicum site's administrative functions may be limited. As a practicing social worker, you will have opportunities to learn about and be involved in the operations of your organization in such areas as practice liability, facilities, personnel, and the budgeting process. Having knowledge of these areas is critical should you elect to move into an administrative role or private practice. While your access to in-depth information and experience may be limited, you can benefit from taking opportunities to discuss issues with your field instructor and other agency staff. Observing staff, administrative, committee, and board meetings are additional strategies for gaining insights into the way in which your practicum organization functions.

In sum, while this discussion of the "business" of practice with individuals and families has not been exhaustive, you have had the opportunity to anticipate a number of issues that may occur during your field experience. Building on the theoretical frameworks and life experiences that you bring to your practice learning, the issues presented here can serve to allay some of your anxieties, raise new questions, and aid you in preparing for learning the "process" of practice with individuals and families.

LEARNING THE "PROCESS" OF PRACTICE WITH INDIVIDUALS AND FAMILIES

Providing social work services to individuals and families is an eagerly awaited aspect of most students' social work training. Students report a moderate level of prepracticum anxiety related to working with clients, particularly in establishing relationships and working with challenging clients (Gelman, 2004; Gelman & Lloyd, 2008). The following discussion will highlight issues and concerns that are typical and normal for beginning social work professionals in practice with individuals and families.

Theory–Practice Integration: Evidence-Based Practice

Corina is in the midst of her first practicum site visit with her field instructor and faculty liaison. She and her field instructor have given the faculty liaison a tour of the detention facility, have highlighted her practicum activities, and are discussing her progress in completing the learning objectives. The faculty liaison inquires about the theories that Corina is using to guide her interventions with the clients and their families. The liaison then asks Corina to describe the way in which she demonstrates evidence-based practice and integrates the theories with her social work practice behaviors. Corina does not know how to respond to these questions. She and her field instructor have not discussed evidence-based practice or theoretical approaches to practice in the family court. Several issues emerge: How can Corina handle the liaison's questions? How can Corina ensure that evidence-based practice and the theory–practice integration issue are addressed in her practicum? What strategies can help Corina facilitate the integration of theory with social work practice and become an evidence-based practitioner?

Human behavior

Focusing on an issue relevant to your practicum, conduct a literature review to identify evidence-based theoretical practice approaches.

The field experience has long been the intended setting for students to master the integration of theory with social work practice (Teigiser, 2009). Despite changing practice realities, the field experience continues to be expected to connect the theoretical with practice behaviors resulting in the development of competencies (CSWE, 2008). Such a requirement compels the profession to determine a rationale for integration, to define theory–practice integration, and to devise strategies for achieving and evaluating integration (both for the classroom and the field).

Theory, research, and practice are inextricably linked as research is utilized to test and develop theory and practice behaviors and competencies become the operationalization of the integration. Evidence-based integration occurs when you utilize research findings, practice expertise, and client characteristics to inform your selection and evaluation of assessment and intervention approaches and strategies (Thyer, 2009). The responsibility for facilitating this process is jointly shared by the social work program's faculty, your field instructor, and you.

In the student profile just presented, Corina may not adequately have considered this issue or she may not be aware that she and her field instructor have, in fact, discussed the issue. Corina can inform the faculty member that she and her field instructor have not yet addressed this issue. This creates the opportunity for Corina, her field instructor, and the faculty liaison to discuss the applicable evidence-based theories and practices used in this setting (possibly enlightening Corina to the fact that theoretical frameworks are indeed considered and applied) and to strategize about ways in which learning experiences can be designed to meet her educational need. Although the profession places considerable importance on the integration of theory and practice, the realities of daily social work demands in the field sometimes do not permit in-depth discussions of theory. Along with utilizing evidence to inform and guide practice, social workers are in a position to utilize practice to inform research (and theory development) and can provide input on theories that are useful in practice (CSWE, 2008; Homonoff, 2008). If Corina's field instructor has in fact neglected to address theory–practice integration, Corina can take the responsibility for initiating this aspect of her learning experience.

The *integration of theory and practice (ITP) loop* is a model by which the integration of theory with practice can be both understood and achieved (Bogo, 2006a; Bogo & Vayda 1998). The model suggests a repeating, flowing process in which you do the following:

1. Retrieval—Initially obtain information regarding the practice situation.
2. Reflection—Reflect on the retrieved information and examine your personal associations and feelings regarding the information presented to you by the client system, which then leads to an objective and sensitive assessment.
3. Linkage—Identify and utilize your knowledge to explain both the retrieved information and your reflection on the information.
4. Professional response—Analyze the information to formulate a professional response from which a plan is developed.

The identification of appropriate empirical and theory-based methodologies and practice lends itself to the operationalization of the integration. The setting and the supervisory relationship, however, must be established and secure enough to allow both the student and the field instructor to give and receive feedback to facilitate this practice learning, which differs significantly

Practice Application 6.2 Application of Evidence-Based Theory to Practice: Testing Your Knowledge

The following scenarios can serve as triggers for your thought and discussion regarding the application of four commonly used evidence-based theoretical approaches to typical practicum situations.

Corina is working with a 16-year-old female remanded to the detention facility for truancy and running away with her 22-year-old boyfriend. The teen's behavior toward Corina and the other staff is extremely belligerent. The client has no actively involved social support system. Corina and her field instructor believe that cognitive-behavioral theory has merit for application in this case. What information is needed to determine the strategies Corina can employ to integrate this theory?

Ben is working with a family of four who live in the neighborhood served by his community center practicum site. The 33-year-old mother, recently diagnosed as HIV-positive, appears depressed, as evidenced by her unkempt appearance, weight loss, lethargy, and withdrawal from center activities. Her boyfriend's interest in and involvement with her children and her appears to have decreased significantly. The 10-year-old son is failing fourth grade and has been involved in a number of fights at school and on the bus. The mother suspects that her 15-year-old daughter is sexually active and may be involved in a gang. The clients' house is in a serious state of disrepair. Ben wants to incorporate a systems theory approach. What evidence is needed to develop strategies for Ben to consider?

Lauren is working with a 20-year-old woman and her two children, who are residents of a women's shelter. This is the client's third admission to the shelter, and she states that she is certain that she wants to leave the abusive relationship this time. If Lauren uses a problem-solving approach to guide her intervention with this client, what issues arise for Lauren and her client? How can Lauren implement an intervention?

Cameron is working with a 64-year-old retired male corporate executive being treated for alcohol addiction. Cameron feels unfamiliar with the issues that this client is experiencing and realizes that he needs to employ an intervention based in ethnic-sensitive theory. Where does Cameron begin in his implementation of this theoretical framework? How might he work effectively with this client while maintaining ethnic sensitivity? How will Cameron know if he has or has not responded appropriately to ethnic and cultural differences?

Regarding the application of various theoretical approaches, do you find that you are comfortable with the scenarios described earlier? If you are able to identify and determine possible intervention strategies, you can feel assured that you have, indeed, grasped the complex concept of evidence-based theory–practice integration. If you are uncertain or at a loss regarding possible applications of theory to practice in these situations, you may benefit from reviewing theories used in social work practice, consulting with your field instructor or social work program faculty, and raising the issue for discussion in your integrative practice field seminar.

from traditional learning. From the evidence-based theoretical–practice foundation established by you and your field instructor for practice with individuals and families, the learning related to your practice behaviors can flow. Areas related to learning the "process" of practice at the individual and family level is highlighted in the following discussion including working with difficult clients, unique practice challenges, developing appropriate expectations for yourself and your clients, and use of self in your practice.

Working with Challenging Situations with Clients

During the learning process, students often lack confidence for working with any and all clients. Working with violent, suicidal or homicidal, resistive, dependent, or inappropriate clients can prompt a unique set of anxieties. Although not all practicum sites serve client populations that are typically considered difficult, all social service agencies serve clients who can present challenges for social workers. What constitutes difficult for one worker or agency may not be perceived as challenging by others. Most of us consider openly hostile or violent clients difficult, but do you consider the overly dependent client who constantly asks your advice and opinions on life matters difficult? What about the client who seems too familiar or friendly? This client may ask you numerous personal questions, bring you gifts, or ask for your personal contact information. What about the client who is persistently late or misses appointments or who does not follow through with agreed-upon tasks? What about the client who appears to be under the influence of alcohol or other drugs? Do you confront the client, refuse to see him or her at that time, ignore the issue unless the client exhibits blatantly obvious signs of inebriation or altered state? What about the client who seeks to make you a friend on a social networking site? Working with the client behaviors described here can pose challenges for all helping professionals, not just practicum students.

Based on your experiences and your knowledge of yourself (your personality and interactional style), what client issues have been or will be difficult for you? Take the opportunity to talk with your field instructor about this issue and learn about his or her challenging experiences and strategies for confronting the difficulties. Then, consider the responses that may be most effective for you. Although each scenario will require an individualized response, suggestions for dealing with difficult client situations include the following:

Ethical Practice

Challenges present opportunities for values clarification. Identify a client-related dilemma and use the NASW *Code of Ethics* for relevant standards.

- Be able and willing to recognize when a client situation makes you feel uncomfortable (e.g., are you feeling anxious, frightened, or manipulated?).
- Do not minimize or discount your feelings. Instead, conduct a reality check for yourself by talking with your field instructor or other staff member(s). The reality may be that this client's behavior has affected other workers in a similar way. You may simply need an opportunity to process your feelings and develop a proactive response. Or something about your encounter(s) with this client may have triggered a memory or past experience for you. In an extreme case, you may need to terminate your relationship with the client.
- Consider setting clear-cut time, access, and interactional boundaries for yourself with the client in order to minimize the challenging behaviors.
- In the case of a client suspected of being under the influence of alcohol or other drugs, be certain you know the agency's policy regarding contact with such clients and rehearse with your field instructor ways in which you can confront the client in this situation.

Regardless of the client issue that triggered your reaction to the situation, working with challenging client behaviors can result in powerful learning. Often, the most difficult experiences are those that provide the most knowledge, skills, and values clarification needed for your professional growth and development of practice competencies. Even when confronted with a difficult client situation, you have the opportunity to learn valuable practice skills and about the resources available to support and promote that learning.

Ethical Dilemma: In the Best Interest of the Child

Rosa was assigned to follow up on a request from a teacher at the neighborhood elementary school. The teacher had asked for the center's help in convincing the parents of one of her students, who is also a client of the center, to allow her to be evaluated for attention-deficit disorder (ADD). The parents believe that if their daughter is evaluated, it will draw attention to the fact that they are undocumented immigrants. If the girl is not evaluated, she will not be eligible for the school district's special education services. Rosa believes that the child should be evaluated, regardless of the impact on the parents' immigration status.

- *What additional information do Rosa and the agency need to intervene in this situation?*
- *Is Rosa's own experience with ADD affecting her perspective on this situation?*
- *Should Rosa self-disclose her personal experience with ADD?*
- *When a child's best interest is in question, should the parents' right to self-determination be respected?*
- *What are the legal and ethical implications of encouraging the parents to allow the evaluation? To not allow the evaluation?*
- *To be an effective evidence-based practitioner, how can Rosa utilize research findings to guide her assessment and intervention planning?*

Unique Practice Opportunities with Individuals and Families

Although we cannot cover all potential practice situations and responses here, several client issues that may arise for you in your practicum include (1) personal knowledge of or connection to the client, (2) encountering the client outside the agency, (3) conflict with the client, (4) sexual attraction to or from the client, (5) suspected system abuse of or by the client, (6) clients with dual diagnoses, and (7) cultural competence.

Personal Knowledge of or Connection to the Client

Not infrequently, a practicum student finds that a friend, acquaintance, or even family member is receiving services from the agency in which the student is completing his or her field requirement. You may realize that you have knowledge of a client that has bearing on the relationship to the agency (e.g., service eligibility, legal standing, or relationship with an affiliated agency). Particularly in smaller communities with fewer service delivery agencies, you may encounter a familiar face in the lobby, intake office, or on a home visit; review the chart of a friend; or hear about someone you know in a case staffing meeting.

Several questions arise in these situations: Do you acknowledge the client, accept the assignment, read the chart, share the information you have, or participate in the case discussion? First, discuss the situation with your field instructor and inquire about the agency's policy or practice regarding workers having personal knowledge of a client. Depending on the agency setting in which you are placed, the services provided, and the community, working with persons you know may be routine *or* may be completely unacceptable. You must also consider your own feelings about the situation. Are you comfortable working with a casual acquaintance from high school around the intense issues of spousal violence, for instance? Can you work with your parents' friend to place her mother in a residential care facility? Consider not only agency culture, your ability to work with such a client, and the client's feelings about working with you or knowing that you are familiar with his or her case.

Encountering the Client Outside the Agency

You may find that you will meet your clients outside the practicum setting at the grocery store, mall, or even a social event. Do you acknowledge or ignore the client? Waiting for the client to acknowledge you is considered appropriate. Some clients may be comfortable meeting and talking with you outside the agency setting, while others will be mortified, particularly if they are with family or friends who do not know that they are receiving services from your agency. Some clients are so comfortable that they will introduce you to their companions or attempt to engage at length with you about their case. Although you can certainly be friendly when this occurs, it is prudent to keep the encounter brief and superficial, leaving case-related discussions for a more appropriate time and location.

Conflict with the Client

What should you do if you find either that you do not like the client or that the client does not like you? Like can mean many different things to each person. You may find the client's philosophy, attitudes, personality, behaviors, language, or lifestyle so foreign or offensive to you that you feel you cannot be an effective practitioner. Differences can range from the client's beliefs regarding abortion to his or her practice of discriminatory behaviors to his or her inflicting physical harm on others.

What can you do, should this challenge arise in your practice learning or later in your career? It presents you with the opportunity to examine your own feelings about diversity and to explore your ability to be a competent social worker when you do not agree with a client's beliefs or choices. You may have considered your thoughts and feelings about diversity during earlier social work courses or in your volunteer/work experience. Until you find yourself face to face with an individual who espouses a belief or behavior that contradicts your own *and* you must provide services to him or her, you may not have fully considered the implications of such a situation.

An in-depth examination of your own beliefs, your commitment to social work values, and your ability to identify self-worth and strengths in all people can guide you in developing the skills needed to confront this difficult practice issue. Seek out these challenging situations to help clarify your values, confront issues of diversity, and through engaging in appropriate practice behaviors, identify those populations with which you may *not* be as effective.

Consider that the client may find your presentation of yourself equally offensive. Ideally, the client should have very limited information regarding your personal situation but may, based on physical evidence and assumptions, decide that he or she cannot relate to you in a productive manner. Important learning can occur for both you and the client in this situation. By addressing the client's resistance and openly confronting his or her perceptions of you and of your abilities, you and the client can learn to overcome the negative feelings and to work together effectively.

An issue related to conflicts with clients is experiencing a situation or population with which you are not comfortable. In accordance with the NASW *Code of Ethics* (2008a), your social work program will develop practice behaviors that provide guidelines for working with all populations. For instance, students have encountered dilemmas when they strive to meet practice behaviors defined by the social work program within the context of the *Code of Ethics* while being consistent with their own spiritual, religious, or value beliefs. You will need to process with your practicum team if you encounter situations that make you uncomfortable so you can determine if you can support a client even if you do not support some aspect of his or her life.

Sexual Attraction to or from the Client

Sexual attraction directed from or toward clients is not unheard of in the helping professions. When humans share intimate details of their lives that may involve connecting with painful memories, a bond can be created that manifests itself in the form of a physical and emotional attraction. The client may mistake his or her appreciation for the worker's efforts as sexual feelings. The worker or the client may find that the other reminds him or her of another individual, thus triggering sexual thoughts. Regardless of the specific situation, you must, at the first hint of any sexual feelings, comments, or actions, seek consultation with your field instructor. As with other practice challenges, do not ignore or discount such feelings. Left unattended, inappropriate client or worker thoughts can quickly dominate the relationship and result in unwise choices.

The NASW *Code of Ethics* (2008a) clearly states that sexual contact with clients is prohibited. In the case of client feelings being directed toward a worker, the worker can take the opportunity to address the feelings with the client and process with the client the motivations behind the feelings. An open and candid confrontation of sexual issues along with ethical responsibilities and boundaries can be a healthy growth experience for both the worker and the client. Should this situation occur in your practicum, you may wish to role-play the confrontation with your field instructor to increase your comfort and confidence levels.

In the event the worker is experiencing sexual feelings for a client, he or she also has the opportunity to examine the roots of such feelings and to gain insight and skill regarding the appropriate response to the experience. Exploring with colleagues or a supervisor one's sexual feelings about a client can prompt feelings of guilt and discomfort but can illuminate and address the origins of the feelings in order to prevent unethical practice.

Suspected System Abuse of or by the Client

A particular challenge may emerge during your field experience in the form of client abuses of or by the social service system. Clients have been known to take advantage of the social service system through such acts as nonreport of income or information or receiving duplicated services from multiple agencies. Conversely, social service workers have been found to exploit clients through eligibility discrimination or engaging in dual relationships with clients.

Should you suspect or have evidence of such inappropriate activity, do not assume that you should not report the information just because you are a practicum student. The whistle can be blown by anyone. The NASW *Code of Ethics* (2008a) clearly states that social workers are responsible for recognizing and taking action in the event of unethical practice on the part of other social workers, but not by clients per se. Regardless of the specific situation in which you suspect an abuse of some kind, suggested responses include (1) inform your field instructor immediately, (2) familiarize yourself with agency guidelines and culture in such situations (including information needed), and (3) consider the "big picture" from all perspectives (i.e., you may not have all the information or understand the particular dynamics of a situation). What if your field instructor does not believe you or discounts your perception? While each case will differ, consult with practicum faculty at your social work program to determine an appropriate course of action.

Clients with Dual Diagnoses

In practice with individual and family client systems, a client may experience more than one condition that brings him or her into the social service system. Known as *dual diagnosis,* multiple conditions may occur at the same time that impact the client's ability to participate effectively in the intervention. An example may be the client experiencing a mental illness while also being addicted to alcohol or other drug.

Working with clients who are experiencing diagnoses in multiple areas can provide both challenges and opportunities. Practitioners find it challenging to assess both areas at the same time. This dual task requires practitioners to have a broad scope of knowledge in both areas, particularly in terms of understanding the impact of each condition on the other. For example, is the alcohol exacerbating the depression? To fully grasp the effect of one condition on another often requires the social worker to have knowledge of physiological, psychological, and medical functioning. You must have a multifaceted knowledge base to develop an accurate assessment and intervention plan. Your field instructor and other agency staff can be a valuable resource for gaining a working knowledge of this area.

Your systems-based social work training provides you an opportunity to develop an assessment and intervention strategy that encompasses all aspects of a client's life and situation. Uncovering the presence of a dual diagnosis may identify for the client a condition or problem not previously known to him or her. Continuing with the earlier example of co-existing depression and substance use, consider the patient who has known that he felt bad and self-medicated with alcohol to improve his mood. Understanding that using a depressant such as alcohol will worsen his depression may be a turning point in this client's recovery.

Cultural Competence

Being a culturally competent social work practitioner is at the core of the social work value system. The NASW *Code of Ethics* (2008a) and the CSWE standards for accrediting social work education programs (2008) both clearly charge social workers with being culturally competent. To operationalize this professional commitment, NASW developed the *NASW Standards for Cultural Competence in Social Work Practice* (2001) and the *Indicators for the Achievement of the NASW Standards for Cultural Competence in Social Work Practice* (2007).

Issues related to diversity have likely received in-depth coverage in most, if not all, of your social work courses. You have had the opportunity to explore your own awareness of diversity, be exposed to others who are different from you, and develop some beginning skills in culturally competent practice. The issue is raised in this section, not because we feel we can thoroughly address cultural competence here but because your practicum provides you with a unique opportunity to grow into being a culturally competent social work practitioner.

"Cultural competence is more than knowledge about others. Cultural competence requires action" (Simmons, Diaz, Jackson, & Takahashi, 2008, p. 12). You now have the opportunity to apply in your practicum setting the culturally competent knowledge, skills, and values that you gained in your coursework. Actually being a culturally competent social worker can be challenging. Client diversity can occur in many areas, including race, ethnicity, culture, age, gender, sexual orientation, religion, spirituality, political philosophy, socioeconomic class, education, family background, and life experiences. The *Code of Ethics* (2008a) charges social workers to gain understanding, knowledge, and education about client culture and diversity. How can one person or even one agency possibly have adequate knowledge about the varied and diverse client systems with which he or she will work during a social work career? The *Indicators for the Achievement of the NASW Standards for Cultural Competence in Social Work Practice* (NASW, 2007) provides guidance in the form of five essential elements that can apply to an individual or a larger system: (1) value diversity; (2) capacity for cultural self-assessment; (3) awareness of the dynamics inherent when cultures interact; (4) institutionalized cultural knowledge; and (5) programs and services that reflect an understanding of diversity between and within cultures (p.13).

One area that has experienced renewed attention and understanding is the impact of spirituality and/or religion on the lives of the clients with whom social workers work. Social workers need skills that will promote the incorporation of spirituality and religion into our practice from engagement through termination. Specifically, questions to consider include the following:

- How is spirituality and/or religious beliefs and practices handled at your practicum agency?
- Are spirituality or religious practices included in the agency's assessment process?
- Is it permissible to include issues of spirituality and religion in your assessment and intervention?
- If the practicum agency supports inclusion of spirituality and religion into social work practice, are you clear about the appropriate way in which to acknowledge and discuss the issue?
- Does the potential for a value and/or ethical conflict exist if the client's spiritual or religious beliefs are different from your own?

"As a practicum student in the role of learner, you can solidify your commitment to strive for all areas of cultural competence, understanding that this is a lifelong challenge and opportunity."

As a practicum student in the role of learner, you can solidify your commitment to strive for all areas of cultural competence, understanding that this is a lifelong challenge and opportunity. Also of importance is the awareness that cultural competence differs from one area and level of practice to another (Simmons et al., 2008). During your practicum, you can proactively seek out opportunities to interact with others whose life experiences differ from yours, so that you can better understand ways in which you can be helpful to those individuals or groups. While you may feel intimidated upon leaving the "comfort zone" of working with those client systems that are most like you, you are particularly encouraged to broaden your understanding of those individuals or groups with whom you have little or no experience. Those opportunities may provide the most valuable learning of all.

Developing Appropriate Expectations of Yourself and Your Clients

What are realistic expectations of yourself and your clients regarding the parameters of your relationship? Should you be available to the client 24 hours a day? Establishing and maintaining clear parameters with your client regarding all expectations for the relationship is critical. Communicating your mutual expectations serves to build rapport and trust, clarify misassumptions, and prevent disappointments or frustrations that may occur if expectations are not met.

Your practicum agency, field instructor, and other staff are a resource for you in developing appropriate expectations for relating to your clients. For example, based on the services provided by your practicum site, the agency may have specific guidelines for such issues as accessibility (e.g., can you be reached during office hours only or through the answering service, beeper, or cell phone?). If your agency does not provide a directive, you and your field instructor can negotiate reasonable expectations based on your practicum responsibilities.

Use of Self in Practice with Individuals and Families

As a social worker, you cannot separate your personal self entirely from your professional self. Just as the client does, you bring your attitudes, beliefs, and life experiences to the relationship. Unlike the client, however, you are responsible for balancing the personal with the professional. Therefore, you must determine the amount and scope of integrating yourself into the client relationship.

Two issues emerge as you consider the integration of self into the professional encounter. First, sharing information with your client about your experiences can be both a positive and a negative use of self. You may feel that you have experience and insights to share with your clients that will aid them in the change process, but make sure that the encounter does not become a testimony of *your* life. A client may experience increased trust, normalization, hope, or insight regarding his or her situation if he or she learns that the two of you share similar experiences. On the other hand, the client may assume that he or she must resolve his or her situation just as you did and may experience a sense of failure if his or her outcome differs from yours.

When considering the use of self-disclosure in a social work relationship, consider the following pros and cons associated with self-disclosure (Linsley, 1998):

Pros	Cons
1. Therapeutic for the client	1. Burdensome for the client
2. Useful tool for "joining" with the client	2. Can disrupt the worker–client work and relationship
3. Can normalize the client's perception of the situation	3. Can make the client feel abnormal
4. Can serve to aid the client in healing old and new wounds	4. Can serve to open old wounds
5. Can create mutuality, hope, and attachment	5. Can create discomfort and possible physical harm
6. Can aid in achieving desired outcomes due to shared experience	6. Can impede progress toward desired outcomes due to the discomfort of shared experience

The decision to self-disclose personal information in a professional relationship is likely to be a difficult and unclear one (NASW, 2001). Some information (e.g., marital status, home of origin, and schools attended) may seem benign, but you should seriously consider the implications of sharing such information with your client. Deciding whether to divulge more personal information (e.g., traumatic or life-threatening illnesses or experiences) requires considerable thought. Information that you should *not* share under any circumstances includes political views and sexual information (Linsley, 1998).

Infusing your life experiences and beliefs into the engagement, assessment, and intervention process can prove inspirational for you. To develop such *practice wisdom*, you can begin by regularly reflecting on your own experiences, professional knowledge, and their impact on your practice behaviors (Chu & Tsui, 2008). You must be careful, however, not to project your own experience onto your client's situation. For example, just because your parents' divorce affected you in one way does not suggest that your client experienced his or her parents' divorce in that way or that you should build your intervention around your experience. Consider that the focus must remain on the client; any disclosure must be for the benefit of the client. Examining your own life

---

Practice Application 6.3 Handling Ethical Dilemmas

As discussed throughout this text, confronting ethical dilemmas is a routine part of social work life. The following scenarios bring to light a number of issues this chapter has raised. Review each of the 10 scenarios and discuss each with your field instructor, other staff, and fellow students to identify the challenges and potential solutions for you:

1. You are at a party, and one of your clients approaches you and begins a conversation.
2. You are discussing a topic in a class that is directly related to your practicum experience. How are you supposed to discuss a case example?
3. Your client happens to mention that an older member of his or her family is being "pushed around" by another family member. How are you supposed to address this with the client?
4. Your client states that he or she does not have the ability to pay for services from your agency.
5. Your field instructor assigns you to obtain a client's records from another agency. What is the procedure for accomplishing this task?
6. What are you supposed to tell clients *before* they begin the process of accessing the services of your practicum agency?
7. You are physically attracted to one of your clients. How are you supposed to deal with this situation?
8. What are you to tell clients about your status at the agency, including length of service and duration of remaining service, authority, and access to information and resources?
9. You hear another worker talking about a client during a lunchroom conversation.
10. You hear another worker telling a racial or ethnic joke.

Developed by Ellen Burkemper, PhD, LCSW, MFT

Practice Application 6.4 Case Re-Enactment

Students will orally re-enact a client system interaction for the class and facilitate a discussion. Students will also turn in a written description of the re-enactment one week prior to the presentation. The purpose of this assignment is to (1) promote integration of theory and practice; (2) assist others in integrating theory with practice; (3) develop work group skills with students in the class; and (4) hone case presentation skills.

Oral Re-enactment

▶ Choose a case scenario of a client system (individual, group, family, or community) from your

practicum agency that either you or your field instructor found challenging. The case can be challenging for a variety of reasons. Some suggested ideas involve challenges concerning the following:

1. Student inexperience/competence
2. Client resistance
3. Client noncompliance
4. Cultural difference
5. Values/ethics
6. Theory–practice integration

▶ Work with a resource group of three or four students to provide feedback, support, and guidance to each other. Class time will be allowed for group work (three meetings); however, students may need to meet outside class to prepare and rehearse/film. Each student will conduct a re-enactment in addition to serving as a group member. In addition to re-enacting a case for discussion, students will serve at least once in the following roles for other members of their groups:

1. Member of a client system
2. Feedback/suggestions/discussion questions in the planning process prior to the actual re-enactment

▶ Develop a 5- to 10-minute re-enactment of a client system interaction. The re-enactment can be live or videorecorded and shown to the class. It can include as many members of your resource group as needed. Introduce the re-enactment by briefly discussing any background (assessment) information that may be needed to understand it. Actors should know their parts and should avoid reading notes verbatim during the presentation. Only information that would identify the client(s) should be changed to maintain confidentiality; otherwise, the interaction should be presented as it actually occurred.

▶ Discuss integration of theory and practice for the interaction re-enacted. The presenting student shall choose at least one theory from a list of theories and present for five minutes on the integration of theory and practice with the client system presented. The presenting student should do these things:

1. Briefly summarize each theory utilized
2. Describe the theory/practice integration with the client system presented

▶ Numerous theories are used in social work, many of which have been covered in your coursework. Discussing theory selection, application, and integration with practice with your field instructor can be an illuminating and productive use of supervision sessions.

▶ Facilitate a 5- to 10-minute discussion of theory–practice integration. Generate two questions about theory–practice integration that will serve to generate discussion, and be prepared to answer the questions.

Examples:

1. "I tried to use the problem-solving approach to working with this client. How might I have done it better?"
2. "How might a social worker implement a mezzo-level intervention with this client?"
3. "I had a lot of trouble using person-centered theory in this interaction. Does anyone have any suggestions?"

Written Requirement

The written description will include these elements:

▶ A brief (one- or two-paragraph) description of the re-enactment, including (1) client system assessment information, (2) summary of the interaction, and (3) list of the participating actors and a description of their roles.

▶ A description of the presentation of theory–practice integration. Provide a one-paragraph summary of the theory(ies) discussed and a one-paragraph description of the interface of the theory with the case.

▶ List the two questions to be used to begin discussion.

experiences as they relate to those of your clients may elicit both elation and pain. Success comes from the outcomes that you derive from this introspective analysis. You and your clients can benefit from your continued efforts to know and understand yourself and the way in which you perceive yourself as a competent social work professional.

In sum, learning the "process" of social work practice with individuals and families is a complex and ongoing endeavor that changes with the client population and setting in which you work. You can begin to unravel this puzzle by considering and experimenting with the issues presented here.

Practice Application 6.5 Learning from the Client: When Listening Is Not Enough

In a future client encounter, spend five minutes at the end of the session really learning from your client. Ask your client to describe to you three pertinent details or bits of information that he or she believes you understand about the presenting situation. Without comment or editorial, write down or record (with client's permission) the client's exact statements.

Following this client encounter, but before the next time you see the client, complete the following:

▶ Compare your formal assessment statements (contained in the client's file) with those of the client. Look for differences, particularly noting the client's language and context use.

▶ Discuss with your field instructor, colleagues, and classmates any words or phrases (client's, agency's, or other disciplines') that are unfamiliar to you. Clarify how the staff and agency define or understand these words or phrases.

At the beginning of the next encounter with your client, do these things:

▶ Compliment the client on "the lesson learned" and discuss and agree to begin to use "mutual language" that ensures that your client and you are communicating clearly and effectively.

▶ With your client's permission, share phrases and culturally diverse language usages with staff during staff meetings, training sessions, or your integrative practice field seminar.

Developed by Carole Price, LCSW

Practice Application 6.6 Developing the Critical Self: Taking the Pain Out of Feedback

Once you have established a working relationship with your client (possibly at the beginning of the second encounter/session), routinely ask the client for his or her feedback about the session you have just completed. Allow approximately five minutes for this experience during each meeting with your client. Listen carefully for the client's perception of your relationship with him or her. To grasp this critical information, you may pose the following questions:

▶ What happens in our sessions/meetings that you find helpful?

▶ What happens in our sessions/meetings that you find not helpful?

After you have collected this information from your client, you can do the following:

▶ Discuss with your field instructor or colleagues the feedback provided by your client and seek constructive strategies for interacting with the client in future encounters.

▶ Discuss with your client the feedback that you have received from your field instructor or colleague(s) and mutually agree on interactions that will enhance your worker–client relationship.

▶ Regularly journal your feelings about this experience, and use a timeline to note your increased ability/progress in using feedback as an effective practice tool.

Developed by Carole Price, LCSW

PRACTICE APPLICATION 6.1 FOLLOW-UP

The documentation exercise could be efficiently rewritten as follows:

S—Ms. Jones is interested in adoption. She wants an African American girl or boy, age birth to 5 years, with mild to moderate challenges. Ms. Jones believes that she is financially and emotionally prepared to adopt.

O—Ms. Jones is a 32-year-old single, African American woman who lives in a three-bedroom home with her 8-year-old daughter. Her annual salary is $42,690.

A—Ms. Jones appears to meet the minimum criteria for eligibility to adopt.

P—I provided Ms. Jones with a description of the adoption process and an application form. She will review the materials and determine if she would like to continue the application. We will meet on August 11 at 3:00 P.M.

SUMMARY

This chapter has been aimed at helping you gain insights into the "business" and "process" of social work practice with individuals and families. Consistent with the concept of generalist social work practice, the issues highlighted here are applicable across all levels of social work practice and will be discussed within the context of practice with groups, organizations, and communities in subsequent chapters. The foundations of practice that you establish as you develop practice behaviors and competencies at the individual and family level will also enable you to function competently as a social work professional.

Lauren responded to the angry client at the shelter initially by feeling defensive about the client's demeaning remarks regarding her status as a student. She was then able to acknowledge to herself and to the client the client's feelings that professionals were not helping her. Lauren offered the client the option to work with another social worker, but she assured the client that she was open to listening to the client's thoughts and feelings regarding resolution of her situation. Lauren was able to apply a strengths-based approach and encouraged the client to collaborate with her to identify the client's assets and resources and develop a plan of action. The client's frustrations were defused and the client agreed to give it a try. The situation appears to be on the way to a positive resolution, but do you have additional strategies that Lauren might have considered?

Corina became flustered when attempting to respond to the faculty liaison's questions regarding evidence-based practice and theory–practice integration. She stated that theories had been discussed in some of her classes but never in terms of actual use in her practice. She suggested that faculty who teach those courses focus on applying research and literature or theories. She was mindful of her field instructor's presence in this meeting, so she tried not to direct the blame for her lack of knowledge to the supervisor. Corina agreed to review her theory texts and readings and engage in discussion of evidence-based theory–practice integration during supervision sessions, but she continued to believe that the faculty and field instructor were responsible for this deficit in her knowledge and preparation. Corina's response is one alternative. Can you think of additional (possibly less defensive and closed) ways in which she might have handled this situation?

Succeed with PEARSON **mysocialworklab**

Log onto **MySocialWorkLab** to access a wealth of case studies, videos, and assessment. (*If you did not receive an access code to **MySocialWorkLab** with this text and wish to purchase access online, please visit* www.mysocialworklab.com.)

1. Click on Interactive Cases for Practice. Select Domestic Violence and complete the module.

2. Click on My Social Work Library and select Domestic Violence: Mikki's Story. Review the case information provided and respond to Questions #3 and 4 included in the first set of questions on pages 31 and 32.

PRACTICE TEST
The following questions will test your knowledge of the content found within this chapter. For additional assessment, including licensing-exam type questions on applying chapter content to practice, visit **MySocialWorkLab.**

Ethical Practice

1. Which of the following is not a violation of a client's confidentiality?
  a. Present client information in agency case conference
  b. Talk about a client in public location (e.g., restaurant)
  c. Discuss a client situation in agency's public spaces
  d. Discuss client with referral source

Critical Thinking

2. Effective documentation of client interventions includes:
  a. Social worker opinions
  b. Verbatim reporting of client statements
  c. Chronological record of client-social worker conversation
  d. Client statement of needs

3. In striving for practice autonomy and competence, practicum students should:
  a. Show initiative by handling case and reporting on outcome in supervision
  b. Negotiate with field instructor appropriate level of independence
  c. Check with field instructor before each client encounter
  d. Utilize staff members when field instructor is unavailable

4. When asked to provide coverage of others' cases, you are responsible for all of the following except:
  a. Provide evaluation of other worker's intervention skills
  b. Review case materials
  c. Ensure you are qualified to provide service required
  d. Provide transition when case is returned to original social worker

Engage Assess Intervene Evaluate

5. The most important aspect of evaluating your practice is:
  a. Make a audio- or video-recording of a client encounter
  b. Obtain client input
  c. Link learning objectives to measurable outcomes
  d. Complete process recordings

6. The best response to a conflict with a client is:
  a. Transfer case to another social worker
  b. Examine your own belief and value systems

  c. Terminate client's services
  d. Ask another social worker to accompany you when you see client

Diversity in Practice

7. Which of the following is not an element of culturally competent practice?
  a. Cultural self-awareness
  b. Value diversity
  c. Programs that embrace cultural diversity
  d. Fluency in client's language

8. Select the grouping of items that best describes the benefits of disclosing personal information to a client:
  a. Promote joining with client, open up earlier trauma, and is therapeutic
  b. Promote joining with client, open up earlier traumas, and achieves outcomes
  c. Promote joining with client, normalize client experience, and provide hope
  d. Promote joining with client, normalize client experience, and prompt discomfort

Engage Assess Intervene Evaluate

9. In conducting an assessment with a client who you find challenging, the most effective strategy may be to:
  a. View challenge as professional growth opportunity
  b. Consult agency policy regarding the handling of challenging clients
  c. View this as a sign that you are not prepared for practice
  d. Delay assessment process until you have more information

Engage Assess Intervene Evaluate

10. A client values the inclusion of her or his religious beliefs and traditions in the intervention. You are not familiar with the client's religion. The best <u>first</u> action may be to:
  a. Inquire if there is another social worker who practices client's religion
  b. Learn more about client's religious beliefs and traditions
  c. Explore conflict potential between your religious traditions and those of the client
  d. Ask field instructor if you must incorporate religion into intervention

Log onto **MySocialWorkLab** once you have completed the Practice Test above, to access additional study tools and assessment.

Answers

Key: 1) a 2) d 3) b 4) a 5) c 6) b 7) d 8) c 9) a 10) c

Social Work Practice in the Field

Working with Groups

Core Competencies in this Chapter (Check marks indicate which competencies are covered in depth)				
Professional Identity	Ethical Practice	Critical Thinking	✓ Diversity in Practice	Human Rights and Justice
✓ Research Based Practice	Human Behavior	Policy Practice	Practice Contexts	✓ Engage, Assess, Intervene, Evaluate

Group work can be powerful, intimidating, chaotic, and immensely rewarding—all at the same time. As Margaret Mead stated, groups can change the world—whether a group of children, a neighborhood, or society. Groups come in various shapes, sizes, and formats and have vastly differing goals and agendas. *Group practice* is defined as "goal-directed activity that brings together people for a common purpose or goal" (Toseland & Horton, 2008, p. 298).

"Group work can be powerful, intimidating, chaotic, and immensely rewarding—all at the same time."

Growing out of the settlement house movement, group work is now one of the three primary areas of social work practice (Toseland & Horton, 2008). Increasing societal complexities, changing delivery of social services and health care, diversity, and technological advances provide social workers with opportunities to utilize both traditional group practice skills along with developing new skills to respond to client needs (Garvin & Galinsky, 2008). In the performance of nondirect service responsibilities, the need for collaboration, coalition building, and issue-based task forces has heightened the need for well-trained group facilitators. Even with increasing needs, only 18 percent of social workers report that group work is their primary practice area (Whitaker & Arrington, 2008). Most social workers, however, engage in some form of group social work practice as a part of their social work positions and view group work as just one of many activities in which they engage.

As outlined in the National Association of Social Workers (NASW) *Code of Ethics* (2008a), the mission of social work is to enhance human well-being and promote social justice and change for individuals, families, social groups, organizations, and communities. Once they gain group experience, many social workers find group practice exhilarating. By facilitating interactions among members, group work builds on individual strengths to actualize the power of the group dynamic that occurs when they share and bring new insights to the experiences of others.

Social work educators and practitioners agree that group work skills are important to the development of a social worker, but practicum students may find skill acquisition challenging. While approximately 80 percent of practicum students report being exposed to group work, only half feel prepared to practice (Clements, 2008). Having group practice experience is predictive of perceptions of preparation and plans for future practice, and gaining skills in practicum in critical (Clements, 2008). Should you find that gaining group practice is not possible, consider seeking a group experience outside your agency in an affiliated agency or related area. Such an arrangement might be negotiated by your field instructor. If group participation is not readily available, an alternative is to develop a student support group composed of students in your practicum site or social work program. Each student can assume responsibility for facilitation of one or more sessions, and the group can use itself to gain group work skills, process group dynamics, and be supported by peers.

Students may be intimidated by group facilitation, particularly if they do not have group leadership experience. Most of us have voiced (maybe not out loud) anxiety about a negative group experience: What if the members of the group do not bond with one another or me, or—worst case—join together to rebel against me? These fears are not uncommon among fledgling group leaders. If this describes you, you may want to begin to learn group skills by observing a group or by serving as a co-facilitator of a group.

If students plan to work with individuals and families, they may not envision group work in their future. Facilitating a support group, chairing a quality assurance committee, or organizing a group of neighbors can be a part of practice with individuals and families. Generalist social work practice encompasses considerable involvement in groups—client, interprofessional, community, and staff—and achieving competence in group work will prepare you for that unexpected opportunity. Talking with your practicum team or seminar classmates can help you work through your questions and concerns about group practice.

This chapter will operationalize group practice within the context of your practicum experience, beginning with your student role and expectations followed by a focus on the "business" and "process" of group practice. The unit will close with a discussion of nondirect service group work, including facilitation of a group meeting, guidelines for presenting information to a group, and working with a task-focused group.

EXPECTATIONS FOR STUDENT LEARNING IN PRACTICE WITH GROUPS

Whether the group is a task or treatment group, group practice shares a commitment to a systemic perspective, group dynamics, common intervention concepts and processes, and evaluation (Garvin & Galinsky, 2008). Following is a brief description of three models, with examples of group types and of the roles a social worker may fulfill.

Social Action/Goals Model

Based on problem-focused interests and goals, examples include neighborhood safety group, parent–teacher association, community development task force, and coalition advocating for improved welfare legislation. The social worker can function as an initiator/convener/organizer (e.g., social worker may respond to a community need and convene a group), facilitator, advocate, and resource (e.g., information, financial support, or access to data or people).

Reciprocal Goals Model

Based on mutual aid and self-help premise, in which members support one another through sharing common experiences, examples include 12-step programs (e.g., Alcoholics Anonymous, Overeaters Anonymous, Al-Anon, and Alateen), grief support group, caregiver support group (e.g., caregivers of persons with chronic illnesses), and disease-specific patient support group (e.g., cancer support group). In this model, the social worker can provide facilitation, mediation, education, and support for resources, education, and referrals.

Remedial Goals Model

Based on the philosophy that group member interactions facilitate change, examples include psychotherapy group for persons with similar diagnoses (e.g., depression, bipolar disorder, and schizophrenia), marital therapy group, child abuse perpetrators group, and survivors of a trauma (e.g., child abuse, sexual abuse, rape, and criminal action). The social work can serve as a therapist/clinician, educator, or mediator.

Your style as a group leader is important to consider as you begin your role as a group facilitator or therapist. Yalom and Leszcz (2005) categorize leader behaviors as (1) emotionally stimulating—challenging, intrusive, and personal risk taking; (2) caring—supportive, affectionate, warm, and genuine; (3) meaningful attribution—interpretation, explanation, and translation of feelings; and (4) executive function—establishes rules and limits and manages the group.

Group leader skills should also include flexibility; awareness of client issues; insight into group process; ability to confront, clarify, interpret, and support; and ability to respond appropriately to frustration and resistance (Yalom & Leszcz, 2005).

Building on key leader behaviors, Yalom and Leszcz (2005) suggest that group leaders have two primary roles—technical expert and model-setting participant. The technical expert assumes a clear-cut leadership role that includes establishing the group membership, rules, and direction. The model-setting participant form of leadership involves the group leader modeling behaviors desired for group members. While these leader functions are rooted in group psychotherapy, they are applicable in any group type and, in some situations, one style may be more appropriate than the other.

To adapt to their style and to respond to the situation, effective group leaders draw behaviors and skills from multiple areas. Take a few moments and consider your previous group leader experiences. Which of the behaviors and styles best describe you? Consider your group successes and less-than-successful experiences, and identify strengths and areas for growth related to your group skills.

Although we all utilize a mixture of different styles and behaviors to meet the needs of the situation, we typically align with one predominant style (which likely mirrors the behaviors and styles that we use at other levels of practice). As you complete your practicum experience, you will be well served by seeking out as many group work experiences as possible. Regardless of the type of group experience, you have the opportunity to apply group theory to practice, to develop group facilitation skills, and to develop group documentation skills.

Engage, Assess, Intervene, Evaluate

To begin developing group skills, identify group-related strengths you bring to engagement, assessment, intervention, and termination.

Practice Application 7.1 Groups, Groups, Groups

This application will enable you to gain familiarity with group process from the perspective of an observer. An observer is often able to perceive group dynamics and process from a different perspective because he or she does not have a vested interest in the agenda or the outcome of the group's work. To facilitate your increased awareness:

▶ Select a group that is a part of or affiliated with your practicum agency. The group may be a problem-solving group, committee, board, staff meeting, therapeutic group, or other group that meets on a regular basis. If your agency does not have such a group, consider asking your field instructor or faculty member for options outside the agency.

▶ Attend the group at least two or three times.

▶ Journal on your group observation experiences and address the following areas:

   ▶ Purpose(s) and goals of the group (explicit and implicit)

▶ Summary of group processes you observe, including reference to the stages of group development

▶ Summary of the contribution of each group member, including both leader(s) and participants

▶ Your observations of the effectiveness of the group

▶ Aspects of group process or outcomes that were successful or could be addressed differently

▶ Summary of new learning in group process, interpersonal communication, and group content/goals

▶ If you have co-facilitated a group, reflect on your experiences. Were you prepared? What did you learn about your facilitation style?

▶ Share your observations with your field instructor, focusing on any changes in your perceptions regarding the role of mezzo social work practice in your agency and your professional development.

Developed by Suzanne LeLaurin, LCSW

LEARNING THE "BUSINESS" OF PRACTICE WITH GROUPS

Group social work practice differs significantly from individual- and family-focused practice. This section highlights the "business" of group practice: orientation, group work assignments, identifying yourself as a student, role transition, confidentiality, documentation, collaboration, and ongoing evaluation.

Orientation

Group activities that occur within the practicum setting may or may not be a regular, ongoing facet of the agency's operations. Clinically focused groups may be time limited, cyclical, or even one-time offerings, or a regular part of the schedule. Opportunities to engage in group work may be dependent on timing, client needs and interests, funding, political agendas, agency administration, or physical space issues. Because of the uncertainty involved with group work opportunities, group work orientation can be part of the formal orientation or it may be on-the-job training that occurs when a group need arises. Whether group work is planned or is spontaneous you can assert yourself to ensure that you receive as much orientation as possible.

Practicum students are often asked to identify a need, develop a proposal for initiating a group, recruit members, and establish and facilitate the group (and make coffee). Your preparation for group work may include reviewing information from coursework on group interventions; observing the leadership of existing groups; interviewing co-workers about strategies for developing a new group; and, certainly, brainstorming with your field instructor on an implementation plan.

Students may also be invited to join new or ongoing groups as co-facilitators. Preparation for this type of group involves discussions with the current facilitator

to learn about the impetus, mission, and goals of the group and to learn his or her role, leadership style, and information about the group members. Your participation also involves observing the group you will be joining or a similar group and gaining insight regarding your role in the group.

As a result of group dynamics, content, continuity, or billing issues or agency policy, students may be unable to assume a facilitator or co-facilitator role. Should you find yourself in this situation, discuss with the group's leader or your field instructor ways to optimize your learning. Despite a passive role, you can observe the group interactions and process your observations with the group leader or your field instructor to gain an understanding of group facilitation, application of group theory to practice, and management of group conflicts. It may be helpful to document statements and group interactions and compare notes with the group leader.

Group Work Assignments

Opportunities for group experiences may arise unplanned and you may be organizing and leading a group in addition to your current workload. If your field instructor asks you to be involved in a new or ongoing group, be certain to discuss with him or her the realities of managing this new assignment along with your other responsibilities. Options for juggling this additional task may include restructuring your current workload, adding hours to your weekly schedule (and completing your practicum earlier if this is an option), or not accepting any additional assignments for a period of time.

To meet your learning plan obligations, you may need to consider the type and level of group experience(s) you need. Often, students cannot be involved in the inception, implementation, and termination of an entire group experience. If this is the case, will developing a group (i.e., recruiting, marketing, and selecting/forming a group, but not leading the group) or co-facilitating a group suffice, or must you facilitate a group by yourself? If you are co-facilitating a group, is there a minimum number of sessions you must co-facilitate to fulfill the group work requirement? These are questions to be addressed with your faculty liaison.

Identifying Yourself as a Student

Identifying yourself as a practicum student was discussed in chapter 6, but it presents a unique challenge in group practice. If you join an existing group, you may be viewed as a disruption or outsider. Depending on the focus of the group, adding a new member can raise issues of confidentiality, trust, bonding, and continuity. As you know from the systems perspective, a change in one part of the system stimulates change in the entire system, and your presence may affect just that outcome. Learning that you are a student whose participation is time limited may create challenges to your entry. With the support of your field instructor and co-facilitator, you can address the issues of your participation and role as a student with the group members, a strategy that can allay group members' concerns.

Role Transition

The transition you make from group observer or co-facilitator to facilitator can be easier by anticipating role changes. The typical initiation to group work for a practicum student is observing a group, minimally participating, and processing the experience with the group leader, focusing on group dynamics and leadership issues. Following a period of observation, the student may become a co-facilitator and assume greater responsibility for the group (e.g., organizing, planning the agenda, identifying and procuring resources, completing group notes/documentation, and presenting information to the group). The final phase of group orientation is assuming full responsibility for facilitating a group. As noted, this opportunity may not be an option, but if the opportunity for sole facilitation presents itself, you can use agency and social work program personnel to debrief the group experience to hone your group skills.

Confidentiality

Defining and maintaining confidentiality in group work is similar to that at the individual and family levels but present several unique challenges. You are now accountable for maintaining confidence of not just one person but an entire group of clients. Questions to consider may include:

- What rules regarding confidentiality should be established for a group? How is confidentiality defined in the group? What (if any) information can be shared outside the group? Is confidentiality violated if group members discuss group information with one another outside the meetings or if members discuss group information with other therapists or family members?
- Do confidentiality rules differ depending on group type (e.g., mutual aid, task-focused, or therapy group)?
- If a group member is a client of a co-worker, am I obligated to share information with that co-worker? How do I respond if asked by the staff person about the client's participation in the group?
- How can I respond if a group member(s) tells me information about a fellow group member?
- Are legal implications possible if certain types of information are shared in a group?
- Do laws about privileged communication protect me if I learn of legal violations or criminal acts?
- What is the appropriate response to a breach of confidentiality by a group member(s)?

The answers to these questions are complex and dependent on several factors: previous norms established by an existing group, the context of the specific situation, agency culture and policy, and legal mandates. The agency's philosophy may be that all information regarding an individual should be shared with all workers involved. Conversely, the agency may adhere to a stringent policy of informed consent, by which the information can be shared only with the express (and, possibly, written) consent of the client.

Technologically related issues may also be involved. (Review related material in chapter 6.) For instance, can a group be conducted electronically? If so, what are the confidentiality issues related to group interactions that use synchronous or asynchronous communication? How can you facilitate a virtual group when you cannot read members' nonverbal cues? While virtual group work may improve access and anonymity and reduce stigma, there is no definitive research on the effectiveness of virtual group work (Toseland & Horton, 2008). The *Standards for Social Work Practice with Groups* does, however, urge social workers to rely on ethical standards to guide virtual group practice (Association for the Advancement of Social Work with Groups, Inc. (AASWG), 2006).

You must also examine confidentiality within different types of groups. Although the commitment to maintain confidentiality is critical to the functioning of any client service, the legal implications differ based on the purpose and leadership of the group. Social workers are mandated by law to report potential harm to self and others regardless of the way in which this information is obtained. Should this occur in your practicum, immediately consult with your field instructor to clarify the legal and ethical implications.

Having a clear understanding of the confidentiality rules established by any group you establish or join is critical. Group members may have pointedly discussed their preferences for sharing information inside and outside the group. You are responsible for obtaining this information, which may not be recorded in any official agency documents. Specific details of a situation are critical to determining the parameters of confidentiality and must be considered if a violation is anticipated. For instance, if a group member informs you that another group member has expressed suicidal or homicidal ideations, you are obligated to intervene because the client may be a danger to himself or herself or others. If you learn from a group member that another group member is engaged in an extramarital relationship, you are not obligated to confront the client with this information but may encourage the first group member to raise the issue (assuming it is relevant) with the other group member within the group session.

In sum, the guidelines for confidentiality in group work are essentially the same as in any other area of social work practice, and similar judgments should be employed. However, the issues may be more complicated by virtue of the presence of multiple persons.

Documentation

You have learned the basics and importance of accurate and effective documentation. Documenting group work is just as important as with individuals and families for capturing and analyzing information and monitoring progress. Documenting information obtained from an individual emphasizes facts, thoughts, feelings, and planning, while the focus of group interaction recording is on group exchanges, dynamics, and planning.

Your practicum agency may or may not have a structured format for documenting group information. The more formalized the group (i.e., therapeutic, mandated, or third-party reimbursed), the more likely that a required documentation process is in place that may involve note keeping on the group as a whole and recording in individual client files. Self-help groups do not typically involve extensive record keeping. Clarity is essential regarding the philosophy of group documentation. Are you documenting events and observations only, or are you including assessment and evaluative statements as well (T. Sullivan, personal communication, September 24, 1998)? If your agency's practice is to include assessment in group documentation, you can report the client's behavior and provide your thoughts regarding the possible origins of or reasons for the client's comments or actions.

Documentation of client group activities should be completed immediately following the session. Verbal debriefing with your co-facilitator, if applicable, or your field instructor is optimal and should encompass such information as

Date _____ Group Day _____

Group Leader(s) _____ Group Time _____

Group Members Present _____

Group Content/Process _____

_____

_____

_____

_____

_____

Group Members—Individual Comments

_____

_____

_____

_____

_____

Figure 7.1
Group Process Form
Form provided by Kids in the Middle, Inc., St. Louis, Missouri. Used by permission.

group membership, content/process, and comments regarding individual members. A sample form for documenting group process is provided in Figure 7.1 (T. Sullivan, personal communication, September 24, 1998).

To aid in documenting and evaluating group interactions, consider including the following (Shulman, 2009):

- Group Description (type, member characteristics, session number)
- Summary of issues discussed during the meeting
- Way in which the problem came to the attention of the leader and current status of the problem(s)
- Strategies for intervention and plans for future groups

Practice Application 7.2   How Do Documentation Styles Compare?

The documentation sample presented in Figure 7.1 is offered as a model for recording a client-centered group experience. Compare this format with that used in your practicum agency, and answer the following questions in a journal entry:

- How do the two documentation formats compare? Do they cover similar areas? If not, how do they differ?

- Are there areas of the format that do not meet the needs of your client population?

- If your current format does not meet the needs of your client population, how might you revise your documentation system to fit the type of group that you facilitate better?

If you are required to document group encounters in each individual client's record, a word of caution regarding confidentiality is in order. As a general rule, you should not refer to another client by name or include significant identifying information.

In sum, you may find that documentation of group social work practice may not be as clearly defined and structured as is documentation of practice with individuals and families. You can attain important critical thinking and writing skills by synthesizing group interactions and committing such information to a written summary.

Collaborative Practice

The very definition of group work includes collaboration. As a group leader, you strive to establish a collaborative relationship with the agency administration, group members, your co-facilitator, referral sources, and agency staff working with the group members outside the group. As a group member, you engage in ongoing collaboration with the other members of the group through your exchanges. You can use the knowledge and skills you have gained regarding collaborative practice to promote effective collaboration and enhance group process, including:

- Ensure that your group has the support (e.g., financial and practical) of the agency's administration. Does the administration provide staff, supplies, space, budget, transportation, and/or child care for this endeavor? If the group is being offered on a trial basis, what is the timeframe for determining a successful outcome?
- Clarify on a regular and ongoing basis *your* roles and responsibilities related to the group.
- Regularly, clarify *group members'* roles and responsibilities.
- Identify terms and professional/popular jargon to ensure that all parties are speaking the same language.
- Determine mutually agreed-on goals for the group.
- Mutually establish clear ground rules for group functioning, including norms for attendance and participation, parameters of appropriate discussion/content, logistical issues (e.g., meeting time, place, room arrangements, refreshments, materials, and clean-up), and boundaries for confidentiality.
- Commit to practicing mutual respect for all members and leaders.
- Engage in clear and effective oral and written communications with all parties.
- Provide appropriate feedback to relevant persons on a timely basis.
- Follow up on commitments made to group members, referral sources, and other persons.

Your relationship with a co-facilitator is also a collaboration. Building on the previous guidelines, strategies for achieving effective collaboration with your co-facilitator include discussing your individual philosophies, theoretical frameworks, and styles, establishing clear and realistic roles and responsibilities, and identifying the group purpose, goals, format, and evaluation. If you begin to feel that the collaborative relationship is not progressing in a positive or productive manner, you are advised to address the problems or concerns as soon as possible. Do not wait for the issues to resolve themselves. Depending on the nature of your concern, you may opt to approach the individual(s) involved or process the problem with your field instructor. Regardless of the method you choose, the important point is to assert your role as an adult learner and to take action.

Ongoing Evaluation

Routine evaluation of the group process and of your role as a facilitator/ co-facilitator is particularly important. Due to the number of persons involved in any group intervention, monitoring and understanding the interactions and dynamics are more complex tasks than evaluating individual interventions. Evaluating the group's purpose and goals, dynamics, format, and outcomes is essential to the effective functioning of the group as well as to the development of your group work skills. You may opt to evaluate individual group member's progress and outcomes, the group process itself, your leadership style and effectiveness, or the effectiveness of the group intervention. You can utilize an evidence-based approach to evaluation by maintaining current knowledge of research on group interventions and practices. Evaluation strategies can include:

- Audio- or videorecording
- Process recording
- Group member pre- and post-tests (e.g., single-system design analysis)
- Group member feedback (e.g., satisfaction with group experience)
- Facilitator debriefings (verbal or written)
- Program evaluation to determine whether group goals are being met, the functionality of the group, and any changes needed

Effective group evaluation includes (1) identifying areas to be evaluated before the group begins; (2) establishing how the evaluation results will be analyzed and distributed (e.g., with clients on an individual or group basis, with parents of children in a group, with referral sources, or with other staff members [Yalom & Leszcz, 2005]); (3) determining evaluative tools; and (4) involving your field instructor or co-facilitator in the review and analysis of the evaluative data.

Outcome evaluation is important with all group work. Reciprocal (self-help) groups may not require as high a level of accountability as remedial (therapeutic) groups, but evaluation is important for determining the viability, dynamics, and future of the self-help group. Some types of groups lend themselves more easily to evaluation. Time-limited (e.g., parent education), goal-focused (e.g., weight loss), and behavior change (e.g., smoking cessation) groups are easier to evaluate as each has tangible goals, parameters, and outcomes. Open-ended, mutual aid groups may be more difficult to evaluate as the members at each meeting may determine the group's agenda and the group focus may not be on a specific behavior change but on quality-of-life issues (i.e., improving the members' life satisfaction or providing support related to an event, developmental stage, or trauma). An appropriate tool for determining the impact of the group experience on the members may be to assess quality-of-life/life satisfaction issues and obtain feedback regarding members' perceptions of needs (and whether they are being met). You may also want to assess if the group experience is contributing to the individuals' goals are being met.

In sum, to develop competency in group practice, be aware of factors that impact the group experience:

- Groups can have powerful effects with both positive and negative outcomes.
- Confidentiality must be negotiated and maintained.

Practice Application 7.3 Group Facilitator Self-Assessment

This application will aid you in conducting an assessment of yourself as a group leader. Consider the following questions (and add any others that you think may be relevant). Follow up this exercise with a discussion with your field instructor, a staff member, and classmates about your facilitation skills.

▶ Was I adequately prepared to facilitate a group (theoretically and practically)?

▶ What were my goals for the group, and have they changed?

▶ Do my goals match the group members' goals?

▶ Am I attending to members in a balanced way?

▶ Does the group see my role the same way I do?

▶ Am I comfortable in a group setting?

▶ Am I able to manage group issues (e.g., conflicts, needs, interactions, and difficult members)?

▶ Am I able to move the group forward, or has the group stagnated?

▶ Does my leadership style fit with this group?

▶ What do I need to change and how can I achieve this?

▶ A group experience may not be the most appropriate or effective intervention for all clients or may be effective when paired with an individual intervention.

▶ While time and cost effective, a group intervention may not be the most efficient means of providing services.

LEARNING THE "PROCESS" OF GROUP PRACTICE

Learning the "process" of group practice means mastering a range of knowledge and skills. This section will highlight practice behaviors to aid in developing competency in group practice, including theory–practice integration, working with difficult clients, unique group practice challenges, appropriate role expectations of yourself and your clients, and use of self in group practice. The *Standards for Social Work Practice with Groups* (AASWG, 2006). presented in Box 7.1 provide a helpful guide to understanding and implementing the concepts and skills discussed in this section.

In group practice, each group develops a personality of its own. Groups can be verbal or nonverbal, interactive or passive, compliant or rebellious, and bonded or fragmented. The personality assumed by the group can have a positive or a negative influence on the work of the group. A positive effect can serve as a powerful mechanism for group members to receive feedback and support and to engage in reality checking, while a negative, conflictual atmosphere can become contagious and infect the work of the group.

Theory–Practice Integration: Evidence-Based Practice

Integration of evidence-based theoretical frameworks and practice applications is an integral part of generalist social work practice at all levels, but it presents unique challenges in group work. First, you must be knowledgeable about and able to apply theoretical concepts focused on the individual. Second, you must be equally competent in the area of theoretical concepts, focused on the interactions of group members. You can develop and hone your techniques and skills for use at the individual and group levels while

Research Based Practice

In facilitating group intervention at your practicum, what empirical evidence guides your approach?

BOX 7.1 Standards for Social Work Practice with Groups

Developed by the Association for the Advancement of Social Work with Groups, the Standards serve as a guide for effective social work practice with groups. By design, the Standards are general, rather than specific and are applicable to the types of groups that social workers encounter in the full range of settings in which they practice. The standards allow the individual practitioner to apply a variety of group work models within the more general mutual aid framework.

Section I identifies essential knowledge and values that underlie social work practice with groups. Sections II through V identify worker tasks in the pre-group, beginning, middle, and ending phases of the group, as well as specific knowledge that may be needed by the worker in each phase. Following are excerpts from the Standards (the entire document is available at www.aaswg.org):

I. Core Values and Knowledge

  A. Core Values: (1) Respect for persons and their autonomy and (2) The creation of a socially just society

  B. Core Knowledge: Knowledge of (1) individuals, (2) groups and small group behavior, and (3) function of the group worker

II. Pre-Group Phase: Planning, Recruitment, and New Group Formation

Tasks: (1) identify aspirations and needs of potential group members; (2) obtain organizational support for group; (3) using an evidence-based approach, select group type, structure, processes, and size; (4) recruit potential group members; (5) obtain consent for participation; (6) clarify and assess member goals and expectations; (7) establish meeting place and time that promotes member comfort and safety; (8) prepare group members for participation; (9) select group members; (10) develop a clear statement of group purpose that reflects member needs; (11) consider potential contextual, environmental, and societal impact; (12) explain group purpose and process to non-members; (13) consider group content; (14) identify tracking methods; and (15) debrief following first session.

III. Group Work in the Beginning Phase

Tasks: (1) establish a beginning contract; (2) cultivate group cohesion; and (3) shape norms of participation.

IV. Group Work in the Middle Phase

Tasks: (1) assist group to make progress in individual and group goals; (2) attend to group dynamics/processes; and (3) identify and access resources.

V. Group Work in the Ending Phase

Tasks: (1) prepare members for group ending; (2) identify member gains and changes; (3) discuss group impact; (4) discuss group movement; (5) discuss member reactions to ending; (6) share feelings about ending; (7) help members share feelings; (8) evaluate achievement of group goals; (9) connect member to resources, as needed; (10) help members apply new knowledge and skills; (11) invite member feedback; (12) help members apply new knowledge and skills outside group; and (13) prepare documentation of group.

VI. Ethical Considerations

From the Association for the Advancement of Social Work with Groups, An International Professional Organization. Used by permission (AASWG, 2006).

exploring their overlap and integration from both the theoretical and the implementation perspectives.

In all levels of social work practice, theory is critical for guiding our work and, eventually, becomes a part of our practice wisdom. However, until you move easily and comfortably from theoretical concepts to practice behaviors, you can benefit from processing group issues as much as possible with your colleagues, faculty, and agency staff. A strategy for gaining this competency may be to routinely require yourself to identify an empirically grounded guiding theoretical premise as you complete your assessments, documentation, and case presentations.

Practice Application 7.4 Application of Evidence-Based Theory to Group Practice: Testing Your Knowledge

Corina, Ben, Lauren, and Cameron are each responsible for facilitating or co-facilitating a group. Read the following descriptions of their group experiences and journal your response to the questions posted.

Corina is responsible for leading a daily teen group at the detention center. The staff subscribes to a cognitive behavioral approach with this client population. Although Corina is gaining comfort with administering the token system on a one-on-one basis, she finds that she has difficulty identifying and implementing a fair, equitable, and appropriate consequence system for violations of group rules in the group setting. How can Corina apply the tenets of the cognitive behavioral approach in a just manner?

Ben facilitates an after-school group for elementary school children. In order for Ben and the children to learn more about one another, Ben decides to have the students complete a sociogram of group interactions. What theoretical premise is Ben utilizing in this exercise?

Lauren co-facilitates a support group for residents of a shelter for women who have been abused. Although the group meets daily, the number of times any one resident attends varies due to length of stay in the shelter, work schedules, and outside appointments. The shelter staff feel strongly about the need to use an empowerment perspective in working with the clients who have experienced some form(s) of domestic violence. Given the typically limited opportunities to engage with an individual client, Lauren feels challenged regarding strategies for empowering women to view options for themselves other than abuse. Within the time constraints, what strategies can Lauren employ that are consistent with the empowerment approach?

Cameron co-facilitates an after-care group in the chemical dependency treatment program. The members are struggling with re-entering their worlds while adhering to a commitment of abstinence. Having grappled with the same problem in his own recovery process, Cameron has insight into the way in which he eventually overcame his re-entry problems, and he knows that he was unaware of any theoretical framework being involved. Cameron is unsure about the existence of or need for a theory to guide his clients in coping with recovery. When Cameron raised this issue with his field instructor, the field instructor stated that he does not use any theory. Is this possible?

The four scenarios presented here address situations frequently encountered by practicum students. Corina's problem is gaining the skills needed to translate theory into practice for individuals within a group. Lauren is frustrated because she feels that she has such limited time with her clients, and questions whether she can adequately convey the value of the empowerment model. Because staff members may not verbalize their decision-making processes regarding the selection and use of theoretical frameworks, students (Ben and Cameron, for instance) are not always able to make the connections between theory and practice strategies. Do any of these situations sound familiar to you? What theoretical framework do you use in your group work? What evidence exists to support your practice approach?

Working with Challenging Client Behaviors in the Group Setting

Chapter 6 emphasized the need to individualize your response to challenging client situations as they arise in your practice. In addition to those client behaviors, attitudes, or situations that you find challenging to address at the individual and family level, group interactions can give rise to another layer of difficult issues. Remember that any group is composed of individual members who bring their individual issues, needs, and characteristics to the group experience. Individual group members can be hostile, violate professional–personal boundaries, display inappropriate behaviors, and resist your attempts to alleviate their crises.

These challenges may be heightened when an individual is placed in a group, particularly if the individual perceives that his or her behavior is being supported or encouraged by other group members. A difficult behavior exhibited by one member can be contagious. If one member is angry with you, he or she may be able to convince the others in the group that they, too, should share and act on his or her agenda. A difficult behavior can be defused or ameliorated through the group's feedback to the individual. This reality check may let the individual know that his or her behavior is unacceptable, at least in the group.

Each group includes its own unique members, and *difficult* means different things to each worker, but group work experience provides client categories that commonly challenge group leaders. There is much to be learned from those group members who make you dread going to group! Each group leader perceives difficult behaviors differently, but commonalties exist regarding member behaviors that have a negative effect on the worker. The following is a list of possible challenging group member characteristics (adapted from Shulman, 2009):

▶ **No-shows and floaters.** *No-shows* verbally commit to regular attendance but rarely attend, while *floaters* attend erratically. The group leader can address such behaviors by emphasizing the importance of attendance to group process and establishes consequences/options for nonattendance. If floating is an accepted feature of the group, such behaviors are not problems.

▶ **The obnoxious member.** Confrontation, constant criticism, and aggression are difficult to deal with, but can serve a useful purpose within the group. Group leaders can take advantage of the obnoxious member's willingness to participate by asking other members how they feel about an offensive comment, encouraging more reserved members to work on their assertiveness skills by responding to inappropriate remarks, and using the power of the group to let the obnoxious person know that he or she is exhibiting offensive behaviors.

▶ **The nonparticipant.** *Nonparticipants* regularly attend the group but do not engage in the group process. Nonparticipants may not interact with the other group members or leader at all or may interact only one on one with the group leader. As group leader, you can explore the nonparticipant's behavior outside the group setting. His or her reticence may be because of shyness, anticipated ridicule or rejection, fear that his or her problem is more severe than other members, or resistance from being forced to join the group. Increasing the nonparticipant's involvement with the group may be a significant intervention made at the individual level.

▶ **The rabble rouser.** The *rabble rouser* can be the most difficult as he or she may persuasively engage the other members in mounting a rebellion against the leader or the agency. The rabble rouser seeks recognition as the group's unofficial or internal leader but unfortunately chooses to gain that role through aggression or intimidation. The rabble rouser can be invited to address group concerns and mobilize the group in a positive way.

▶ **The phantom.** The *phantom* group member arrives late or leaves early, thus creating disruption for the group. Investigating reasons for his or her nonconformist behavior may reveal that he or she is overextended and could benefit from using assertiveness skills to prioritize activities. The phantom may also enjoy the attention resulting from this behavior or is placing limitations on the commitment made to the group or individual problem resolution.

▶ **The know-it-all.** The *know-it-all* appears to have experienced more than the other group members or the facilitator. Others (even the group leader) can see this person as condescending and elitist. Should you encounter a know-it-all, consider the origins of such behaviors before you respond negatively. Might this person be (over)compensating for feelings of inadequacy, staving off intimacy, or exhibiting anger that he or she has to be in the group? Whatever the source of the know-it-all's feelings, you can allow the behaviors to be a detriment to the group's functioning (i.e., other members are likely to feel anger, intimidation, and, ultimately, disgust for the know-it-all), or you can use the group process to break down the know-it-all's interaction style. If the know-it-all's behavior is directed at educating you, monitor your feelings, and react professionally.

▶ **The monopolizer.** The *monopolizer* dominates the group's conversation and probably does not listen well to others (Shulman, 2009). The monopolizer's behavior can be an effort to avoid feelings, problems, or concerns and should be addressed directly by the group leader or the group.

▶ **The scapegoat.** The target for the frustrations and anger of another group member(s), the *scapegoat* role can serve a function for the group (Shulman, 2009) by enabling group members to vent and displace feelings. The scapegoat can engender sympathy or antipathy from the group and the leader, but the worker must confront the scapegoat and the group about the necessity for this role in the group. Once exposed, the scapegoat and the group may be able to dispense with the need for such a function as they can discuss issues more openly (Shulman, 2009).

▶ **The enmesher.** One type of *enmesher* is the member who seems to be involved in every facet of the group's experience (i.e., the busybody). A second type of enmesher is the member who develops an unusually close relationship with one or more other group members. In either instance, the enmesher can impact the group's functioning in an unhealthy manner. The origins of the enmeshment may stem from a need for closeness, acceptance, or intimacy. The group leader can address the enmesher's behavior, preferably within the group but may choose to do so outside the group setting.

▶ **The defender.** The *defensive* member may have been mandated or coerced into the group or may be unable to admit to having the problem/issue for which he or she is seeking help (Shulman, 2009). The group leader can intervene by first acknowledging that defensiveness serves a purpose for that individual client and then defusing the need for continued defensiveness through supportiveness and offering alternative behaviors (Shulman, 2009).

Although these descriptions are useful and interesting ways to categorize group members, you are cautioned against stereotyping through either your use of labels or your responses. These behaviors can be identified as deviations from the group norm, but you should recognize that any and all behaviors can fulfill a function for the group. The behaviors described here should be addressed promptly and fairly by the group leader and potentially the members, but each member deserves to be viewed as an individual who has joined this group in an effort to resolve a problem and improve the quality of his or her life.

Ethical Dilemma: Culture Clash

As part of her practicum at the Hispanic Outreach Center, Rosa is co-facilitating a personal enrichment group with adolescent girls ages 12 to 15. The girls represent the range of ethnic diversity of Latina groups from Central and South America. Rosa has noticed increasing tension within the group related to the countries and regions of origin from which the girls and their families immigrate, that is, she has noticed tension between the girls born in the United States and those who immigrated, which has resulted in bickering at the group sessions, self-segregating by nationality, and a general breakdown in group cohesiveness. Rosa's co-facilitator thinks if the girls refuse to get along with one another, the group should be disbanded. Is this an ethical dilemma? While Rosa wants the girls to feel pride in their heritage, should she try to force the girls to get along with one another? What might Rosa do to rebuild the group cohesion? Since Rosa is a student and her co-facilitator is a social worker at the agency, what are the implications of a disagreement?

Unique Group Practice Opportunities

Corina has the opportunity to co-facilitate a daily teen group at the detention center. During one group meeting, the issue of sexual abuse is raised by a group member. As the discussion unfolds, Corina becomes aware of the fact that the group includes both victims and perpetrators of sexual abuse. The discussion soon becomes extremely heated and emotional, and the session ends explosively with the teens being forcibly returned to their rooms. Anticipating the next day's group meeting, Corina has the following questions: (1) How does she address the previous day's exchanges—does she ignore the incident or encourage the members who are sexual abuse survivors to confront the members who have perpetrated sexual abuse? (2) Should the group be disbanded and reformed, ensuring that survivors and perpetrators are not assigned to the same group? (3) Should the group be broken into smaller, mixed groups? (4) Should she ask the group members what they think should occur?

As a result of the meshing of people, issues, and group process, group work presents a variety of challenges that do not occur at other levels of social work practice. Corina's situation represents several challenges that commonly arise in the application of group interventions. First is the issue of group membership (recruitment and ongoing membership). Second, group dynamics can be a powerful force for the individuals in the group. This discussion is intended not to replicate your previous study of group interventions but to translate the knowledge gained through your practice theory/methods coursework into actual practice behaviors.

"When considering group dynamics, the group is viewed as two clients—the individual and the group"

When considering group dynamics, the group is viewed as two clients—the individual and the group. The social work role in this arena is to mediate individual–group interactions and guide the group members to relate to and support one another (Shulman, 2009). The worker's role in this situation is specific to group work and presents opportunities for competency development and intervention unmatched in other areas of social work practice.

Once you have been invited or assigned to a group or received approval to develop a group, you must begin the process of operationalizing your plans. The following discussion highlights four common issues in group development that you can anticipate—marketing and recruitment, membership/structure, "process" versus "content," and group dynamics. For an in-depth retrospective, you can review your practice theory text(s).

Marketing and Recruitment of Group Members

Critical to the marketing and recruitment activities of voluntary group development (regardless of the type of group) is determining that the group will meet the needs of the individual (Shulman, 2009). Consider timing, location, group composition, purpose, and commitment required by the group member as you begin. Questions that potential group members will raise may include:

- Is the group being offered in a timely manner for my particular need (e.g., will a grief support group be as helpful to me if my son died two years ago as it would be to me immediately following my loss)?
- Is the location of the group convenient and accessible?
- Will the other members have issues, problems, and needs like mine?
- Is the purpose of the group appropriate for my needs at this time (e.g., will an Alzheimer's caregiver support group be a means of obtaining information on physical care, research findings, and available treatments)?
- What is the extent of the commitment? Can I attend as I feel the need, or am I expected to participate regularly?
- Will I have to stop my individual or family treatment if I join this group, and will my therapist be given information about my group participation?
- Will my insurance company pay for my group treatment?
- Can I be assured that the other members of the group will maintain confidentiality?
- Has this type of group been shown through research to be effective for my needs?

Imagine that you are a potential group member. What additional questions emerge as you weigh the option of joining a group? What do you need to help you determine if group intervention is the best option for you?

Group Membership/Structure

Competency in group work focuses on understanding group membership and structure. If you form a group during your practicum, you may have input into determining:

- Group purpose and goals—Is the group aimed at providing support, treatment, or education?
- Time limits—Will the group be open ended (i.e., the members can attend as they desire for as long as they desire) or closed ended (i.e., group members commit to regular attendance for a specified period of time)?
- Group membership—Will the members join the group voluntarily, require a referral from a professional, require approval (if approval is required, who determines approval), or be mandated to attend by an authority?

◗ Location—Will the group be held at your agency, requiring clients to come to you for group activities, or is there a location more convenient for members (e.g., school, workplace, or residential care facility)?

If you are not involved in forming a group, you can still explore these issues by discussing such decisions with the person(s) responsible for making them. If the founder is not available, discuss group formation issues in your agency with your field instructor. If your field instructor is not engaged in group work, he or she may refer you to other staff who can share their experiences and insights related to group development.

Group Dynamics

Groups typically evolve through phases of development—beginning, middle, and termination. Depending on group purpose and structure, these stages can be fluid, undistinguishable, and overlapping at times. Basic group dynamics to consider may include (1) establish mutually agreed-on ground rules (e.g., group purpose and desired outcomes, attendance, boundaries, sharing appropriate and sensitive information, management of confrontations, conflicts, and rule violations, confidentiality, and leadership); (2) clarify the leader's role, particularly as it concerns authority and intervening in group member disputes and problems; and (3) strive for cultural competence in your group work knowledge, skills, and values.

Diversity in Practice

Identify cultural competency skills important in engaging a group of adoptive parents of foreign-born children.

How Do You Fit into the Group Process?

How involved should you be in the group sessions you facilitate? Monitoring your participation in the group can serve as a mechanism for developing appropriate expectations of yourself as a group leader. What is your responsibility as a facilitator in each of these situations?

◗ The group's members do not bond or relate well to one another.
◗ Members engage in unproductive interactions.
◗ The group includes disruptive members.
◗ Members' attendance is sporadic.
◗ The group disbands entirely.

These are several issues a new group leader should address. Just as you cannot accept credit for all your clients' successes, you cannot assume responsibility for what you may deem nonsuccesses. As a group leader, you have an obligation to address your concerns with the group and facilitate possible responses. You are not responsible for the group members, individually or collectively, exercising their right to self-determination if they choose alternative courses of action. You can identify your feelings about the issue, process those feelings with a colleague, and consider your response options. You can then frame the experience as a valuable learning exercise and move on.

Use of Self in Group Practice

In group practice, you will incorporate your own attitudes, beliefs, and life experiences along with those of *all* the group members. This can, at times, seem a daunting task for a group leader, regardless of his or her experience level. The group leader has to maintain a balanced and appropriate level of interpersonal disclosure and exposure.

The worker's use of self is similar across all levels of social work practice, but new and different concerns occur in group work. First, you are motivated to invest as much of yourself as possible into your role as a group leader; but you must consider the impact of your group role on your own well-being. Issues that can affect your group leader role include self-disclosure, boundary limitations, prior group experiences, and termination issues.

Social workers often facilitate groups based on a personal interest or experience, as in the case of Cameron, whose status as a recovering alcoholic led to his interest in substance abuse treatment. If you have personal experience or knowledge related to the group's purpose, you must consider the issue of *self-disclosure.* Is it appropriate to share with the group your personal experiences? What is the purpose of sharing? When and how much do you share and how often do you relate group members' situations to your own? In determining the extent of self-disclosure, rely on your professional judgment and that of others who have faced this decision. Consider self-disclosure only in those instances in which the group member(s) (versus you) will benefit.

Second, establishing and maintaining appropriate boundaries between you and the members of the group can be a difficult task. Group leaders may oversucceed in building rapport and group cohesion if the group members and the leader begin to perceive the group leader as a *member* of the group. By clearly assuming the role of the professional, you will be better able to avoid exploitation and inappropriate interactions while preserving credibility and integrity with the group members.

Last, practicum students in group leader roles may have to leave their groups before the official or natural termination of the groups' work. Some students feel such a strong commitment to their groups that they continue as group leaders on a voluntary basis. Continuing with the group is a positive action in most cases for both the clients and the student. However, nontermination may mask the student's investment of self in the group and enable the student to avoid confronting his or her feelings about the group. Effectively facilitating a termination enables you to reflect on your own feelings about and involvement with the group and serve as a positive model for the group members regarding appropriate endings. What do you think?

To maintain an appropriate use of self in group work, spend time thoroughly processing or debriefing following each group session to gain insight into your group experience. Methods include sharing your observations and reactions with a co-facilitator, reviewing audio/video recordings and process recordings, and processing with a supervisor.

In sum, the skills you gain in facilitation of client-focused groups have implications for your social work professional development in other areas. Grasping the intricacies of establishing and facilitating a client group can aid you as you move into facilitation of nonclient groups. As a facilitator for a committee, task force, board of directors, or consortium/coalition, you will find that the knowledge and skills highlighted here also apply to this new area of work. Although the competency required for facilitating client and nonclient groups overlap, leading nonclient groups does necessitate specialized attention and will be the focus of the following section.

WORKING WITH TASK GROUPS

> *Cameron's field instructor chairs an interprofessional agency com-*
> *mittee and has asked Cameron to chair a committee meeting*
> *because he has another obligation. Cameron feels honored that his*
> *field instructor has entrusted this important committee responsibil-*
> *ity to him. A new committee member, a psychiatrist, joins the group*
> *at this meeting and dominates the meeting. Cameron perceives that*
> *she has her own agenda (one that is not consistent with the group*
> *mission or purpose). During the meeting, the psychiatrist interrupts*
> *other members, is verbally aggressive, and attempts to force deci-*
> *sions to be made that conflict with the views of other members.*
> *Cameron, mindful of his position as a student and substitute chair,*
> *does not know if he should confront her in the meeting or privately,*
> *ignore her, or attempt to gently redirect. The other committee mem-*
> *bers do not acknowledge or confront her behavior during the meet-*
> *ing and appear uncomfortable. What should he do?*

Just like leading a client group, facilitating a task group can be a powerful, gratifying, and challenging experience. Cameron is experiencing the powerful
impact of one member's behavior on the group, the gratification of the leadership role, and the challenges of leadership and having to contend with a difficult group member.

Task group interventions assume a variety of forms, serve a myriad of purposes, and entail the use of a diverse range of practice skills. The emphasis of
work in task groups is typically on "problem solving, making decisions, and
achieving mutually agreed-on goals based on a shared understanding of the
problem or task facing the group" (Toseland & Horton, 2008, p. 303). Also
known as *social action groups*, goals encompass constituencies outside of the
group itself, and the work of the group is aimed at collaborating for the purpose
of a larger objective (Toseland & Horton, 2008). Effective leadership of a
task/work group can impact policy and program development, funding decisions, and client services. Gaining exposure to nonclient group dynamics,
process, and leadership is a valuable and necessary skill for you as a social
worker. Regardless of your current or future career plans, you will inevitably
find yourself a member and possibly a leader of such a group.

Learning the business and process of task group can build on your work
with client groups. Tropman (2003) offers seven principles for effective meeting management:

1. *The Orchestra Principle*—Preparation, rehearsal, and expertise are
   essential and the leader is a facilitator.
2. *The Three-Characters Principle*—Meetings should include announce-
   ment of events and decisions; decisions about options; and brainstorming for future issues.
3. *The Role Principle*—The leader can change the behavior of the group
   by changing his/her own behavior.
4. *The No New Business Principle*—New business can be introduced
   prior to the meeting and packaged appropriately within the agenda.
5. *The No More Reports Principle*—Invoking the three-characters
   principle (#2 in this list) replaces "oral newsletters" with items that
   spark discussion.

6. *The Proactivity Principle*—Raising issues early and with preparation so that participants derive "psychic income" (emotional reward from a task completed well).

7. *The High-Quality Decisions Principle*—High-quality decisions occur when views are "heard, disassembled, and reassembled in combination with the views of others to construct a decision that advanced the interest of all the stakeholders" (p.18–19).

The remainder of this chapter focuses on issues and skills for your development as an effective leader of task groups. We will highlight group member and leader roles, techniques for group meeting facilitation, and management of difficult group dynamics.

Group Member and Leader Roles

You may become a member of a task or work group by appointment, election, or selection by a supervisor or constituency, or you may volunteer. Regardless of the route you take to join a group, clarity about individual and leader roles and expectations is key, particularly those of your supervisor, agency, or group. What are you expected to bring *back* to your primary group from the work group? What do the other group members expect of you? What are you expected to bring to the work group *from* your primary group?

Practicum students often have the opportunity to participate in non-client groups in a variety of roles—observer, note taker, group member, or co-facilitator/facilitator. If you are asked to observe a group, you can orient yourself by consulting with others about group culture and rules, particularly related to observers. If you are invited to take meeting minutes or provide a summary of the session activities, you can review copies of minutes from previous meetings, notes, or summaries to determine style, content, and format. Students may perceive that assuming this secretarial function is not a valid or meaningful learning experience for a new social work professional. On the contrary, taking minutes and compiling summaries is an excellent method for observing, absorbing, and analyzing group interactions and process. Documenting meeting activities requires you to develop and hone your professional writing skills in yet another area necessary for your future practice.

As a group member, you are obligated to be engaged, active, and ethical. If you are representing your practicum site on a committee or ad hoc group, you are further responsible for presenting and possibly advocating for the organization's needs and contributions. If you have the opportunity to co-facilitate or facilitate a work group, your role is more expansive and requires particular clarity. Groups involved in developing and implementing policy may impose more formality and structure on the group leader role than do groups engaged in networking, event/program planning, or educational activities. Tropman (2003) suggests that an effective group leader is responsible for managing structure and procedure; participant trust; pre- and postmeeting tasks; rehearsals, performances, and audiences; emotions; ideas and proposals; decision rules; decision and choice; positions and roles; tasks and functions; value conflict; and evaluation.

If you are involved in a work group from its inception, you have the opportunity to define your own participation and role. In most cases, students are asked to join existing groups, represent staff members at meetings, or assume vacant positions for the duration of their practica. You can prepare for your role in these ways:

1. Request to observe the group before you become a member.
2. Observe the group's rules and roles. Does the group follow parliamentary procedure (see Box 7.2), and, if so, are you familiar with this procedure?
3. Interview current or former members regarding their experiences with the group.
4. Review any documentation that pertains to the group's mission, goals, and previous accomplishments.

Facilitating Group Meetings

Skills for facilitation of client and nonclient groups overlap, but effective facilitation of task groups can require more attention paid to preparation and detail and management of time and dynamics. The following list of techniques, compiled from the literature and our experiences, provides a helpful guide to

---

Box 7.2 Parliamentary Procedure: What? Why? How? When?

Ben receives approval to observe the monthly board of directors meeting. He realizes almost immediately the board adheres to parliamentary procedure, with which he is unfamiliar. He finds the style of meeting facilitation using parliamentary procedure difficult to follow and realizes that he must familiarize himself with it. Tips for Ben include:

What Is Parliamentary Procedure?

Robert's Rules of Order (2004), also known as *parliamentary procedure,* establish in considerable detail a democratic (majority rules) mechanism whereby formal groups engage in efficient and fair decision making. Parliamentary procedure includes: (1) use of *motions* to introduce proposals; (2) *seconding* of a motion to move it forward for a vote; (3) *debate/discussion* to enable members to present differing perspectives and ask questions about a motion; (4) *amendments* to reflect revisions to an original motion based on the debate/ discussion; and (5) *majority votes* (i.e., a minimum of 51 percent of members agreeing) to establish a motion as policy (Kirst-Ashman & Hull, 1998).

Why Do I Need to Know about Parliamentary Procedure?

Most formal groups (e.g., boards of directors, committees, and policymaking bodies) use a form of parliamentary procedure. They may embrace the spirit of the rules while not adhering religiously to each and every minute detail.

How Do I Learn about and Use Parliamentary Procedure?

In addition to reviewing Robert's Rules of Order (Robert, Evans, Honemann & Balch, 2004), you can visit the website (http://www.robertsrules.com/). You can also observe meetings in which the procedure is used to gain insight into the variations employed.

When Do I Use Parliamentary Procedure?

If you join a committee, advisory group, or board that has been in existence prior to your entry, the group likely has a routine established for decision making, but you can raise questions regarding the rules for decision making: Does the group use parliamentary procedure in its literal form? If not, what liberties and deviations are acceptable?

If you chair a newly founded group, you have the opportunity and responsibility to establish with the group the methods to be implemented to ensure the professional management of issues and decisions.

ensuring smooth and productive meetings (Kirst-Ashman & Hull, 1998; Sheafor & Horejsi, 2008):

- ⬧ Preparations should include:
  - ⬧ Purpose and membership—Identify appropriate purpose and group membership and ensure that you know the identity, title, and role of each member.
  - ⬧ Logistics—Select a noncontroversial, accessible, and appropriately sized location; a convenient time for the number of participants expected; and arrange the room for optimal achievement of purpose.
  - ⬧ Materials—Develop a clear, well-organized, and realistic agenda and handouts and distribute prior to the meeting.
- ⬧ The beginning of the meeting should focus on introduction, announcements, "housekeeping," and clarification of purpose, goals, roles, rules, decision-making processes, and outcomes.
- ⬧ The work phase of the group encompasses:
  - ⬧ Following the agenda or amending it if determined by the group
  - ⬧ Keeping the group on task by managing the time and discussion (with flexibility) within an environment that is conducive to open, cooperative, and interactive discussion.
  - ⬧ Periodically summarizing discussion and decisions.
  - ⬧ End the meeting at the appointed time, and determine any tasks (with timeframes) to be completed outside the meeting, person(s) responsible for the outside assignments, and future meeting times, places, and agendas.

Challenging Group Dynamics

As with any collaboration, the work group is a compilation of different people, resources, and philosophies. Although the work group pools resources that can produce an outcome greater than that possible for an individual, the road to that outcome can be full of potholes.

Similar to challenges in client group practice, nonclient group behaviors can include members who are disruptive, nonparticipative, consistently late or absent, or uncooperative. Group leaders are often faced with the need to manage and mediate conflict. Conflict is not necessarily bad: A calm meeting without disruption or conflict may seem productive when, in fact, the group's goals go unfulfilled because needs were not heard or met. When members represent other groups, they can be passionate and strong willed regarding their positions and goals for their group involvement; as a leader, you are required to maintain an atmosphere in which members can express their views, feel they have been heard by the other members, and leave the meeting/group experience with a sense of productivity. As a result, conflicts may emerge as a result of disagreement over interpersonal, resource, representational, or intercessional issues (Kirst-Ashman & Hull, 1998). These conflicts may be productive or unproductive. Strategies for managing productive conflict include the following (Kirst-Ashman & Hull, 1998):

- ⬧ Anticipate and recognize potential conflicts.
- ⬧ Attempt to reframe conflict as it relates to the entire group.
- ⬧ Invite all members engaged in the conflict to share their views.

> ▶ Avoid win–lose outcomes.
> ▶ Encourage members to strive cooperatively for compromise and consensus.

An effective group leader does not take sides in a conflict, misuse his or her power, avoid the conflict altogether, use covert means to resolve the conflict, or co-opt other members in an attempt to solve the problem (Kirst-Ashman & Hull, 1998). Have you found yourself in the role of an arbitrator of conflict? What strategies have been effective and ineffective for you? Providing leadership for a work group is essential for your professional development. The NASW *Code of Ethics* (2008a) urges us, as social workers, to serve as leaders for our communities and our profession. To be effective advocates and representatives who can make strides for our clients and discipline, we must be able to function competently as leaders.

Practice Application 7.5   Facilitating Your Own Interprofessional Group Meeting

This application provides you with an experience in facilitating an interprofessional team meeting. You and your fellow students will role-play an interprofessional team meeting from the perspectives of multiple disciplines. To complete this application, you may use the case in the Social Work from Many Perspectives (Practice Application 2.3) or create your own case. After you have identified a scenario, use the following guidelines for your experience:

▶ Develop a summary of the case and identify the disciplines of the players involved in the role-play.

▶ Identify the role and position for each professional involved. Provide a brief synopsis of each player's

role, and develop scripts for the players who will role-play the team meeting (do not share the various players' parts with the other members involved in the role-play). Assign roles to each student.

▶ Using video- or audiotaping, role-play the meeting. Encourage each role-player to stay in his or her character's discipline as much as possible. You may assign the roles prior to the actual role-play to enable the players to research their disciplines' perspectives and possible positions on an issue.

▶ Review the tape with the players, facilitate a discussion, and address such issues as group dynamics, interprofessional issues, the social work perspective, and other issues that arose for individual group members.

Practice Application 7.6   Documenting Group Process: When the Obvious Isn't So Obvious

This application will help you further develop your group documentation skills. Using a style/format/tool of your choice (e.g., your practicum agency's, the sample provided in this unit, or another tool), document your impressions of the described scenario in a journal entry and share with your field instructor. Keep in mind the issues that have been raised in this unit regarding the confidentiality of documenting client/patient information in single and multiple client records.

The Scenario

You are a co-facilitator of a group of patients hospitalized in a psychiatric unit. Due to the short duration of

the hospitalizations, group membership is fluid and changes frequently. Today's group includes the following members:

▶ Clarissa—a 27-year-old female hospitalized for a suicide attempt. She was severely depressed prior to her suicide attempt and has not responded well to medication and therapeutic interventions during the week she has been hospitalized. Clarissa's family initiated this hospitalization against her will.

▶ John—a 65-year-old male with a history of schizophrenia who requires hospitalization when he does not comply with his medication regimen. Once he is regularly taking his medication, he is noncombative and does not experience delusions or hallucinations. John is responding well to treatment and is ready for discharge.

▶ Jennifer—a 22-year-old female with a history of self-mutilating behaviors and anorexia. She rarely has periods in which she functions well enough to attend school or hold a job. She requires frequent hospitalizations and is viewed by staff as extremely difficult because she does not respond well to treatment or relate appropriately to staff or the other patients.

▶ Jeffery—a 32-year-old male court ordered into inpatient treatment for evaluation and treatment for aggressive behavior. He has made numerous appearances in court for fighting with his girlfriend, family members, neighbors, and motorists who he perceives to have intentionally "cut him off." Staff report that his aggressive behavior has continued during this hospitalization, requiring physical restraint on several occasions.

▶ Gordon—a 36-year-old male, hospitalized for the first time, with a diagnosis of bipolar disorder. Gordon is currently in a manic phase and is extremely agitated most of the time. He attempts to dominate any conversation in which he participates and incurs the wrath of group members during each group session.

You start today's session by asking the group to share any issues they would like to discuss. You turn to Clarissa, who is sitting next to you, and ask her to begin. Clarissa refuses to talk. She begins to cry when Jeffery makes fun of her for not talking. Jennifer attempts to come to Clarissa's aid, and Jeffery then turns his vengeance on Jennifer, demanding that she let the "crier" fend for herself ("after all, what does a 'kook' like her know about these issues?"). John begins to assault Jeffery verbally for picking on these "poor, helpless girls" and tells Jeffery that he does not understand what it is like to have "real problems." Jennifer begins to scream at both Jeffery and John, at which point Gordon launches into a speech about how you, the group leader, have allowed the group to get out of control. He demands to know what you are going to do to "get a handle on this bunch of loonies."

Your Turn

Document your impressions of the interactions that have occurred during this session. Prepare progress notes for both the group process and individual client records.

Practice Application 7.7   Need a Group Work Practicum Experience? Start Your Own Group

In this application, you have the opportunity to develop plans for your own group. As a component of your learning plan, you and your field instructor have agreed that, in order to gain group practice experience, you will co-facilitate the agency's new parent education/support group. Your agency was concerned that workers spent too much time and resources individually teaching young parents basic parenting skills and supporting their efforts in the areas of parenting, nonabusive punishments, and consistency. The agency determined that a group effort would benefit clients and increase work efficiency. When you began your practicum, your field instructor informed you that the worker who originally intended to form this group has abruptly left the agency. Your field instructor suggested that you take this plan on and form and facilitate the group yourself.

Using your own agency context or creating a context appropriate to this scenario, develop a plan for forming such a group and share it with a member of your practicum team. Your strategy should include the following:

▶ Eligibility criteria for group members
▶ Marketing and recruitment plans
▶ Arrangements for location, schedule, and needed supplies and resources
▶ Research of the evidence to identify group format and structure
▶ Group goals and objectives (including format, open versus closed group membership, frequency, timeframe, and length of group and other structural issues)
▶ Plans for the first session and beyond
▶ Evaluation criteria

The group worker's a social worker too (sort of). The group worker's a social worker too (guess so). Why they use Scotch tape and adhesive? To make their groups cohesive. So I guess the group worker's a social worker too.

—Excerpted from the chorus of "The Group Worker's a Social Worker Too" by Harvey Bertcher

SUMMARY

These lines describe the plight of the social worker interested in group practice. Fortunately, we have come to view group work as an integral and valuable part of the repertoire of generalist social work practitioners. This chapter has provided insights into the rewards and challenges that come with developing competencies in group practice. Proficiency in the implementation of group intervention is more important than at any point in social work history. Economic challenges and third-party payer constraints create increasing need for group work skills. Critical to the nondirect service area are the emergence of agency–community collaboratives and interprofessional service delivery teams and the increasing role of social work in administrative, corporate, and nontraditional settings.

Despite the fact that **Corina's** initial inclination was to avoid the issue or to disband the group, she consulted with her field instructor regarding strategies for responding. Together, they agreed that the issue could not be ignored and that Corina would open the next meeting with a brief summary of the previous day's events, establish guidelines for a discussion of the event, and ask for the group's thoughts about the future of the group. Having spent the evening processing the experience, Corina returned to the agency the next day and asked her field instructor to listen to her proposed presentation and to provide feedback from the teens' perspectives. This exercise bolstered Corina's confidence, and she was able to approach the group, regain her role as a leader, address (and learn from) an extremely difficult issue, and move the group forward.

Cameron opted to confront the psychiatrist calmly during the meeting, despite his concerns about the reactions of his field instructor and other staff, about his student role, and about the functioning of the committee. He believed very strongly that he had a right and responsibility to confront this person, regardless of her position and/or the potential implications for his practicum. Immediately following the meeting, the psychiatrist found Cameron's field instructor and demanded that he be removed from the agency. The field instructor tried to defuse the situation. The psychiatrist relented and agreed to participate in a meeting with the field instructor and Cameron. The field instructor facilitated the meeting, during which Cameron and the psychiatrist agreed to work together in the future. At present, Cameron and the psychiatrist are civil and professional when they encounter each other in the agency, but they co-exist with considerable discomfort.

Succeed with PEARSON **mysocialworklab**

Log onto **MySocialWorkLab** to access a wealth of case studies, videos, and assessment. (*If you did not receive an access code to **MySocialWorkLab** with this text and wish to purchase access online, please visit* www.mysocialworklab.com.)

1. Click on Interactive Cases for Practice. Select Group Work and complete the module.

2. Click on Core Competency Videos and select Human Behavior. As you review the first video, document the practice behaviors being demonstrated by the social worker.

PRACTICE TEST The following questions will test your knowledge of the content found within this chapter. For additional assessment, including licensing-exam type questions on applying chapter content to practice, visit **MySocialWorkLab.**

1. A student group formed to raise awareness about homelessness is an example of a:
   a. Reciprocal group
   b. Remedial group
   c. Social action group
   d. Psychoeducational group

2. A social worker-led group for adolescent females experiencing eating disorders is an example of a:
   a. Social action group
   b. Reciprocal group
   c. Task group
   d. Remedial group

3. A volunteer-led group for the caregivers of persons with a head injury is an example of a:
   a. Reciprocal group
   b. Social goals group
   c. Therapy group
   d. Remedial group

4. A technical expert leader assumes all of the following roles except:
   a. Determines group membership
   b. Establishes group rules
   c. Models desired group behaviors
   d. Establishes group purpose and goals

Ethical Practice

5. As a mandated reporter, a social worker leading a group is required to intervene in which of the following situations involving group members?
   a. Extramarital affair
   b. Threat of assault to estranged spouse's new boyfriend
   c. Payment for sexual acts
   d. Use of illegal drugs

Human Behavior

6. The best response to an "obnoxious" group member is to:
   a. Confront the individual about the inappropriate behavior
   b. Eject individual from the group
   c. Ignore the inappropriate behavior
   d. Elicit input from other members of group

Professional Identity

7. Engaging the group members involves the social worker's use of self. Which of the following is an inappropriate use of self?
   a. Sharing life experiences of a member of one's therapy group
   b. Sharing a similar life experience
   c. Sharing a personal coping strategy
   d. Sharing a personal relapse

8. The "high-quality decisions principle" of task group leadership entails:
   a. Leader behavior can change group behavior
   b. Issues are constructed in the best interest of the group
   c. Meetings include announcements, decisions, and brainstorming
   d. Leaders exhibit preparation, rehearsal, and expertise

9. In Robert's Rules of Order, amendments are used:
   a. Following a motion
   b. Following a vote on a motion
   c. Following a discussion of a motion
   d. Following a seconding of a motion

Engage Assess Intervene Evaluate

10. The "work (intervention) phase" of a task group does not include:
    a. Summarize progress
    b. Follow agenda
    c. Manage time
    d. Review "housekeeping" items

Log onto **MySocialWorkLab** once you have completed the Practice Test above, to access additional study tools and assessment.

Answers:

Key: 1) c 2) d 3) a 4) b 5) b 6) d 7) a 8) b 9) c 10) d

8

Social Work Practice in the Field

Working with Organizations, Communities, and Policy

Core Competencies in this Chapter (Check marks indicate which competencies are covered in depth)				
Professional Identity	✔ Ethical Practice	Critical Thinking	Diversity in Practice	Human Rights and Justice
Research Based Practice	Human Behavior	Policy Practice	✔ Practice Contexts	✔ Engage, Assess, Intervene, Evaluate

167

Although many social work practitioners focus on direct practice with individuals, families, and groups, the social work profession is also heavily involved in macro practice, or organizational, community, and policy practice (Netting, 2008) and have the goal of benefiting large groups of clients or general society. Macro practice presents opportunities for practitioners to induce large-scale positive change in the lives of many clients through systemic solutions.

Given the growing complexity of client problems, becoming immersed in the practice issues that present themselves on the individual, family, and group levels is understandable. However, attention to the broader organizational, community, and policy issues that frame individual problems is important. The issues that individual clients present to social workers are often rooted in problems that affect large numbers of people in their communities. Some of these problems can, at least in part, be addressed at the individual, family, and group levels within social service agencies and neighborhoods (but others are best addressed at the macro level). The Council on Social Work Education (CSWE) accredits social work programs, and requires programs to include content that prepares students to "advance human rights and social justice," "engage in policy practice to advance social and economic well-being and to deliver effective social work services," and "respond to contexts that shape practice" (2008, pp. 5–6). Further, the National Association of Social Workers (NASW) *Code of Ethics* (2008a) requires social workers to embrace the value of social justice and to be socially and political active. By this point in your coursework, you may have the opportunity in the practicum to apply your macro knowledge and skills.

Macro practice is a broad concept that covers a wide range of social work activities. Those social workers involved at the organizational level shape the way that human service policies are implemented, as well as inform and influence the policy formation process (Patti, 2008). The skills needed for administrative social work practice include (Netting, 2008; Patti, 2008):

- Budgeting and financial management
- Working with boards
- Organizational design, development, assessment, and diagnosis
- Computer information systems and other technology
- Human resource management (selection, training/staff development, supervision, and compensation)
- Management (including use of affirmative action principles)
- Marketing management techniques
- Networking and building partnerships with collaborators
- Financial resource development
- Media relations
- Policy Advocacy

Community practice social workers are engaged in development, organizing, planning, and action for progressive social change (Weil, 2005). Community practice skills include the following (Weil, 2005):

- Program development, implementation, and evaluation
- Fundraising (grantwriting and other techniques)
- Coalition formulation and maintenance
- Planned change techniques
- Macro-level advocacy
- Community analysis
- Interorganizational planning
- Leadership development and citizen participation

- Small-group decision-making techniques
- Community organizing
- Task force membership
- Membership development and retention
- Social and economic development techniques
- Computer information systems and other technology

Finally, social policy practitioners analyze policy alternatives using data and research, select a preferred policy, advocate for preferred policy, and are involved in policy implementation (Iatridis, 2008). Policy practice skills include (Iatridis, 2008):

- Legislative (advocacy and lobbying skills, including mobilizing citizens, organizations, and communities)
- Policy analysis and management
- Issue analysis techniques
- Social policy research
- Legal (including judicial and regulatory skills)

Although these skills are grouped under discrete headings here for illustrative purposes, the three areas of macro practice share a symbiotic relationship in practice; practitioners in one area often need skills in other areas. For example, community planners, organizers, and developers often work with boards and engage in lobbying; policy practitioners may engage in leadership development and citizen participation; and administrators of social service agencies are often involved in social policy development.

This chapter will address the breadth of topics contained in macro practice, including student involvement in community planning, development, and organizing; administrative activities; and policy practice. Rather than review macro content that is covered in your practice courses, this chapter will build on your knowledge of community, administrative, and policy practice to help you apply ethics to macro practice and clarify expectations for your learning. This chapter will also discuss the business and process of organizational, community, and policy practice.

Ethical Dilemma: Engaging in Advocacy

Rosa has approached her field instructor several times with questions about how she can implement her social work program's requirement to engage in some form of macro practice. Her field instructor has deferred discussion of any specifics for vague reasons but during the last supervision session admitted that she did not want Rosa to do any sort of advocacy because it might "take away from her commitment to her clients" and/or "rock the boat." Rosa knows that she must gain macro experience and would like to engage in advocacy at some level regarding immigrants' rights. What should she do? Is this an ethical dilemma?

ETHICS IN PRACTICE WITH ORGANIZATIONS, COMMUNITIES, AND POLICY

Rosa is experiencing the tension between her concern about the welfare of her individual clients and the societal and environmental structures that shape her clients' lives. While she wants to offer her clients as much assistance as

Ethical Practice

What are the ethical dilemmas that arise at the macro level can foresee at your practicum site? How might you resolve an ethical dilemma that pits the best interest of an individual client with the best interests of an organization or community?

possible, she is right to recognize the mandate of the social work profession to "promote the general welfare of society" (NASW, 2008a) and to struggle with the need to also focus on the larger issues in clients' lives.

According to the NASW *Code of Ethics* (2008a), social workers have many ethical obligations that apply to work at the organization, community, and policy levels. These include ethical responsibilities in the practice settings, to the social work profession, and to the broader society. You might experience or observe situations in which social work ethical responsibilities must be carried out, despite their difficulty. For example, you might experience a situation in which the policies or procedures of your practicum agency do not allow staff to work toward the client's best interest. You might also observe a situation in which effort taken to organize a community could result in harm to another part of the community, when for example, drug activity moves from one part of a neighborhood to another part. You are encouraged to become familiar with the sections of the *Code of Ethics* that relates to macro social work, and to keep a copy of the *Code of Ethics* available throughout your practicum so that you can begin to recognize challenges in any of these areas, and discuss them in supervision with your field instructor (Reamer, 2006).

EXPECTATIONS FOR STUDENT LEARNING IN ORGANIZATIONAL, COMMUNITY, AND POLICY PRACTICE

Generalist practice requires a wide range of skills for helping individuals, groups, families, organizations, and communities. Therefore, building on practice skills with individuals, families, and groups, social work practitioners must have both a clear understanding of the community and agency contexts for service delivery and the ability to intervene in order to deliver effective services. Unless you are in a practicum setting that focuses primarily on macro practice (i.e., is involved solely in administrative work, community organizing, community development, or policy practice), you will likely assume fewer macro practice responsibilities as compared to responsibilities at other practice levels. Even if you consider yourself to be primarily a direct practitioner, you may find it necessary to engage in certain macro-level activities in order to meet your clients' needs effectively. Such activities may include:

1. Giving a fundraising speech about your agency to a local church
2. Testifying before a local mental health funding board
3. Organizing an interagency group to develop needed services for homebound seniors
4. Working with a neighborhood group to rid the area of abandoned apartment buildings
5. Organizing a group of public housing tenants with the goal of persuading the local housing authorities to hire tenants to provide maintenance to the buildings
6. Conducting policy research to learn about policy position papers and current research in preparation for policy advocacy
7. Using the Internet to track legislation and sending e-mails to local or state-level legislators or the White House regarding legislation

8. Signing an e-petition and forwarding it to others for their action (McIntosh, 2004)

9. Presenting a budget to the board of directors of an agency for approval

10. Lobbying a legislator in person to support a piece of social legislation

Social work practitioners working in wide-ranging contexts must be prepared to use the various client system levels to address client needs. Practice skills with individuals, families, and groups provide a solid foundation for and must be utilized in macro practice (Weil, 2005). Just as you must know how to work with people as individuals to work effectively with them as a group, you must possess the ability to work with individuals, families, and groups to work with people as members of organizations, communities, and policymaking entities. In your interaction with individuals, groups of clients, agency administrators, community residents, other community agencies, and politicians, you may use such direct skills as effective verbal and nonverbal behaviors, warmth, empathy, genuineness, and other communication skills (such as rephrasing, reflective responding, and clarification) (Kirst-Ashman & Hull, 2009). Furthermore, the mezzo skills of networking, effectively functioning as a team member or leader, planning and conducting meetings, and group conflict resolution are frequently utilized by macro practitioners (Kirst-Ashman & Hull, 2009).

Which skills distinctive to macro practice are needed by social work students in practicum vary widely depending on the assignment and the agency context. Indirect skills you may wish to consider learning in the field include community planning, community organizing, use of social action techniques, conducting a community needs assessment, policy analysis, coalition building, program development, lobbying, grantwriting, fundraising, public relations, staff and board of directors development and training, supervision, organizational policy development, and strategic planning (Weil, 2005).

The following sections will discuss (1) the "business" of macro practice—administrative and task-related issues; (2) the "process" of community, administrative, and policy practice—commonly encountered issues related to student implementation of macro assignments. Additionally, the impact of recent social policy changes on social work practice and the student role in practicum will be examined.

LEARNING THE "BUSINESS" OF ORGANIZATIONAL, COMMUNITY, AND POLICY PRACTICE

Although many social work practitioners engage in community and organizational practice, recent research shows that most social work practitioners define their primary practice as direct practitioners (Weisman & Whitaker, 2008). Therefore, unless you are among the small percentage of students specializing in community organization, community development, social strategies, social justice, or political social work, your field instructor is probably a direct practitioner or an administrator. Direct practitioners are often involved, at least minimally, in some administrative-level responsibilities or may be involved in macro-level activities outside of work time. In many cases, students must be proactive if they wish to incorporate macro-learning activities into the practicum experience.

Practice Application 8.1   Gathering Information

If your agency-based field instructor engages primarily in micro- and mezzo-level service delivery, interview him or her about his or her involvement with macro-level activities. Among other questions, ask the following: With what administrative activities are you involved? With what macro-level (policy) advocacy efforts are you involved? Does the agency encourage or support these efforts? What involvement in macro practice (organization, community, and policy work advocacy) would you prefer? Do you find involvement in macro practice rewarding? Do you see these types of activities as falling within your professional role within the agency? Or within your professional role outside the agency? Journal on your discussion, and compare and contrast the roles of your agency-based field instructor with those of other students in practicum in your integrative practice field seminar.

Receiving a Macro Assignment

> *Thus far, Cameron is very pleased with his practicum experience in the substance abuse treatment center. However, he realizes that he would, at some point, like to assume some administrative duties in a social service agency. He was discouraged from pursuing this further at the interview with his field instructor, when he was told that the agency director has never worked with a student and was very "cautious" about delegating administrative responsibilities. He feels stymied and frustrated. What might he do to pursue this interest further?*

Cameron is discovering institutional barriers that prevent him from becoming involved in social work within larger systems. Like Cameron, you will likely need to engage in negotiation and dialogue with your field instructor about your interests in and needs for macro practice, the types of skills you wish to develop at this point in your curriculum, and realistic possibilities for involvement in the agency. Even if your agency is eager to allow you to assume macro-practice responsibilities, planning and forethought are important to ensure that you have a meaningful and positive experience. Beyond your preference for an assignment and that of your field instructor, consider the following strategies for gaining macro-level experiences:

1. Work at the macro level in communities, in organizations, and with policy can have profound effects on the operation and the reputation of the agency. Therefore, permission from an administrator may be needed prior to launching into a macro assignment. The extent of your experience in macro practice may play a part in the assignment of activities. If you are inexperienced at macro practice (as many students are) and will need a significant additional amount of task guidance and supervision, you may find that you are offered only a modest number of macro practice choices.

2. You may find that your involvement in macro-level activities is highly dependent on forces outside the control of your field instructor or practicum site (e.g., lobbying may be possible only within a seasonal legislative session in your state, fundraising events may already be scheduled, or a community organizing opportunity may occur only after a crisis). You might seek those opportunities available during your practicum timeframe, even if not those that are your first choice.

Despite these barriers, exposure to all three client-system levels is critical so that you can be prepared for social work practice at the conclusion of your studies. The following sections identify possible activities you can perform as a practicum student. Some of these activities may be possible within your practicum agency, while participation in others may entail the involvement of another agency, group, or a coalition.

Administrative Practice

Many Master of Social Work (MSW) field instructors are involved in the administrative structures or procedures of their employing agencies in addition to having direct service responsibilities to clients. Therefore, you will likely find exposure through your field instructor to administrative practice to occur naturally throughout your practicum. However, taking an active, responsible role in administrative activities will offer you the greatest rewards relative to your learning goals. This may require you to make an explicit request of your field instructor. Consider requesting one or more of the following administrative tasks/responsibilities:

Engage, Assess, Intervene, Evaluate

Most social workers primarily work directly with at the micro level with individuals, families and groups. How might you generate ideas about administrative, community and policy practice that would benefit your clients through micro level work?

- Assuming an active role with the board of directors (e.g., presenting a report, facilitating client representation on the board, or participating as a member of a board committee)
- Preparing part or all of the agency's annual report (e.g., contributing to the preparation of the budget, developing a description of the program in which you are most heavily involved and interviewing clients to gain their perspective, or drafting the cover letter to be edited and signed by the executive director)
- Working with a staff member to develop and gain approval for a new program for the agency (examples of program ideas: use of students and volunteers for a summer low-income teen leadership camp or jobs programs, or use of students to train homebound seniors to participate in a peer-to-peer telephone support network)
- Participating in advancing the technology/communications resources of the agency (e.g., researching and presenting information about needed computer hardware and software, participating in the creation or modification of a website or webpage, training staff in the use of a new software program to provide services online, or training staff about the use of social networking sites for agency promotion)
- Participating in staff recruitment and retention activities (e.g., participating in the selection of a new staff member, participating in the design and delivery of staff training on diversity issues, or supervising short-term volunteers for the agency)
- Participating in media relations and marketing efforts (e.g., drafting a new program brochure that targets an immigrant population; drafting an op-ed piece focusing on a timely issue and, after approvals, submitting the piece to a local newspaper; or working with others to create a brief video about the agency to be used as a promotional piece
- Participating in agency networking efforts (e.g., attending a local chamber of commerce meeting, networking with local politicians at a legislative breakfast, or participating as a volunteer in a local United Way's allocations process)
- Participating in the agency's resource development efforts (e.g., completing the literature search, needs assessment, project goals and objectives, and/or a portion of a grant proposal; researching new

funding possibilities for a program; assisting to research potential major donors or serving as an active member of a committee planning a fundraising event for the agency)

Community Practice (Planning, Development, Organizing, and Social Action)

Because a relatively small number of social work students specialize in the areas of community development, organizing, or social action (Weisman & Whitaker, 2008), you may find incorporating learning experiences encompassing this area of macro practice more challenging than integrating administrative activities. Unless you have secured a practicum site with the goal of learning these skills, you may find that your field instructor has more difficulty offering a venue for you to observe, engage in, and receive resources needed to implement community planning, organizing, development, and social action skills. Opportunities to engage in community-practice activities in direct service agencies may be very seasonal (i.e., prior to, during, or after the state legislative session), random (e.g., during an unexpected community crisis), or highly dependent on the orientation of the members of the board of directors or agency administrators (i.e., the board's or administration's philosophy regarding the importance of involvement in political activities on behalf of clients). Many community planners, organizers, and developers, and those involved in social action are from disciplines other than social work. The goal of practice within these areas is to empower people affected by policy in order to effect change on a scale wider than a single agency can hope to do. In addition to the administrative activities listed earlier, the following activities can help you learn community practice skills:

- Participating in coalition formulation and maintenance (e.g., taking responsibility for researching organizations that may be interested in working with a coalition on a particular issue, attending a coalition meeting as a representative of your practicum agency (Bobo, Kendall, & Max, 2001), or integrating technology [the Internet, e-mail lists, databases, and social networking sites] into coalition-building efforts (Lohmann & McNutt, 2005)).
- Participating in planned change techniques and interorganizational planning (e.g., assisting in organizing community hearings to allow community input into a new employment project sponsored by local government, supporting efforts to arrange meetings of community professionals to solve problems around a communitywide public transportation issue, or working with government officials to plan a new summer employment and mentoring program for the county)
- Engaging in macro-level advocacy efforts (e.g., organizing a large meeting of neighborhood residents and inviting local elected officials to the meeting to hold them accountable for their voting records on key issues in the last legislative session (Bobo, Kendall, & Max, 2001), participating in a demonstration, working with a group drafting legislation to fight against the building of a superhighway through the neighborhood of your clients (Kirst-Ashman & Hull, 2009), or lobbying a state legislator on a particular bill)
- Participating in a community needs assessment/analysis (e.g., interviewing key members of the community using a structured interview to ascertain the most pressing community needs, engaging in community

mapping, using a capacity inventory tool with individuals involved in your agency to ascertain the strengths and capacities inherent in local community members (Kretzman & McKnight, 1993), or attending neighborhood public meetings to learn more about the issues most affecting the neighborhood)

▶ Participating in leadership development and citizen participation (e.g., conducting a leadership training session on the legislative process with low-income residents, organizing a letter-writing campaign by neighborhood residents, assisting clients with voter registration efforts, or assisting in planning a conference (Younes, 2003))

▶ Participating in community organizing (e.g., organizing and recruiting for a neighborhood meeting to discuss the problem of absentee landlords in the neighborhood; participating in the recruitment, training, and organizing of a group of low-income clients to testify at a county hearing on local spending priorities for federal funds; or inviting people to join in your organization's efforts to reform health care for the poor)

▶ Participating in membership development and retention (e.g., engaging in door-to-door canvassing to recruit new members, gathering signatures for a petition drive at a central location in the community and recruiting new members, or planning a volunteer recognition event)

▶ Engaging in economic development activities (e.g., working with low-income women to start a small business sewing infant baptismal dresses, recruiting low-income minority men to join in a worker-owned cleaning company, or providing technical assistance to teen parents in their development of a cottage industry)

Policy Practice

Social policy impacts and shapes the lives of clients. Social workers must advocate for clients within the policymaking process. Even though it may constitute a small portion of your time in practicum, seek avenues for incorporating policy practice into your field experience. Consider the following options for gaining policy practice experiences:

▶ Participating in the legislative process (e.g., researching, preparing, and testifying in support of or in opposition to a bill during a public hearing; meeting with legislators individually to lobby for more funding for human services; or strategizing with a coalition of advocates regarding the defeat of a harmful bill)

▶ Participating in policy analysis and management (e.g., assisting others in providing an analysis [fiscal or human cost] of proposed legislation to a local legislator (Haynes & Mickelson, 2006), assisting others in analyzing the impact on vulnerable populations of proposed regulations issued by a governmental entity, or writing an article for the agency newsletter relating the effects of new legislation on agency clients)

▶ Participating in social policy research (e.g., participating in an evaluation of a new Medicaid outreach program by appraising and synthesizing multiple sources of information, compiling the results, drafting a report, and sending the final report to decision makers for advocacy purposes; researching the development of government policy related to homelessness to assist in advocacy efforts; or assisting a professor in analyzing the impact of welfare reform on rural elderly caretakers)

◗ Participating in legal proceedings or issues relevant to policymaking (e.g., helping a social worker from your agency to prepare testimony as an expert witness for a legislative committee, providing testimony to a legislative committee, or communicating with an administrator of the county human service agency to request clarification on a policy negatively impacting your clients (Haynes & Mickelson, 2006))

Orientation

After learning about the services your agency provides, your task is to orient yourself to the macro-level work (administrative, community practice, and policy practice) implemented by the agency. Second, you will need to be oriented to the resources needed to carry out a macro assignment. Many macro assignments entail large projects that can be time consuming. You will likely find that you are able to work on a small macro project at the same time that you carry out your direct practice responsibilities. You may find that your work with individuals, families, or groups provides you with an issue or with case scenarios that you can (with permission) use in advocacy efforts. If, however, you would like to be involved in a large project, you may consider either (1) transferring most or all of your direct practice responsibilities to another staff member so that you can devote most of your time to the project or (2) negotiating a role within a large project under the direction of a staff member. Consider these issues concerning orientation to a macro-level project:

◗ What level of access do you have to the resources needed to carry out this task (i.e., administrators or staff, financial resources, or multiple sources of information)?
◗ Do you have the permission, support, and guidance from the agency (administrators, board of directors, or staff) that you need to carry out this task?
◗ Does the task you are completing involve a significant risk (public relations, political, or otherwise) to the agency? Are you prepared for this risk?
◗ How much time and energy will the task take? If needed, will you be able to carry out your direct practice activities and your new task effectively?
◗ How can you influence the degree to which other organizations with which you will be working take your role seriously and treat you as a professional?

Practice Application 8.2 Socialization into Macro Practice

Because many social work programs devote more time to direct practice skills than to indirect practice skills, many students feel unsure of their macro skills and experience anxiety contemplating a macro project. Discuss any anxieties and questions you may have with a member of your practicum team while you are arranging for task guidance to assist you throughout your macro-level work. Questions to consider include these:

1. What knowledge and skills will I need for a macro assignment?

2. Do I feel that my social work program has prepared me with the knowledge and skills that I need?

3. What resources will I need from the agency and the social work program, and are they available?

4. What challenges do I anticipate as I engage in macro work?

5. How will I evaluate my work in this area? How would my field instructor evaluate my work?

6. What competencies and practice behaviors would I gain by involvement in a macro activity?

- What is your ability to be an effective team player on a large project, in which you may receive little to no recognition for your contribution to the larger project?
- What is your ability to contribute to a project for which you may not see evidence of a resolution which you are involved?
- How will you be able to maintain appropriate boundaries and avoid triangulation if different members of a group try to "recruit" you to advocate for their position about next steps?

Identifying Yourself as a Student

Your student status can be both a strength and a limitation in macro-level activities. As a student, you can explain the limits of your experience in macro-level activities to others with whom you will be working and ask whether you can turn to them for assistance. Being forthright about your rookie status can allow you to question strategies, tactics, procedures, and assumptions within the framework of learning; you will not necessarily appear to be challenging the wisdom of experienced staff members. However, your student status may also limit the possibilities for tasks for which you may take responsibility. For example, you may wish to assume complete responsibility for a new marketing brochure but may be given permission only to draft certain sections.

Practice in Smaller Communities

Developing your community practice skills is critical to becoming a competent generalist practitioner. However, if you are working in a nonurban or smaller community, you will likely find that these skills are of even greater importance. Smaller communities generally have fewer formal resources to which you can refer clients, and many services are provided on an informal basis by family, friends, neighbors, or church members. As a social work professional (may be the only social work professional in the community), you may find that you must learn about and use this informal network. Moreover, you may find that you must creatively access, utilize, and develop resources to meet client needs.

In addition to understanding the dynamics of service provision in a rural setting, you must focus on developing your relationship with key people within the community. While knowing the elected officials, business owners, bankers, and health care providers in an urban area may enhance your ability to provide services, you will learn that such knowledge is absolutely essential in a smaller community. These groups can prove to be assets in your efforts to obtain funding, influence policy, access resources, and organize and deliver services.

Practice Application 8.3 Professional Socialization in a Smaller Community

If you are completing a practicum in a smaller community, this practice application will assist you in the process of socialization into the community, an essential aspect of macro practice.

Ask your field instructor to help you meet other human service professionals. Some possible avenues include (1) spending a few hours being introduced around the town or county, (2) attending interagency meetings, (3) participating in "Law Day" at the courthouse, (4) having social lunches with professionals from other agencies/organizations/churches, and (5) attending office openings or parties. To gain credibility as a professional, make certain to accompany another professional known by the community when being introduced.

Developed by Ellen Burkemper, PhD, LCSW

"Working with social work staff from other areas of the agency or staff from other disciplines, other agencies, or other sectors of society (such as public agencies, businesses, private agencies, and schools) can constitute a significant portion of practice with communities and organizations"

Practice Contexts

How might working in collaboration and coalition with other social workers and staff assist in your effort to provide leadership in promoting sustainable changes in service delivery to improve the quality of social services? What barriers might exist for you to exhibit leadership in this area?

Confidentiality and Self-Determination

Client empowerment and involvement in macro-level activities are important elements of social work practice. An essential component of client empowerment is emphasizing the situational, environmental, political, and organizational solutions to problems in an effort to raise clients' consciousness about the limits of personal solutions and to avoid blaming the victim (Haynes & Mickelson, 2006). Although encouraging clients to share their experiences with agency programs and social policies is essential to competent social work practice, equally important are the basic social work principles of confidentiality and self-determination. If you are sharing information about an individual client with other agencies or decision makers, you must be careful to protect his or her privacy. Unless you have received permission from the client to use identifying information outside the agency, you should share information only in the aggregate. Likewise, clients should be encouraged but never be pushed to be involved in macro-level activities inside or outside the agency. The choice to be involved must be a product of the client's free will.

Collaboration/Coalitions

Working with social work staff from other areas of the agency or staff from other disciplines, other agencies, or other sectors of society (such as public agencies, businesses, private agencies, and schools) can constitute a significant portion of practice with communities and organizations. Working with other disciplines who may have different perspectives, philosophies, and skills can make reaching agreement on strategies and tactics for initiating change challenging (Aronoff, 2008). As noted in chapter 6, encountering different jargon, different professional socialization practices, and lack of clarity regarding roles and expertise can challenge even the most dedicated practitioner (Moxley, 2008). Although collaborative practice with professionals with a diversity of interests, education, background, and perspectives in collaborative practice or within a coalition can bring the most comprehensive analysis and approach, as well as strength and power, to change efforts (Lawson, 2008), it can also mean that a group has to make too many compromises to work together and cannot accomplish a worthy goal (Bobo, Kendall, & Max, 2001).

Facilitation of coalition or interagency meetings often requires a high level of facilitation skill. Because interdisciplinary work is central to macro practice and is growing in importance, try to be involved in a collaborative, coalition, or interdisciplinary effort if possible. Even if you are only able to observe meetings, note the facilitation style, how conflict is handled, and the methods by which consensus is built and agreements are made. Learning from an observation role will serve you well in the future.

Writing/Documentation Skills

Strong writing skills are as important at the macro level as in practice with individuals, families, and groups. Effective writing skills are needed for such activities as grantwriting; preparation of budgets and agency annual reports; conducting policy research and policy analysis; developing flyers and action alerts; public relations materials (e.g., agency newsletters, press releases, press packets, and brochures); reports for the board of directors; program evaluation reports; minutes of meetings; policy position statements; and written testimony for public hearings. You may be asked to engage in process recordings for your macro-level work, to include documenting your weekly progress on activities and assignments, challenges encountered and strategies utilized to address challenges, personal insights gained, key persons with whom you interacted, theory/practice integration, future plans for the projects and other topics (Ward & Mama, 2006).

Many of the rules regarding documentation presented in chapter 6 also hold true for macro practice. These include the use of accurate grammar and punctuation, focused writing, appropriate client information, and inclusion of only nonjudgmental and factual information. Macro-level writing often involves condensing and organizing a large amount of information into a useful, efficient, and easily readable document. If your project involves a written product, review previous editions of similar documents to guide you. Additionally, you will need to know the completion dates for drafts of the document, the completion date for the final document, the editing process (who will need to review the document?), and the audience (who will receive or approve the final document?). Even if no review process by others is involved, ask that someone review and give critical feedback to you. You will gain a higher level of writing skills if you receive feedback.

In addition, documentation of unmet needs and needed services is an important task for advocacy for policy changes. Most agency documentation systems of direct service work with individual clients, groups, and families are designed to capture information needed for reimbursement, clinical interventions and progress, and administrative purposes (Haynes & Mickelson, 2006). If the documentation system of your agency is designed to inject information into the political process, you may wish to take advantage of the opportunity to engage in this process. Ask to be involved in working with data to be used in the policymaking process. Another way to gain experience is to provide testimony at a legislative hearing. To increase the effectiveness and impact of your testimony, use the statistics, scenarios, and case illustrations that have emerged from documentation efforts.

The documentation efforts of other practitioners may also enable clients themselves to be involved in advocacy. Effective documentation can help identify clients who may be willing to share their stories for media or legislative testimony purposes. Personal stories from clients can make a dramatic and effective impact on the policymaking process, both at the administrative and legislative levels (Haynes & Mickelson, 2006). Macro-level social workers can assist clients to prepare for legislative advocacy by rehearsing testimony and role-playing the follow-up questioning process. This rehearsal can help prepare clients for the possibility of an intimidating atmosphere, questions about their personal lives, or an adversarial process.

Ongoing Evaluation

As you develop your plans for involvement in macro practice, identify points at which your work will be evaluated. Due to the lengthy process typically involved in these activities, using benchmarks to assess your growth and development is critical for your success in macro-level activities. For example, if you are writing an annual report for the agency, consider negotiating due dates for sections of the product so that you can receive feedback along the way. If you are working with a group of rural farmers to fight development of condominiums in the area, develop benchmarks in your plan to assess progress, such as obtaining meetings with important people and gathering signatures on petitions. This discussion of the business of macro practice has touched several key issues commonly encountered in the process of assuming macro-level responsibilities. Once these decisions have been made and you are engaged in obtaining macro skills, the "process" of implementing macro activities raises new issues.

LEARNING THE "PROCESS" OF ORGANIZATIONAL, COMMUNITY, AND POLICY PRACTICE

This discussion of the process of organizational, community, and policy practice will focus on theory–practice integration, managing adverse relationships and conflicting goals, and developing reasonable expectations for completion and effectiveness of a macro practice assignment.

Theory–Practice Integration

Just as integrating theory in practice with individuals, families, and groups is imperative for effective social work practice (see Chapters 6 and 7), theory must provide the framework for macro practice. As discussed earlier, macro practice entails the use of individual, family, and group practice skills; therefore, you should consider theories you have learned at both of these levels within your macro activities (Gamble & Weil, 2008). Furthermore, if you have not already done so in your curriculum, you may wish to investigate community practice theories (Streeter, 2008), management theories (Patti, 2008), and policy theories (Haynes & Mickelson, 2006) and to discuss the theories that relate to your

Source: Saint Louis University.

activities with your field instructor. In your discussions with your field instructor, consider the following questions:

1. In what way do the perspectives offered by the various theories in macro practice help frame your work?
2. Does a particular theory help guide your work?
3. Does a combination of theories best explain the development of the organization, community, or policy with which you are working?

Managing Adverse Relationships and Conflicting Goals

Ben has been working on an assignment from his field instructor since the second week of the practicum and feels stuck. The community-based outreach program in which he works is located in a low-income community with poor-quality housing stock. A developer, with the support of the county government, wishes to purchase a significant amount of real estate in the area (displacing low-income residents in the process), rehabilitate the buildings, and sell them as owner-occupied buildings. Ben's field instructor, at the prompting of the agency administrator, has assigned him to organize a group of neighborhood residents to oppose the gentrification efforts. Ben is facing at least two problems: (1) The developer has a great deal of power and money and the support of the county, and Ben wonders whether he will be wasting his time fighting the development; and (2) Ben is unsure whether he is well suited to engaging in neighborhood advocacy that involves confrontation and politics. Should he ask to be released from the assignment?

Like Ben, you may experience issues that are unique to macro-level practice. You may doubt that advocacy efforts are worthwhile given your resources, the length of time you will be placed in the agency, and the influence of your opponents. You may also doubt whether you can assume the role of agitator. As a social worker, you are accustomed to seeing the various perspectives involved and working toward conflict resolution and unaccustomed to an adversarial role that may involve confrontation. The inertia, fear, and anxiety raised by these issues can be significant barriers to involvement in community practice.

Social workers have a professional responsibility to "act to expand choice and opportunity for all people" (NASW, 2008a) and must work through their struggle with confrontation (Reisch, 2005). As a social worker, you have a professional responsibility to work to strengthen the community's capacity to respond to injustices and promote change. The power of a group of concerned, organized citizens may surprise you. The integration of the right information, timing, and strategy (and a little luck!) may enable even a group of marginalized people to affect social policy (Haynes & Mickelson, 2006). Although conflict resolution techniques and consensus building are important parts of social work (Mayer, 2008), conflict is often the essential ingredient for social change (Bobo, Kendall, & Max, 2001). If conflict is difficult for you, you may wish to role-play with and receive feedback from your field instructor on situations that involve expression of differences and tension. To learn about the important historical role conflict has played in social change efforts, you may also want to read about early unionizing efforts, the civil rights movement, the women's rights movement, and other social change efforts that used conflict techniques successfully.

"As a social worker, you have a professional responsibility to work to strengthen the community's capacity to respond to injustices and promote change"

Interview a social worker involved with social policy advocacy efforts about working with or promoting conflict and adversarial relationships. Among other questions, ask the following:

1. What type of techniques do you use to work toward social change?
2. Does conflict play a role in the efforts?
   a. If so, how? Do these efforts produce adversarial relationships? As a social worker, how do you come to terms with contributing to adversarial

relationships? How successful have your efforts to promote social change been? How do you define *success*?

   b. If conflict does not play a role, why is conflict not an element of your efforts? How successful have your efforts been?

Discuss the results of your interview in a journal entry, and share them with a member of your practicum team or with other students in your integrative practice field seminar.

Developing Reasonable Expectations

Macro practice often entails long-term projects. Administrative tasks can be lengthy, policy practice activities can entail several months of work, and achieving community practice goals can take several years. Successful engagement in macro practice involves the ability to accept that your efforts may not result in a desired outcome for a long time, perhaps long after your involvement has ended. Macro practice efforts often involve teamwork, and there may be little to no recognition of individual efforts.

What can you expect to achieve as a student? Setting realistic goals and objectives (achievable within a semester or two) is imperative to your sense of accomplishment and your learning. Having unrealistic expectations can lead to frustration, a loss of self-confidence and perspective, as well as burnout. You may consider choosing several pieces of one large project if your macro-level interests lie in only one particular area, or select small portions of several projects in order to gain skills in different areas of macro practice. In the negotiation process, be clear about your interests in macro practice so that appropriate, reasonable activities can be planned that meet specific competencies and demonstrate appropriate practice behaviors.

POLICY CONTEXTS THAT SHAPE PRACTICE

Managed care, current administrative trends, and the recently developed asset development field are policy contexts that shape and affect contemporary social work practice. These topics and their impact on social work practice and social work practica are discussed in the following sections.

Managed Care

The onset of managed care in the private and public sectors has created turbulence in many sectors of society, including health care, mental health care, and the management of nonprofit and for-profit organizations. *Managed care* is a term used to describe the prepaid health sector in which care is provided under a fixed budget (Karger & Stoesz, 2006). It includes health maintenance organizations (HMOs) and preferred provider organizations (PPOs), which are used to control costs (Karger & Stoesz, 2006). Managed care has a growing influence on the lives of clients as well as on the delivery of social services, and a wide diversity of opinions about managed care exists among social workers and other health providers. Managed care has been the subject of both praise for care coordination and promotion of evidence-based practice, and criticism for withholding needed medical services to control costs. Managed care will likely undergo significant changes in the next five years (Vandiver, 2008).

Impact of Managed Care on Social Work Practice

The impact of managed care on social work practice depends primarily on the type of agency, services provided to clients, and client populations. In addition to serving as mental health providers, social workers exist in a variety of roles within the framework of managed care—for instance, as case managers, executives, administrators, and utilization management staff (Vandiver, 2008). In general, social work has experienced increases in the following areas from managed care (Simmons & Enguidanos, 2006; Vandiver, 2008):

1. Emphasis on short-term, behavioral modalities of mental health practice
2. Emphasis on evidence-based practice
3. Emphasis on documentation and evaluation of practice
4. Use of less costly services
5. Presence in primary health care settings

Box 8.1 shows a list of managed care terms used in social work practice.

Box 8.1 Guide to Managed Care Terms

As social workers are increasingly influenced by managed care, you may encounter some of the following terms in your practice (Karger & Stoesz, 2006; Moniz & Gorin, 2007; Vandiver, 2008):

- **Capitation**—A monthly payment to a health care provider that is paid prior to service delivery. The provider agrees to provide certain services as needed for a certain length of time (usually a year) and to accept this flat fee, regardless of service usage.
- **Case management**—The comprehensive management of a person's health care needs.
- **Employee assistance programs (EAPs)**—Counseling and referral programs sponsored by employers that are designed to offer treatment for problems that affect workplace performance (such as chemical dependency and family issues). Employees may voluntarily consult an EAP manager or may be referred by their supervisors as a condition of their continued employment. EAP managers may offer assessment and intervention or may refer to a provider who offers specialized services.
- **Fee for service (FFS)**—A system in which the health care provider is paid a fee for each service delivered.

- **Gatekeeper**—The primary care physician whose responsibility it is to authorize all medical services and referrals for a patient in order for those services to be covered under the patient's managed care plan.
- **Health maintenance organizations (HMOs)**—Corporations that offer health insurance and medical care. Patients in these systems can receive reimbursable care only from providers employed by the HMO organization.
- **Preferred provider organizations (PPOs)**—A network of providers who are in individual practice and receive payment on a fee-for-service basis. If a patient chooses to see a provider outside the preferred provider network, the patient assumes a higher cost for the services of the provider.
- **Utilization review**—A process whereby the provider typically must provide written documentation of the need for and progress of care to a utilization reviewer employed by a managed care company. To be eligible for reimbursement, services and products provided to the patient must be authorized by the reviewer.
- **Carve-out plans**—Specialized mental health and chemical dependency care plans.

Impact of Managed Care on Practicum Experiences

The impact of managed care on the practicum experience can vary widely. Some programs have lost a modest number of placements due to managed care, and programs have also experienced a loss of supervision time because supervisors are required to bill for all of their time and student hours may not be reimbursable. Furthermore, while some organizations have opened new opportunities for students as a result of managed care (for example, utilization review, authorization of services, and case management), others have eliminated some learning experiences for students (by not allowing students to carry their own caseloads or restricting group work). Changes in organizations due to managed care may require changes to programs and services, as many agencies have merged with or been purchased by other agencies. To prepare for the field impacted by managed care, students are encouraged to learn about financing and insurance (Kane, Hamlin, & Hawkins, 2000).

If the effects of managed care have not been discussed in your supervision, take the opportunity to discuss this topic with your field instructor. The pace of change in managed care is rapid, and you may find that your knowledge about managed care is already outdated. Even if your practicum site (or practicum activities) has not been directly involved in managed care, you will benefit from a knowledge of the topic as one that will continue to affect both social work practice with clients and the organizational context of practice.

Administrative Trends among Social Service Agencies

The organizational context for social work practice is also undergoing significant changes. The catalysts for change among nonprofit, for-profit, and public social service agencies include a context that is increasingly competitive, privatized (or contracting with private agencies to deliver services), requires increased use of technology, and is outcomes oriented. Some areas are experiencing a growth of collaborative arrangements to share information and resources, and the merging and consolidation of smaller agencies into larger agencies (Patti, 2008). Another trend of note is the increasing numbers of nonprofit agencies engaging in for-profit commercial activity. For many agencies, the development of for-profit businesses helps offset deficits that might otherwise result from their nonprofit activities (Mort, Weerawardena, & Carnegie, 2002). Last, due to continued federal and state budget cuts for social services (and other factors leading to decreased revenue), many nonprofit agencies are spending more resources on fundraising (Gronbjerg, 2008)).

You may notice some evidence of these trends and their effects in your practicum. For example, your agency may be experiencing transition in the structure of the agency, resulting in increased or decreased opportunities for roles for students. You may notice staff members discussing increased workloads or that the organization is considering a collaboration or merger. In the face of budgetary constraints, some agencies may strongly encourage you to spend a significant portion of your time assisting with fundraising. In some public social service settings, services previously delivered by staff and students are now contracted out to private agencies or performed by volunteers. Organizational changes can occur suddenly (the closing of a practicum site mid-semester), or slowly.

Asset Development

Since the late 1980s, asset development programs to address poverty have been promoted on the state and federal levels. Since the 1990s, *individual development account (IDA)* programs have begun as the implementation of the asset development approach. These programs, which encourage clients to save for purposes such as post–high school education, home ownership and repair, starting a small business, and other similar activities through matched savings accounts, are the implementation of a social policy shift to encourage savings and investment among the poor. IDA programs emphasize potential, opportunity,

---

Practice Application 8.5 Community Analysis through Observation

This practice application will provide a structure by which you will become familiar with the neighborhood in which your practicum site is located. Information gathered may provide insights into the issues most affecting neighborhood residents and the resources available in the community.

Walk through or sit/stand on a corner in the community in which your practicum site is located. Then drive slowly through the community. Record your answers to the following questions in a journal entry.

Community Geographic Information

1. What are the main geographical boundaries and natural barriers?
2. Is the community geographically isolated, or does it border other communities?

Economic Characteristics

1. Do you see evidence of unemployed community residents?
2. What types of commercial enterprises exist in the community? Are they locally owned businesses or large chains?
3. What type of transportation is available locally? Is it public or private? How available is public transportation?
4. What types of employment do community residents have? Is the employment mainly blue or white collar?
5. Do you see evidence of an underground economy (i.e., illegal economic activities)?

Social Characteristics

1. How would you describe community residents in terms of age, gender, ethnicity, race, family composition, sexual orientation, and social class?
2. How do community residents react to you (e.g., hostile, friendly, indifferent, curious)?

3. Does the community contain places of worship?
4. Do public meeting places exist in the community (e.g., meeting halls, clubs, coffee shops, bakeries, associations, or a community center)?
5. Does the community contain any parks and recreational areas/buildings? What type? What are the conditions of the recreational facilities?
6. How would you describe the housing stock? Is the stock mainly rental or family owned? How would you describe the upkeep of the stock?
7. Is there housing for sale? Is it dispersed through the community or clustered?
8. Are there distinct social subcommunities within the larger community?

Political Characteristics

1. Are there any signs of political activity/activism (e.g., yard signs, bumper stickers, political offices, and political meetings)?
2. What are the conditions of the roads and sidewalks? Is garbage collected regularly?

In a discussion with a member of your practicum team or in integrative practice field seminar, reflect on the information you have gathered. Additionally, discuss the following reflection questions:

1. What appear to be the most pressing needs of the community?
2. What appear to be the resources that exist in the community to address the needs?
3. How responsive do public officials appear to be to meeting the needs of the community?

Developed by Melford Ferguson, MSW, adapted from Sherraden, M. S. (1993). Community studies in the baccalaureate social work curriculum. *Journal of Teaching in Social Work, 7*(1), 75–88.

and investment, rather than just the transfer of income, and are designed to produce a range of positive social, economic, and civic effects. Social welfare programs have historically discouraged the poor from saving by enforcing eligibility rules for assistance programs that disallowed such savings. IDA-type savings accounts are monitored by agencies, and participants can only access the funds for specific predetermined purposes. Many community-based programs and federal demonstrations currently exist. IDA programs also often involve a mandatory education component to teach participants about such matters as increasing credit scores, buying used cars, accessing affordable credit, and other related matters (McBride et al., 2004). Other types of asset development work include first-time homebuyers and housing counseling programs and micro-enterprise programs (Green & Haines, 2008).

These programs provide an opportunity for social workers to be involved in the economic and social development of clients. Many agencies offer practicum experiences working in such programs. If you are in an agency that has such a program, you may want to learn more about the philosophy and operation of such programs in general. Otherwise, you may want to become aware of the asset development programs in your area as potential resources for your clients.

Practice Application 8.6 Community Analysis through Illustration

The completion of this practice application will provide a graphic representation of the relationships between the community in which your practicum site serves and outside entities.

Create an eco-map of the community in which your practicum site is located or serves and include the following:

1. All entities external to the community with which the community (as a whole) interfaces (e.g., governmental entities, other communities, social service agencies, businesses, and community institutions and organizations)

2. A graphic description of the relationship between the community and outside entities using different types of connections (e.g., broken lines, thin lines, thick lines, and curving lines)

3. A legend/key that explains the types of connections

Explain and discuss your eco-map with a member of your practicum team or in integrative practice field seminar.

Practice Application 8.7 A Macro Approach to the Educational Needs of Children Who Are Homeless

Imagine that you are a social work student in a homeless shelter. When children come to the shelter, many must change schools and many miss a number of days before they are enrolled again in school. You have been directed to work with a group trying to draft state legislation to remedy the situation. The group will also try to find a sponsor of the legislation and will work to pass the bill. Answer the following questions in a journal entry and share your answers with a member of your practicum team:

1. What might be some solutions to the problem?
2. How would you begin to work on this issue within your practicum site?
3. What people or groups would you identify as important to this effort?
4. How might you go about engaging important people or groups in this effort?
5. What kinds of activities might be needed to pass this legislation?

Developed by Marian Hartung, LCSW

> ### Practice Application 8.8 Role-Play: Social Advocacy
>
> Choose a pressing social issue that you have encountered in your practicum. With a group of students, role-play a macro approach to the issue in integrative practice field seminar. Options include (1) holding a press conference; (2) testifying before a legislative or funding body; (3) conducting a demonstration with picketing, songs, and slogans; (4) meeting with an elected official to request a specific action; (5) holding a sit-in; and (6) staging a rally and leafleting.

> ### Practice Application 8.9 Contact with an Influential Person
>
> Identify an issue (political, social, policy, or legal) that is relevant for your practicum work. Identify a key player that has affected/could affect your issue. Contact this person/body through a letter, phone call, or personal visit. State your position (reasons you are concerned, who is affected, and how and what can be done to rectify/improve this situation). Be sure to recognize other perspectives on the issue and other possible means of addressing the problem. Ask the person to follow up with you regarding the action you are requesting (e.g., cosponsoring legislation, contacting other influential persons, or introducing an amendment to legislation) to let you know whether he or she will comply with your request. Provide documentation of your key points (e.g., a copy of a letter or a fact sheet) to a member of your practicum team and discuss your contact.

SUMMARY

This chapter discussed both the "business" and "process" of macro practice in practicum. Issues such as expectations for student learning in macro practice, receiving a macro assignment, identifying yourself as a student, role transition, confidentiality and self-determination, collaboration and coalition, writing and documentation skills, and ongoing evaluation were explored. Examples of administrative, community organizing and development, and policy practice activities students may engage in were provided. Furthermore, theory–practice integration, managing adverse relationships and conflicting goals, and developing reasonable expectations were "process"-oriented issues discussed in this chapter. Last, the impact of managed care, administrative trends among social service agencies, and asset development on social work practice and student learning in practicum were explicated.

After further discussion with his field instructor about his frustrated attempts to gain some administrative responsibilities as part of his practicum, **Cameron** asked the field instructor about her administrative duties within the agency. She discussed her grantwriting, administrative reports, and coalition meetings. They agreed that Cameron will take responsibility for many of her administrative duties under close supervision and that the field instructor will sign off on all the work.

Ben, after much thought regarding his discomfort with a macro assignment that entails use of adversarial relationships with a powerful housing developer and county officials, asked his field instructor to release him from the assignment. The field instructor denied his request, stating that this assignment will be an important learning experience. They discussed Ben's feelings of discomfort that arise with situations involving conflict. The field instructor discussed the importance of the effort to stop gentrification in the area as a contribution to the empowerment of the low-income residents of the neighborhood and as a mechanism for building community between low- and moderate-income residents. The field instructor agreed to work closely with Ben and to assist him in processing his feelings of discomfort along the way.

Succeed with **mysocialworklab**

Log onto **MySocialWorkLab** to access a wealth of case studies, videos, and assessment. (*If you did not receive an access code to* **MySocialWorkLab** *with this text and wish to purchase access online, please visit* www.mysocialworklab.com.)

1. Under the core competency videos, choose Practice Context, then watch Keeping Up With Shifting Contexts. What are some possible community, administrative, and policy responses to the budget cuts for which the social worker could provide leadership?

2. Under the core competency videos, choose Practice Context, then watch Providing Leadership to Promote Change to Improve Quality of Social Services. If this client decides to participate in the advocacy activities about the budget cuts, how could a social worker help the client to prepare for fully participating? What sort of ethical dilemmas could arise through the client's participation?

PRACTICE TEST The following questions will test your knowledge of the content found within this chapter. For additional assessment, including licensing-exam type questions on applying chapter content to practice, visit **MySocialWorkLab**.

Engage Assess Intervene Evaluate

1. Skills needed for administrative social work practice do not include:
   a. Policy advocacy
   b. Computer information systems
   c. Media relations
   d. Community analysis

2. Community practice skills do not include:
   a. Task force development
   b. Human resource management
   c. Planned change techniques
   d. Interorganizational planning

3. Policy practice skills do not include:
   a. Legal skills
   b. Legislative skills
   c. Coalition formulation and maintenance
   d. Policy analysis and management

4. Most social work practitioners define their primary practice as:
   a. Direct
   b. Clinical
   c. Indirect
   d. Therapy

5. The following elements of community practice skills are of even greater importance in smaller communities, with the exception of:
   a. Learning about and utilizing informal networks
   b. Understanding the dynamics of service provisions
   c. Learning about agricultural systems
   d. Developing relationships with key individuals

6. The challenges of working with other disciplines includes:
   a. Different jargon and professional socialization
   b. Different jargon, professional socialization and lack of role and expertise clarity

   c. Different jargon, professional socialization and compensation levels
   d. Different jargon, lack of role and expertise clarity and compensation levels

7. Theories that relate to the following client system levels apply to macro practice:
   a. Individual and community
   b. Individual, family and community
   c. Individual, family, group, community and management
   d. Individual, family, group, community, management and policy

8. Due to managed care, social work has experienced increases in the emphasis of following aspects of practice except:
   a. Cultural competence
   b. Short-term, behavioral models
   c. Documentation and evaluation of practice
   d. Evidenced-based practice

9. The context for agency practice is increasingly competitive, privatized, requires increased use of technology and:
   a. Requires less communication
   b. Is outcomes oriented
   c. Publically funded
   d. Requires increased use of marketing

10. Social welfare programs for the poor have historically discouraged the poor from saving by:
    a. Providing resources for basic needs
    b. Caseworkers
    c. Enforcing eligibility rules for assistance programs that disallowed savings
    d. Supervisors of welfare programs

Log onto **MySocialWorkLab** once you have completed the Practice Test above, to access additional study tools and assessment.

Answers:

Key: 1) d 2) b 3) c 4) a 5) c 6) b 7) d 8) a 9) b 10) c

Social Work Practice
and the Legal System

Core Competencies in this Chapter (Check marks indicate which competencies are covered in depth)				
Professional Identity	✔ Ethical Practice	Critical Thinking	Diversity in Practice	Human Rights and Justice
Research Based Practice	Human Behavior	Policy Practice	✔ Practice Contexts	✔ Engage, Assess, Intervene, Evaluate

The legal system affects many aspects of social work practice. Social workers in a wide variety of roles interface with laws and the professionals who uphold them through employment in the courts, judicial or justice-related entities, probation and parole services, publicly funded social services, law firms, developmental disability services, and victim service offices and as counselors or therapists in correctional settings. Most recently, social workers are working in drug courts and mental health courts, both of which handle the specialized needs of defendants (Tyuse & Linhorst, 2005). Social workers in the areas of child welfare, domestic violence, crime victim counseling, adult protection, housing, immigrant services, youth services, and public policy also have frequent interactions with the justice system as advocates, petitioners, witnesses, and defendants (Kirst-Ashman & Hull, 2009; Madden, 2008; Stein, 2004). Social workers whose primary focus is social policy must have an intimate knowledge of federal, state, and local legislative, administrative, and regulatory processes. However, even social workers whose roles do not involve frequent contact with the legal–judicial or legislative systems need a basic understanding of both systems to enable them to participate in social policy development and to assist clients with issues that have legal considerations (Stein, 2004).

> "Social workers in a wide variety of roles interface with laws and the professionals who uphold them . . ."

Even if you are not currently involved in any aspect of the legal system in your practicum, you should be aware of the legal issues of social work practice that impact clients and practitioners. Knowledge of the legal system will undoubtedly aid you in your work with clients in the future, and knowledge of the professional legal issues will enable you to practice ethically and within the boundaries of the law. Social workers must have a working knowledge of the legal system in order to (1) communicate and work successfully with judges and attorneys; (2) recognize the rights afforded to clients by the law; (3) recognize certain problems of their clients as essentially legal problems or social policy problems; and (4) minimize their legal risk in practice (Madden, 2008; Stein, 2004).

Legally related activities in which social workers may engage include the following (Albert, 2000; Jansson, Dempsey, McCroskey, & Schneider, 2005; Kayser & Johnson, 2008; Madden, 2008; Stein, 2004):

- Testifying in court on behalf of a client
- Testifying in court on their own behalf
- Submitting records after receiving a subpoena
- Providing expert testimony
- Advocating on behalf of or in opposition to legislation
- Drafting regulations in response to legislation
- Responding to draft regulations issued by a governmental body
- Acting as an agent of a court system (i.e., enforcing the policies and mandates of the court)
- Providing mediation to resolve disputes as an alternative to litigation
- Petitioning the court on behalf of an agency in guardianship hearings
- Helping clients participate in class action lawsuits
- Helping clients obtain and enforce an order or protection
- Assisting to draft legislation
- Assisting older adults in hospice and their families

Your social work courses may have provided you with knowledge of the legal–judicial community. The type of agency in which you are completing a practicum, the type of work in which you are engaged with clients, and your student role will determine your opportunities to observe and participate in the legal–judicial system.

Students in clinical settings (particularly agencies that have been sued) may have the opportunity to work with professionals who are keenly aware of legal issues that impact professional practice. Up to this point in your career, you may not have been exposed to the depth of the legal considerations required for social work practice. Knowledge of the following legal issues listed is especially important in settings that involve a high level of direct client contact (Barker & Branson, 2000; Chase, 2008; Stein, 2004):

- Professional liability and malpractice
- Clients' rights to confidentiality and the prevention of inappropriate disclosure
- Clients' end-of-life decisions
- Limits of clients' rights to confidentiality
- Privileged communication
- Defamation of character
- Emergency assistance and suicide prevention
- Placement and supervision of clients in residential settings
- Procedures for obtaining informed consent from clients
- Guidelines for appropriately terminating treatment
- Limitation on intimacy with clients
- Interventions with acting-out clients
- Duty to protect intended victims from a client's violent acts

This chapter will focus on a range of topics (e.g., professional liability and malpractice, limits of clients' right to confidentiality, and several others) that merit further discussion as you obtain more responsibility for clients in your practicum. If you feel that you do not have adequate background on any of these topics, consider reviewing your practice theory texts or including several topics in supervision discussions with your field instructor.

The legal system is a very complex, formal system having highly intricate rules and procedures. Effective social work practice involves learning about relevant aspects of the system, utilizing the legal system for the benefit of your clients, and delivering services in a manner that minimizes your malpractice liability (Reamer, 2003). Although the formality of the system can be intimidating at first, many professionals find their comfort level increasing dramatically with time. If you relish working with the legal system as an exciting aspect of your practicum, you may consider shaping your employment choices after graduation so that you have ready access to the legal–judicial system. Possible sites include legal aid, the public defender's office, a correctional facility, or the local, state, or federal court system.

LEGAL TERMS

Just as social work has a unique set of terms, the legal–judicial system possesses an extensive, unique set of terms (or jargon) that can be difficult to learn. Some legal–judicial terms that you may encounter include those defined in the following (Albert, 2000; Barker & Branson, 2000; Black, 2004; Kirst-Ashman & Hull, 2009; Stein, 2004):

Allegation—An assertion, claim, declaration, or statement of a party to an action that the party expects to prove.

Arbitration—Private decision making by one or more individuals with a neutral third party to develop a binding decision for disputing parties.

Civil offense—A noncriminal offense punishable by restitution or payment of a fine

Court process—Two phases: (1) adjudication phase—facts presented and charge determined by a judge or a jury; and (2) disposition—determination of sentence.

Criminal case—An action to identify and punish a defendant for the act of committing a crime.

Defendant—One who is charged in a crime or sued in a civil action.

Emancipation—A surrender of part or all of the rights of a child. A client can become emancipated through parental permission, court order, or, depending on the state, by taking certain actions (such as marriage, childbirth, independent living, or enlisting in the armed forces).

Evidence—Proof legally presented at a trial through witnesses, records, documents, exhibits, or concrete objects to convince the court or a jury.

Family court—A type of court system that has jurisdiction over the following proceedings: (1) child custody; (2) child support; (3) determination of paternity and support; (4) termination of parental rights; (5) juvenile delinquency and whether a person is in need of supervision; and (6) divorce.

Felony—A crime considered serious enough to be punishable by imprisonment (e.g., murder, kidnapping, first-degree sexual assault).

Guardian ad litem—Under the laws of many states, all children and any adult judged legally incompetent may have a special guardian, or guardian ad litem, appointed to represent that person's best interests, as determined by the guardian ad litem. For example, a guardian ad litem may recommend a finding of incompetence of an elderly man to a court. In some states, the guardian must be an attorney, while in others, the guardian may be any member of the community in good standing (including a family member, a professional, or any other citizen). The guardian may question witnesses on the stand on behalf of the client.

Informed consent—The client's granting of permission for intervention services based on complete information of the facts, risks, and alternatives. Such consent must be documented.

Jurisdiction—The authority to act (may be based on offense, age, or location).

Juvenile justice system—A separate justice system having jurisdiction over children 17 years of age or younger involved in the legal system.

Liability insurance—Insurance that transfers financial risk from the provider, agency, or school to an insurance carrier.

Malpractice—Any act of professional misconduct or unreasonable lack of skill resulting in harm to a client.

Mediation—Participation of an impartial third party to resolve a dispute, plan a transaction, or assist in negotiations.

Misdemeanor—A less serious crime generally punishable by a fine or imprisonment (e.g., battery, negligent operation of a vehicle, or carrying a concealed weapon).

Plaintiff—A person who brings an action or sues in a civil action and is named on the record.

Privileged communication—Communications between a social worker and a client that may be kept out of legal proceedings.

Standard of proof—The burden of proof required in a particular kind of case; the level or degree of certainty needed to prove an allegation in court. Types include (1) beyond a reasonable doubt, which applies in criminal or delinquency cases; and (2) fair preponderance of the evidence, which applies to most civil cases.

Witness—One who is called to testify in a court proceeding. Persons may be classified as *lay* (factual) or *expert* (rendered qualified by the judge to give opinions in a particular area of expertise).

GRIEVANCE PROCEDURES AND LEGAL RESOURCES FOR CLIENTS

"Advocacy on behalf of or with clients as they encounter the legal system or work with grievance procedures can be rewarding"

Advocacy on behalf of or with clients as they encounter the legal system or work with grievance procedures can be rewarding. Whether you work with clients interfacing with the legal or judicial system on a regular or an infrequent basis—and whether a client is a victim or a witness—you can prepare a client for court in several ways. Preparation for court proceedings can make a client more comfortable throughout the process. Clients who encounter the legal or judicial system as victims or witnesses will often prepare their testimony with an attorney. Possible roles for social workers in the preparation process include the following (Kirst-Ashman & Hull, 2009):

- Advising clients of the formality of the proceedings (i.e., dress, titles, and process), adversarial nature of the process, and the importance of nonverbal behavior
- Preparing clients for the courtroom experience by defining terms, taking them to visit the courtroom prior to the proceedings to familiarize them with the arrangement and the role of participants, procedures, and other details
- Informing clients of their rights and helping them obtain their rights (e.g., the right to be notified of all charges against them, the right to legal counsel, the right to face accusers, the right to cross-examine all witnesses, the privilege against self-incrimination, and the right to invoke privileged communication if helping professionals are called to testify in court about clients)
- Accompanying clients to court during trials as a support and an advocate

Another advocacy role for social workers occurs when they support clients through grievance, review, or appeal processes. Providing verbal support and physically accompanying clients through such processes can make a significant difference in the outcomes. Providing support, encouragement, advocacy, and resources for clients enables them to pursue and persist through often complex and burdensome processes. In your work with individuals, families, and groups, consider exploring issues with the clients concerning public assistance or disability benefits, housing issues, and other resources. Are your clients experiencing difficulties receiving government- or agency-administered benefits or other assistance to which they may be entitled? Your referral to legal resources or involvement as an advocate in grievance or appeal procedures can enhance the quality of life for your clients and their families.

Increasingly, social workers use types of conflict resolution techniques, such as negotiation, arbitration, and mediation for resolution of their professional conflicts and for disputes between clients and others. As an alternative to often costly litigation, a social worker may serve in the role of *conflict practitioner,* performing such activities as facilitation of decision making, evaluation of and assistance in defining problems, and provision of suggestions and solutions. Conflict resolution techniques, such as mediation, are widely used in child custody and divorce disputes, decisions about the care of older adults, child welfare proceedings, and special education hearings, and workplace and medical disputes (Kayser & Johnson, 2008; Mayer, 2008).

As a practicum student, you can be a catalyst for identifying civil legal issues for clients and referring them to resources for pursuing legal remedies. Resources through which they might pursue legal remedies for problems include federal, state, and local regulatory bodies for various appeal, hearing, review, grievance, and complaint procedures; community legal services (e.g., Legal Aid and other sources); the American Civil Liberties Union (ACLU); public interest law groups; special interest organizations (e.g., the National Organization for Women); legal clinics within law schools; and private attorneys who take pro bono (free) cases. Common civil legal issues for low-income, vulnerable populations (for which you might refer clients to one of the resources listed) include tenant–landlord/housing issues, obtaining or maintaining public benefits (such as food stamps from the Supplemental Nutrition Assistance Program [SNAP], Temporary Assistance to Needy Families [TANF], Section 8 housing, and Supplemental Security Income [SSI] benefits), and child welfare issues. Clients accused of criminal offenses who cannot afford private attorneys should seek representation from a public defender's office; however, given the high number of cases that many offices carry, the public defender's office may represent only defendants in criminal cases in which incarceration is possible (Barker & Branson, 2000).

As a practicum student, you could also work with others to produce a legal resource guide for clients on a topic pertinent to your practicum setting (e.g., laws and grievance procedures regarding divorce and child custody, mental health issues, accessing public benefits, the rights of tenants in low-income housing, financial issues, and the educational rights of homeless children). Working with attorneys and translating legal jargon to produce such a resource guide could provide an opportunity for you to demonstrate a practice behavior or competency.

You may also help clients identify their issues as ones that also affect others—even as issues that may merit class action lawsuits against an agency or governmental entity. Among the wide variety of issues that bring individual clients to social service agencies, difficulty meeting the basic needs (i.e., food, housing, medical care, and clothing) of a family is a common issue and may be best remedied by a systemic response. If you find many clients experiencing similar issues, consider exploring a systemic response through the legal system by contacting one of the legal resources noted earlier. Class action lawsuits can be an effective tool for providing resources to a targeted population. For example, in an effort to force the city to finance shelter and services for its homeless citizens, social service delivery providers joined in an effort in the mid 1980s to file a class action suit against the city of St. Louis, Missouri. The impetus for the suit

Engage Assess Intervene Evaluate

Engage, Assess, Intervene, Evaluate

Social workers provide conflict resolution services for disputes between clients and others. How might the provision of these services affect the processes of engagement, assessment, intervention and evaluation?

was the city's lack of responsiveness to the needs of its homeless citizens for shelter and services. The settlement of this lawsuit produced city-sponsored short-term and long-term services to homeless persons that continue today (Johnson, Kreuger, & Stretch, 1989). Although legal action can be time consuming and produce results long after the immediate need was felt, the rewards of engaging in this type of action can be felt by a large population.

PROFESSIONAL AND STUDENT MALPRACTICE ISSUES AND LIABILITY

Increased attention is being given to social work practice liability issues due to the increase in number of states that license social workers and provide appropriate discipline for ethical violations and our increasingly litigious society. Although the percentage of social workers sued is small, clients sue social workers over issues such as diagnosis and treatment, confidentiality, documentation, and boundary violations (Chase, 2008). In response to this risk, the social work profession is working to increase knowledge about ethics and legal responsibilities of social workers (Stein, 2004). The issues most prevalent for social workers and practicum students include confidentiality and documentation.

Confidentiality

Corina's confidence in facilitating the evening group in the detention facility is growing. She has received permission from her field instructor to facilitate group tonight without another staff member in the room. However, during group, one of the members reveals that during his most recent escape from the detention facility, he took a friend's car for a joy ride and totaled the car. He states that because of the confidentiality of the group discussions, he knows that the group will not reveal his secret to anyone in "authority." Corina thinks that this information is probably true. She feels trapped. She wants to maintain the rapport with the group that she has worked so hard to build and is tempted not to reveal the information to anyone. On the other hand, she also knows that she may have a legal responsibility to make a report. She is speechless and wonders what to say. What would you say to the group? Should Corina break the confidentiality of the group?

A hallmark of the social work profession, the importance of worker–client confidentiality is an area in which students are usually well versed. Agencies must have procedures to protect client information and records, particularly in recent times with client information increasingly maintained in electronic format only (Stein, 2004). In practicum, special circumstances may leave you questioning the appropriate course of action, particularly in the areas of criminal offenses, AIDS/HIV status, providing services to minors and (documented and undocumented) immigrants. As Corina discovered, even with thorough knowledge of the basics of client confidentiality, no single response is appropriate for all situations, and social workers must make decisions based on their best professional judgment (Barker & Branson, 2000). The following discussion will address some difficult issues around confidentiality.

What Should I Do If a Client Discloses a Prior Criminal Offense to Me?

Corina's situation poses an ethical dilemma. Although the social worker's duty to protect potential victims of his or her clients is familiar to her, the question of whether to disclose a client's alleged past crime leaves Corina in a quandary. Although the National Association of Social Workers (NASW) *Code of Ethics* (2008a) provides guidance for decision making about confidentiality ("Social workers should protect the confidentiality of all information obtained in the course of professional services, except for compelling professional reasons" [Section 1.07(c)]), no specific directions are provided on the topic of reporting past criminal activities. The issue may become one of determining if the client poses a danger to others as a result of past activity, or the activity involved children, elderly, or vulnerable adult victims. If you are unsure if a client could pose a danger to someone, seek consultation with your field instructor or other knowledgeable, experienced staff at your agency. Always maintain written records concerning your resolution of the issue, and seek to learn your state laws governing these areas (Kirst-Ashman & Hull, 2009).

Professional Ethics

How might you assess whether a client who has committed unreported criminal activity poses a danger to others? If the client's unreported criminal activity must be reported, what might be your first step?

What Should I Do If a Client Discloses a Positive HIV Status?

Several issues present themselves when a client discloses information about a stigmatizing health condition that could pose a risk for others, such as a positive HIV status. The issues include who has access to the information, what can be done with the information, and what are the liability issues for inappropriate release of the information. There are both federal and state statutes that can govern your response to this information (Hodge Jr., 2004; Stein, 2004).

Due to the possible consequences of wrongful disclosure of a client's HIV-positive status (e.g., loss of family and friends, loss or denial of employment, and social stigma), social workers must be careful to obtain written informed consent from the individual (or his or her legal guardian) prior to the release of AIDS/HIV-related information. Only after investigating the policy of your practicum agency, examining state and federal law, and obtaining qualified legal advice (as well as consulting with your field instructor) should you consider disclosing the information without informed consent from the client.

Disclosure without informed consent is permissible under specific circumstances, depending on local, state and federal law. Because an HIV-positive status could pose a threat to those with whom the client is sexually intimate (e.g., spouse, partner, or acquaintances) or to those with whom the client might exchange body fluids (e.g., during needle sharing or health care provision), there is increasing pressure to notify those persons at risk for exposure (Stein, 2004). Clients may be informed that many states allow for criminal prosecution if it is deemed that a person has willfully exposed others to potential infection. The appropriate course of action for a social worker is to encourage the client to notify those persons at risk for the disease or to gain informed consent for notification. When necessary and as a last resort, a court-ordered release of confidential information is an option for a situation in which a strong possibility of harm to another exists and the client refuses to notify those at risk. Disclosing the HIV/AIDS status of a client without consent should occur only after serious deliberation and consultation with a knowledgeable professional (Stein, 2004). As always, careful documentation of these actions is essential.

Can I Serve a Minor without Parental Consent? Do Adolescents Possess the Same Confidentiality Rights as Adults?

All states specify an age, generally 18, at which a minor is emancipated and has many of the legal rights conferred on adults. Although the rights of children have increased in recent times, minors, unless emancipated, do not possess all the constitutional rights of adults. However, some states allow the provision of select services to children without parental consent under specific circumstances. Because the right of decision making about the welfare of nonemancipated children resides with their parents or legal guardians, the issue of confidentiality of minors can be confusing to practitioners and students. The rights of minors vary from state to state, as in the areas of contraception, abortion, and consent to substance abuse, mental health, or other health care treatment (Stein, 2004). The following issues are common areas of confusion:

School Records.   Under the federal Family Educational Rights and Privacy Act (FERPA), parents of children under the age of 18 have the right to inspect and review educational records maintained on their children. Students over the age of 18 also have a right to view their own records. Noncustodial parents have the same access to minor children's school records as custodial parents, unless a court order stipulates otherwise. Under FERPA, educational institutions are prohibited from disclosing records without a student's prior consent, except in specific situations. Those schools that are not in compliance with the standards mandated by FERPA are ineligible for federal funding (Stein, 2004).

Social workers within a school setting may be involved in the release of student records to eligible parties. If you are in a school setting when a student or parent makes a request to view the educational record of the student with whom you have worked, consider asking to be involved in the release procedures so that you can learn the process. You may also wish to discuss with a social worker agency or school policies regarding the kind of information that can be included in a student's file.

Limits of Confidentiality with Minors.   Several situations warrant a violation of confidentiality with minors. Depending on state statute, you can disclose information regarding reasonable suspicion of child abuse or neglect and possible suicidal intentions, with full knowledge and permission of your field instructor. If you are working with minors, be certain to explain the limits of confidentiality to clients during the engagement process. For example, a minor should be told that you want him or her to feel comfortable sharing information with you and that you will not disclose any information shared with you without his or her knowledge. You should further explain, however, that you are required to report to the appropriate authorities any information disclosed that you feel could place him or her or others at risk for harm. Ensure that the minor understands that you will not disclose any information without cause. Additionally, explain that his or her parents or guardians may have access to school and agency records. This knowledge will allow a minor to interact with you on an informed basis (Stein, 2004).

Ethical Dilemma: Clients' Legal Status

The agency in which Rosa is completing her practicum does not, as a policy, ask clients about their legal status in the United States. The agency has gained the trust of the Hispanic community, and many clients eventually discuss their legal status with staff members. Clients are beginning to share their legal status information with Rosa, who feels conflicted. While she is not legally compelled to report known undocumented immigrants, Rosa is unsure what to do. The agency has come under some criticism in recent years for serving undocumented immigrants, and there have been staff discussions about the topic. Further, Rosa's parents arrived in the United States legally, and Rosa has been reared to respect the law. Is this an ethical dilemma? What should Rosa do?

Working with Immigrants

Following enactment of the 1996 federal welfare reform law, social workers have struggled with questions concerning their ability to serve immigrants. This legislation eliminated eligibility for undocumented and some documented immigrants for certain federal assistance programs (including TANF and SNAP) and included provisions that direct federal and state agencies to implement citizenship verification procedures with their clients. Some agencies administering federal assistance funds must also report known undocumented immigrants (Stein, 2004).

As a practicum student, you are well advised to keep abreast of the changes affecting immigrants. The fear invoked by citizenship-reporting requirements for some social service programs may dissuade clients from accessing any programs at an agency. Reporting requirements could pose ethical dilemmas for you in your efforts to maintain client confidentiality and to abide by the law. If you are completing your practicum in a federal or state agency or in an agency that receives federal support for a program, check with your field instructor regarding any restrictions to service eligibility for documented and undocumented immigrants.

Confidentiality and Agency Information

As a practicum student, you are required to adhere to all agency policies and procedures (NASW, 2008a). Your obligation to adhere to confidentiality obligations goes beyond that of client privacy. Working at an agency, you will likely learn about personnel matters, agency procedures, agency history, agency gossip, and other information that is specific to your agency. Some of the information that you will learn may be sensitive information that, if shared, could embarrass or prove harmful to current or former staff members or agency administration. Therefore, while the NASW *Code of Ethics* (2008a) does not explicitly state that social workers have an ethical obligation to refrain from sharing employer information, the spirit of the code indicates that social workers should not share sensitive proprietary information.

Documentation as a Legal Record

Documentation concepts are often taught in practice theory courses. Specific education is typically provided in the practicum agency in such areas as methods of documentation, confidentiality of records, and conditions under which the sharing of records with outside agencies is permitted. Documentation provides a record of services rendered and a tool for evaluating the effectiveness of services and reduces practice risk (Chase, 2008). The importance of documentation as a legal record cannot be overstated. You will want to learn as much as possible about documentation in your practicum

(Chase, 2008). For legal purposes, a record should contain the following elements (Stein, 2004):

▶ **Assessment information.** Include methods used to gather information, including interviews, direct observation, number of sessions and other details. Identify whether other professionals were involved in the assessment. The assessment information should form the basis for services provided.

▶ **Information about referrals.** Include whether you assisted clients to obtain services through transportation, and whether you make any follow-up contact to determine whether the client is accessing services.

▶ **Acceptability to the client.** Your documents should show whether services were acceptable to you and the client and that you took client concerns into account in developing plans for the client. Consent forms could include the clients' rights to know agency expectations of them, what activities will be done to assist clients, what clients can expect as an outcome of their involvement, the consequences of client failure to be involved in services, and the process of and handling of confidential information.

▶ **Monitoring of service provision.** Document any treatment contracts and actions resulting from the contacts, progress toward goal attainment, unsuccessful efforts to contact clients, correspondence, and suggestions,

---

Practice Application 9.1 Agency Records as Legal Documents

This practice application will provide an opportunity to critique your practicum site's record format relative to the elements expected of a client file for legal purposes.

Obtain a copy of a client file. Compare and contrast the contents of the file with the list of elements that a file should contain for legal purposes, as noted earlier (Stein, 2004). Discuss your findings with a member of your practicum team.

A practitioner's personal notes can also be used as a legal document in court proceedings. A practitioner's personal notes should contain the following information for legal purposes (Munson, 2002):

▶ Speculation about client dynamics
▶ Impressions about the course of treatment
▶ Problems resolved
▶ Problems being worked on now
▶ Problems to be worked on in the future
▶ Projections about termination
▶ Summary of perceptions of significant treatment session dynamics

---

Practice Application 9.2 Personal Notes as Legal Documents

The personal notes of a practitioner can be used as legal documents in court proceedings, so it is important to review the preceding list with your field instructor. Ask your field instructor or another social worker at your practicum site the following questions:

▶ Do you maintain personal notes on clients?
▶ If yes, will you share the format with me?

▶ If no, why do you avoid taking personal notes?
▶ Have your notes ever been subpoenaed?
▶ Will you share with me the agency procedure for subpoenaed documents?
▶ Will you share with me your suggestions about documentation?

Take notes on the discussion, and share your findings in integrative practice field seminar.

instructions, referrals, or directives made to the client and whether the client followed through with them. Also include any notes about supervision or consultation about the client.

Although documentation is time consuming, practitioners and students must prioritize documentation of their cases in order to optimize service delivery and minimize malpractice liability. In your practicum activities, consider maintaining a log of any outgoing and incoming telephone calls (including the date, time, and content of conversation). In addition, complete documentation as soon after the events as possible. A delay could alter your memory and result in omissions or misrepresentation of critical information.

SPECIAL LEGAL ISSUES IN PRACTICUM

Although you are a student, you are acting in the same capacity as a professional social worker in your responsibilities with clients and, as such, are accountable for upholding the same legal, professional, and ethical standards as other social workers (Kirst-Ashman & Hull, 2009). Although your field instructor is responsible for notifying clients that you are a student, you should take on this responsibility rather than leave clients uninformed (Kirst-Ashman & Hull, 2009). As a helping professional, you are held to the standards of the NASW *Code of Ethics* (2008a) as well as to federal and state law governing professional social work services. If you bring harm to a client during the course of your practicum, your field supervisor, agency, and social work program could possibly be held liable (Reamer, 2006).

Nevertheless, you are advised to ensure the existence of malpractice insurance coverage for your activities in practicum (Chase, 2008). Many social work programs either provide malpractice coverage or require students to purchase it independently. Additionally, your practicum site may provide coverage for you as it does for other staff or volunteers. Last, clarify the extent of all the insurance under which you are covered. Does it cover all types of activities? Would it pay for legal defense fees?

Potential liability exists in any student–client relationship, and you are well advised to follow the same guidelines as nonstudent social workers to minimize your liability. The following duties place social workers and agencies at greatest risk of legal liability: avoid sexual misconduct, warn others when a client discloses intent to harm them, prevent a client's suicide, properly diagnose and treat a client, ensure continuity of service to a client, maintain and protect confidentiality, and maintain accurate professional records and a proper and legal accounting of payments and reimbursements (Sheafor & Horejsi, 2008). As social workers have developed expertise in a wider range of areas, particularly with specialized populations, the expectations for a higher standard of care requiring increased knowledge and skill have also developed in most areas of practice.

> *"As a helping professional, you are held to the standards of the NASW* Code of Ethics *as well as to federal and state law governing professional social work services"*

SOCIAL WORK ETHICAL VIOLATIONS AND GRIEVANCE PROCEDURES

The increased recognition of the social work profession has resulted in increased regulation of the profession. Social workers are responsible legally and ethically for their behaviors to several bodies.

The Employing Agency

As a professional, you are accountable to your employer for your services to clients. According to the NASW *Code of Ethics* (2008a), you are responsible for adhering to commitments you have made to your employer, including following agency policies and procedures. Even as a student, your employer could be held legally responsible for your actions in a lawsuit (Reamer, 2006).

Profession

Various professional organizations have codes of ethics as well as grievance processes that may be utilized for ethics code violations. For example, the NASW *Code of Ethics* (2008a) outlines various roles and responsibilities for professional social workers, and NASW offers a process for reviewing and resolving alleged violations (NASW, 2005). As a result of a *request for professional review* being filed with the National Ethics Committee, a determination will be made regarding whether a dispute meets the criteria for acceptance into the mediation or adjudication process. If the professional review will involve NASW *Code of Ethics* section 1.09 (Sexual Relationships), 1.10 (Physical Contact), 1.11 (Sexual Harassment), 2.07 (Sexual Relationships), or 2.08 (Sexual Harassment), the matter will be referred to adjudication. Matters involving other sections can be referred to the mediation process. This process can occur at the state chapter or national level for any alleged violation of the *Code of Ethics* (NASW, 2005). If serious misconduct is found, sanctions may be imposed, including the following (NASW, 2005):

- Corrective actions (to restore or increase a social worker's competency and ethical functioning) (e.g., supervised practice, consultation, additional coursework, or an apology or restitution to a victim)
- Sanction(s) (e.g., temporary or permanent revocation of NASW membership or the Academy of Certified Social Workers [ASCW] credential, notification of the state regulatory board, publication of action in the *NASW News* or chapter newsletter, or notification of a social worker's employer and credentialing entities)
- A combination of any of the above

Practice Context

How could the increase in litigation against social workers affect the practice context? How could the practice context affect the degree to which social workers are involved in litigation?

State

In addition to the professional review, licensed social workers can also face a review by a state board of regulation and licensing. State regulatory boards can call practitioners before a disciplinary panel for a formal hearing. If the board finds *unprofessional conduct,* such disciplinary actions as a reprimand, public censure, fine, probation, or suspension or revocation of a license could result (Stein, 2004.).

Court (Civil and Criminal)

In addition to being subject to agency, profession, and state entities, social work professionals may come under the scrutiny of federal and state civil and criminal courts. All social workers, even those who are not members of the NASW or licensed (and so do not fall under the jurisdiction of a state licensing board or the NASW), are held accountable to civil and criminal laws governing professional behavior. *Civil litigation* (a lawsuit) can result in monetary damages, while *criminal charges* can result in incarceration as well as loss of license or certification and sanction by the NASW (Barker & Branson, 2000; NASW, 2005).

The increase in the number of lawsuits filed against social workers may be a reflection of factors other than an increase in negligent or unethical activities, including the increased frequency with which clients seek legal recourse for malpractice. Regardless of the reasons, this trend is cause for concern. The most common categories of malpractice claim filed against individual social workers are incorrect treatment, sexual impropriety, breach of confidence/privacy, and failure to diagnose or incorrect diagnosis. Most insurance payments from the NASW-sponsored malpractice insurance policy result from claims concerning sexual impropriety and incorrect treatment (Reamer, 2006; Sheafor & Horejsi, 2008). You are encouraged to take advantage of education in the area of ethics to be fully aware of your ethical and legal duties. As a student, you are encouraged to use your supervisor to discuss difficult issues, and to arrange for ongoing consultation as a practitioner (Chase, 2008).

IF YOU ARE SUED

If a legal action is brought against you, the following is suggested (Stein, 2004):

- Resist the urge to panic. Stay calm. Many lawsuits are frivolous, and you can continue to practice your profession during the proceedings.
- Immediately inform your field instructor and your social work program.
- Discuss your suit only with your attorney. Statements to other professionals, as well as to nonprofessionals (family, friends, and fellow social work students), are generally not considered privileged information and can be admissible in court. Your communications with your personal therapist are considered privileged.
- Refrain from making any self-incriminating statements to anyone.
- Do *not* contact the suing client (plaintiff) or his or her attorney. Your professional relationship ends when the adversarial relationship inherent in a lawsuit begins.
- Assemble relevant documents (e.g., files, case notes, telephone logs, and calendars) and make them available only to your attorney and your attorney's representative.
- Follow the advice of your attorney. Your communications with your attorney are privileged.

Finally, consider this a learning process! Unless you practice social work outside the boundaries of the *Code of Ethics* (NASW, 2008a), you are not likely to be sued. As you go through the process, your involvement in a lawsuit may provide invaluable lessons that may serve you well in the future.

PROFESSIONAL COURT INVOLVEMENT

Ben had a feeling that something was very wrong with the professional relationship between a staff member, Harold, and a client, Regina. Staff members had been talking about Harold and the unprofessional manner in which he was working as a substance abuse counselor with

Regina, but no one had been willing to go to any administrators about the situation. While Ben was conducting a home visit with Regina last week, Harold arrived and confronted her on the front porch. Ben could not help overhearing the nature of the interaction between the two, which clearly bordered on harassment. Harold felt that a rejection of his substance abuse treatment was a rejection of him and told her that "she couldn't live without my services." Ben learned today that the client is suing Harold for sexual harassment. The client has told her attorney that Ben was present during one encounter with Harold, and Ben received a subpoena today. Ben has no idea what to do and wonders whether he should call Regina to let her know that he does not wish to jeopardize his practicum by testifying against a staff member. What should he do?

Receiving a Subpoena

Receiving a subpoena can provoke anxiety for even the most experienced practitioner. Ignoring a subpoena is illegal and could result in a fine or even incarceration, yet inappropriately revealing confidential information could result in a malpractice suit and a soiled reputation that permanently damages your career (Black, 2004). A subpoena could compel the attendance of a witness to provide testimony at a deposition or a trial or order the production of documents or other things, such as records, notes, and files as well as electronic formats (Polowy & Gilbertson, 1997).

Before a social worker can make any response to a subpoena regarding work with a client, the requirements of privileged communication must be fulfilled. *Privileged communication* differs from the concept of *confidentiality* because the client, rather than the social worker, possesses the privilege to restrict the dissemination of information given in confidence in a legal action (Kirst-Ashmen & Hull, 2009). When a court orders disclosure of confidential or privileged information, social workers are instructed by the NASW *Code of Ethics* (2008a) to disclose the least amount of confidential information necessary. If you receive a subpoena (either as a student or as a practitioner) to testify in court, you should immediately inform your field instructor (if student) or supervisor and the agency's legal counsel and work with the attorney to prepare for your court appearance. Carefully read a subpoena to determine the action required, the date for a response, and the issuing court and attorney. Document the steps taken to ensure compliance with the order while protecting the client as much as possible. (Kirst-Ashman & Hull, 2009).

Testifying in Court and Serving as an Expert Witness

Social workers can be called to appear in court either as a fact witness or an expert witness. Examples of activities in which a social worker may be involved that could lead to court appearances include mandatory reporting of and involvement in a case of child or elder abuse/neglect or exploitation, involvement in a client's child custody case or worker's compensation hearing, and civil damage suits or criminal matters (including domestic violence and violation of probation orders) (Stein, 2004). Social workers provide testimony based on personal observations or documentation. Testimony based on personal observation may or may not involve referring to notes during the testimony, while testimony based on documents entails reading reports and possibly explaining the process of producing and storing documents during the proceedings (Sheafor & Horejsi, 2008).

Social workers may also be called to provide expert testimony in cases. Due to expertise and special training, expert witnesses can be asked for both facts and their opinions or conclusions about facts, as well as opinions about hypothetical situations. Examples of cases in which a social worker may be asked to testify include child custody cases, child abuse cases, and adoption placements (Stein, 2004). It is essential that you consult with the attorney for whom you will be called as a witness prior to any court proceedings. Meeting with the attorney will provide an opportunity to learn about questions that you are likely to be asked as well as to inform the attorney of any weaknesses in your testimony (Sheafor & Horejsi, 2008).

The following suggestions will serve to assist you in delivering effective testimony in court (Stein, 2004):

- Take your time answering questions.
- Always tell the truth. Do not guess, speculate, evade a question, or use humor or sarcasm.
- Never answer a question that you do not understand; rather, ask that the question be rephrased.
- Never interrupt the attorney or judge.
- Avoid professional jargon and define terms as needed.
- Offer to explain your answer if necessary.
- Cease talking if an objection is made.
- Answer the question that has been asked.
- Ensure that your nonverbal and verbal behaviors are congruent.
- If arranged prior to the trial, bring and refer to your written notes during your testimony.
- Dress formally and professionally.
- Use a demeanor that is calm, sincere, and detached even under adversarial questioning.
- Consider requesting financial compensation in exchange for expert testimony.

You are well advised to obtain as much knowledge about responding to subpoenas and providing testimony as possible. You may consider talking to your field instructor about your interest in gathering information about social work involvement in the legal system and asking whether you could accompany any agency social workers to court. Consider asking whether any agency

Practice Application 9.3 Noncustodial Parental Rights to Review School Records

Imagine that you are a practicum student at a high school, assisting in a "Rainbows" after-school group for children of divorced parents. A noncustodial father arrives at school and presents a written request for the release of his daughter's complete file, to include all counseling records. The signed request is for "all documentation pertaining to enrollment, admission, student progress, counseling, and any other activity undertaken by this student while on school premises, etc." The secretary is copying the general school file but requests that you pull and copy her counseling records. The secretary informs you that the father has said that he would wait for all copies.

When you pull the counseling file, you notice that a copy of an adult protective order is in the file. The order was issued last summer and is effective until next summer and orders the respondent (the father) to be restrained from any contact with the wife. He is granted supervised visits with his daughter. In addition to this order, you see a note that the mother will bring in a copy of their divorce decree as soon as it is available to her.

The father has not asked to see his daughter, although she is in a class just down the hall. He has asked for a copy of the complete file, including your records, which contain a complete intake form, treatment plan, and progress notes. What are your options? What would you do? (Note: For our suggested resolution, see page 207.)

_____

Developed by Dana Klar, JD, MSW

Practice Application 9.4 Reflections on the Legal System and Vulnerable Populations

Vulnerable populations often experience difficulties with the legal system. Many social workers provide assistance to clients in their dealings with the system. Knowledge of the problems encountered by a particular population can help you become a more effective advocate for clients.

1. With two or three other students, select a population and identify the point at which this population often interfaces with the legal system. Examples include the following:

   ▶ Battered women and the police
   ▶ Single mothers and the child support enforcement system
   ▶ Juvenile offenders and the juvenile court system
   ▶ Families involved in divorce proceedings, to include making child custody and visitation arrangements

2. Interview at least two social workers who serve this population, and identify the body of law with which professionals working with the population need to be familiar. Research and obtain copies of significant, related legislation, regulations, and any available legal resource guides for clients.

3. Interview three or four clients to learn about their experiences with the legal system. After learning more about their particular situations, ask the clients the following questions related to their experiences:

   ▶ What do you understand about the law relevant to your issue(s)?
   ▶ What problems did you encounter in working with the legal system?
   ▶ What would have been beneficial for you in your involvement with the legal system?
   ▶ What changes (if any) do you think need to be made in the legal system to promote fair treatment and justice?

4. In a journal entry, reflect on the interviews, and share your entry with a member of your practicum team.

5. If a legal resource guide for clients is not available or is out of date, compile/revise a legal guide for the population and issue(s) you have selected that would help clients advocate for themselves.

_____

Developed by Jan Wilson, PhD, LCSW

Practice Application 9.5 The Courts: How Much Do You Know?

A variety of levels (federal, state, county, and municipal) and types (civil, criminal, family, and juvenile) of court systems exist. Divide into groups of two or three, and select a level and type of court system. As a group, research the organization and functions of the chosen system. Specify the jurisdiction and the types of cases the court system adjudicates. Identify which client populations are likely to be involved in the system.

As an integrative practice field seminar class, compile a table like the one that follows, showing the variety of levels, types of court systems, jurisdictions, types of cases adjudicated, and client populations likely to be involved in the system. Each group will enter the information about its chosen level and type of court system. As a class, discuss the information your group gathered and the ways in which your particular court system relates to other courts and to clients' issues.

	Federal	State	County/Municipal
Civil a. Organization and Functions b. Jurisdiction c. Client Population			
Criminal a. Organization and Functions b. Jurisdiction c. Client Population			

Developed by Jan Wilson, PhD, LCSW

---

staff member has received a subpoena, and arrange an informal discussion with that person to inquire about steps taken in response to the subpoena.

FOLLOW-UP TO PRACTICE APPLICATION 9.3: SUGGESTED RESOLUTION

In this instance, the release of records to a noncustodial parent is appropriate. However, the response in this situation must be in compliance with state law as well as school and school district policy. Given the situation, the appropriate course of action is (1) consult with the field instructor and the school (or school district's) legal counsel as quickly as possible; (2) inform the school secretary about the order of protection and your need to do some checking; and (3) inform the parent that you will need some time to determine and comply with the school's procedures regarding the release of counseling records and that you will call him within a short time period. After the parent leaves, make every effort to consult all the necessary parties as quickly as possible and respond within the timeframe you specified. You will need to conceal all address information in the student's records and inform the student and his or her parent(s) of the request and your duty to comply with the request.

SUMMARY

Knowledge of legal and judicial matters is an essential part of professional social work practice. As a social work student, assume responsibility for acquainting yourself with the relevant legal aspects of your practicum setting. Familiarity with legal issues will provide you with the possibility of using the legal and judicial system to advocate for your clients on both the micro (individual) and macro (legislative and policy) levels. Furthermore, investigate potential practice liability issues within your practicum site to lessen your legal vulnerability. Knowledge of the legal and judicial system and a heightened awareness of ethical issues in your professional work will enable you to serve your clients better and to deliver your social work services with minimal liability risk (Reamer, 2006).

During the group session, **Corina** asked the group for reactions to the information that the client had shared. Some members of the group lauded the client for his daring and for "getting away with it," while others talked about the importance of integrity and honesty and encouraged him to "come clean" with the friend. Corina echoed the need for integrity and the importance of sincere friendship in maintaining a support system. She also told the group that she may have to break confidentiality and explained the possible limits to confidentiality. Afterward, she checked with her field instructor and discovered that under state law, social workers are required to report criminal activity to the authorities. She did so with great trepidation and enlisted the assistance of her field instructor to make the report and to process the reporting with the clients in the next group meeting.

Ben discussed with his field instructor the encounter between Harold and Regina he overheard and his fears about jeopardizing the integrity of the practicum if he testifies against another staff member in compliance with the subpoena. The field instructor intervened with Harold and told him that Ben was present at the home visit and must testify if he is called. Harold left the agency a week before the case went to court. When the case went to trial, Ben provided testimony about what he had overheard at the home visit.

Succeed with **mysocialworklab**

Log onto **MySocialWorkLab** to access a wealth of case studies, videos, and assessment. (*If you did not receive an access code to* **MySocialWorkLab** *with this text and wish to purchase access online, please visit* www.mysocialworklab.com.)

1. Under the core competency videos, choose Policy Practice, then watch Participating in Policy Change. If the correctional staff was not open to considering changes in the system, what types of responses may be possible using the legal system? What role could the social worker play in the legal responses?

2. Choose the Interactive Cases for Practice, then click on Domestic Violence. Go to page 18 (of 28), and watch Identifying Next Steps. If you were to tell the client about the legal services provided by the agency, what more would you add?

PRACTICE TEST The following questions will test your knowledge of the content found within this chapter. For additional assessment, including licensing-exam type questions on applying chapter content to practice, visit **MySocialWorkLab.**

Professional Identity

1. Social workers can do all of the following, except:
   a. Testify on behalf of a client
   b. Assist to draft legislation
   c. Provide mediation to resolve disputes
   d. Represent a client in court

Professional Identity

2. Possible roles for social workers in the court preparation process includes:
   a. Informing clients of their rights and helping them obtain their rights
   b. Preparing the court paperwork
   c. Taking clients to meet the judge
   d. Taking clients to meet the jury

3. In the role of conflict practitioner, social workers use the conflict resolution techniques of:
   a. Negotiation, arbitration and mediation
   b. Negotiation and arbitration
   c. Negotiation and mediation
   d. Negotiation, arbitration, mediation and court

4. Increased attention is being given to social work practice liability issue for the following reasons, except:
   a. The increase in the number of states that license social workers
   b. The federal licensure of social workers
   c. The increasingly litigious society
   d. The increase in the number of states that have discipline for ethical violations

5. All of the following should occur before client AIDS/HIV information is disclosed except:
   a. Inform the client about possible criminal prosecution
   b. Obtain written consent from partners
   c. A thorough investigation of federal, state, and local law, and agency policy
   d. Consultation with a knowledgeable professional

6. Noncustodial parents of minor children:
   a. Have no right to access their children's school records
   b. Have the right to access their children's school records with consent of custodial parent
   c. Have the right to access their children's school records
   d. Have the right to periodic access their children's school records

7. If a student brings harm to a client during the course of your practicum, the following could possibly be held liable:
   a. Your field instructor, agency and social work program
   b. The agency and social work program
   c. Your seminar instructor and field instructor
   d. Your field instructor, agency and seminar instructor

Ethical Practice

8. A professional review that will involve the following sections of the NASW *Code of Ethics* will be referred to the adjudication process, except:
   a. Sexual relationships
   b. Informed consent
   c. Sexual harassment
   d. Physical contact

9. The most common categories of malpractice claim filed against individual social workers includes all of the following, except:
   a. Lack of informed consent for treatment
   b. Sexual impropriety
   c. Breach of confidence/privacy
   d. Failure to diagnose or incorrect diagnosis

10. As a student, the first thing you should do upon receiving a subpoena is:
   a. Inform the agency's attorney
   b. Inform your attorney
   c. Inform your field instructor
   d. Contact the client

Log onto **MySocialWorkLab** once you have completed the Practice Test above, to access additional study tools and assessment.

Answers:

Key: 1) d 2) a 3) a 4) b 5) b 6) c 7) a 8) d 9) b 10) c

10

Termination

The Beginning of an End
(or the End of a Beginning?)

Core Competencies in this Chapter (Check marks indicate which competencies are covered in depth)				
✔ Professional Identity	☐ Ethical Practice	☐ Critical Thinking	☐ Diversity in Practice	☐ Human Rights and Justice
☐ Research Based Practice	✔ Human Behavior	☐ Policy Practice	☐ Practice Contexts	✔ Engage, Assess, Intervene, Evaluate

You are approaching the end of your current practicum experience. You may be nearing graduation from your social work program, or you may be preparing for your next field experience. In either case, you are bringing closure to this practicum experience—a task that may entail closing cases or ending projects but also requires you to say your farewells, assess your accomplishments, and identify future learning needs. If you are continuing on to a second semester at your current practicum site, this chapter can help to anticipate issues for your upcoming termination.

Throughout your social work training, you have learned about the importance of the termination process for the client. Appropriate termination and closure are essential for an effective social work intervention as the client system is allowed to plan for and participate in the ending of the relationship with you, the worker. Also critical to the effective social work intervention is your own closure with client systems, your supervisor, and your co-workers.

This final chapter is devoted exclusively to the multiple levels and types of practicum-related terminations. To be addressed first are the issues that surround the emotional reactions you may experience as you terminate from this practicum experience. Next, you will explore the practical aspects of terminating from the agency and your field instructor. Last, the termination process provides an opportunity to discuss professional development issues that may now be (or soon will be) relevant to your social work career.

WHAT HAS THIS PRACTICUM EXPERIENCE MEANT?

Termination of any type, but particularly one related to a powerful or meaningful experience, can elicit mixed feelings. You may be feeling a sense of accomplishment, pride, and competence now that you have completed another step in your journey to becoming a professional social worker. Completing the experiential portion of your social work education provides you an opportunity to experience, learn, and practice social work. You have increased your social work knowledge, mastered practice behaviors and competencies and exhibited skills necessary for effective social work practice, identified and clarified personal and professional values, and begun the process of integrating theoretical frameworks with the application of concepts.

The practicum experience may also have evoked a sense of incompetence, fear, or trepidation. Putting your knowledge into practice can result in a realization of how little you feel you actually know. Although you have developed practice competencies for your current setting, you may question if these skills will transfer to a different setting. Although you may have a fear of the future and doubt your ability to be an effective social worker, self-assessment and "reality checking" are important and normal stages of professional development. This period can be an opportunity to assess knowledge, skills, and practice behaviors gained and areas for future development.

Terminations also evoke a range of emotions as you contemplate closing or transferring client cases, wrapping up projects, and saying good-bye to people who have influenced your development as a social worker. You may be feeling reluctance to leave your practicum site, the "I can't wait to get out of here" syndrome, or some combination of the two. Although not all your learning has been "pain free," your field instructor and staff at your practicum site has helped shape your definition of social work practice and guided you through

Source: U.S. Department Of Agriculture.

this phase of your professional development. There may be some colleagues to whom you are ready to bid farewell, but ending your professional relationship with others may be a difficult emotional event in your life.

Two important issues emerge as you enter this final phase of your practicum. First, your learning is far from over as effective social workers are committed to lifelong learning. With the radical and rapid changes that occur in the social work profession, staying current in the areas that affect those we serve is critical. Second, stay in touch with your emotions and feelings regarding this experience. Being able and willing to acknowledge that you may have both positive and negative feelings about the experience and its termination is a normal and expected phenomenon.

An important task at this point in your practicum career is to consider the meaning (personal and professional) of this experience for your life. Along with assessing your learning of knowledge and skills, reflect on the ways in which your practicum has affected you as a person. The termination of this practicum can aid in evaluating your career choice as well as yourself as a social worker. Some students question their career choice at this stage. Your self-examination can include such questions as these:

"Along with assessing your learning of knowledge and skills, reflect on the ways in which your practicum has affected you as a person"

- What are the reasons I became a social worker?
- Am I gratified by being a social worker? Is this profession a fit for me?
- Am I burned out on helping?
- What strengths do I have as a social work professional?
- What do I enjoy about being a social worker?
- What do I *not* enjoy about being a social worker? What can I do to change those things I do not enjoy about the social work profession? If I cannot change them, can I live with them, or might they impede my ability to practice social work?

Practice Application 10.1 What Is Social Work and Where Do I Fit?

The aim of this practice application is twofold: (1) help you begin your termination process from your current practicum site and (2) enable you to review your perception of the social work profession in general and the role of social work at your practicum site. If you have not already done so, begin by developing a written statement outlining your philosophy of social work (i.e., describe your definition and philosophy regarding the social work profession).

Develop a list of termination-related issues to discuss with your field instructor during your final supervisory session. Include items on your list that are relevant for you. We offer the following suggestions to get you started.

▶ Has my perception of social work changed since the beginning of this practicum? If so, how has it

changed, and what factors contribute? If not, why has it not changed, and what factors contribute?

▶ Did I understand the role of social work in my practicum agency at the beginning of my practicum? Has that understanding been strengthened, clarified, or refuted as a result of my experience here?

▶ Regarding my learning plan, where are my strengths and areas for growth?

▶ Do I have a better understanding of the practicum agency's policies and procedures? What suggestions for improvement might I have?

▶ What recommendations do I have for future practicum students to enhance their learning experiences?

▶ Which practice behaviors are my strengths? My challenges?

Professional Identity

Termination provides opportunities for reflection. List accomplishments and growth and discuss with your field instructor.

▶ Was the agency and population at my practicum site one in which I enjoyed working?

▶ What other settings or populations would I like to explore?

▶ Have I identified any settings or populations that I am not well suited to serve?

▶ Where do I go from here in the short and long run (e.g., administration, different population or setting, more intense involvement with clients, or less intense involvement with clients)?

▶ Do I want to continue my education and training, perhaps to obtain another degree or receive training in a specialized area of social work practice?

BEGINNING THE TERMINATION: WHERE DO I START?

Cameron's practicum at the substance abuse treatment program has been a powerful and significant professional and personal experience for him. Professionally, he gained insights into the etiology and dynamics of addictions, learned skills to work with addicts and their significant others, and became comfortable functioning as a professional in this setting (versus his previous role as a client). On the personal side, Cameron is empowered to remain abstinent and to devote his life to helping others overcome their addictions. As a result of these profound realizations, Cameron has decided that he wants to stay on at his practicum site as a volunteer upon completing his practicum requirements. He believes he can continue to help clients by serving as a group leader, individual therapist, or aftercare worker. Cameron has not been invited to continue as a volunteer and his fellow MSW students voiced concerns about his "obsession" with this population. What do you think Cameron should do?

The practicum experience is intended as a training tool and a stepping stone for professional development. Viewing practicum as one component of your education (versus the entire experience) allows you to maintain a perspective on the practicum experience. If the practicum has gone well, this does not mean that you have learned all there is to learn. Conversely, if your practicum was not the success you hoped for, you are not doomed to be a failure as a social worker. Framing your experiences realistically frees you to move to the next chapter of your professional development.

In Cameron's case, he is ambivalent about ending his practicum. Practicum experiences can be so intense and profound that some students feel disloyal or uncommitted if they "abandon" their clients. Others feel unable to separate from their settings because their practicum experiences met a personal need. Students who find it difficult to terminate from practicum may explore continuing their work as volunteers or employees. Should you find that you are experiencing difficulty moving on, exploring your feelings about terminating may be in order. Ask yourself these questions:

- Do I have trouble accepting change or transitions? Why?
- Do I feel I am abandoning my clients or co-workers? Why?
- Do I feel that no one else can work with my clients as well as I do? Why?
- Can I not imagine my life without my work at this agency?
- Am I fearful I will not be able to get a job/another practicum?
- Have I not learned all of the competencies I should have learned in this practicum, and am I therefore feeling unprepared for the next chapter of my professional life?
- Have I had such a powerful learning experience that I am now so passionate about this work that I feel compelled to stay in this setting?
- Am I afraid that the skills I have learned will not be transferrable to the next setting?

Continued involvement with your practicum site as a volunteer or employee is not inappropriate and may, in fact, be a bonus for your personal, financial, and professional situation, but consider examining the reasons for staying or leaving. Your field instructor or faculty members can be resources for processing these issues. Termination provides an opportunity to appreciate the power of mentoring and consultation in your professional growth and development.

Joys and Frustrations: Taking Stock

As you begin to consider your termination, you can identify the joys and frustrations associated with leaving your practicum, clients, co-workers, and field instructor. Termination provides a time for reflecting on these and other important developmental issues. Resist the temptation to romanticize or deromanticize the practicum experience. Being realistic about the practicum experience begins with an exploration of the joys and the frustrations.

The Joys

Consider those events, interactions, and activities that brought gratification, a sense of accomplishment, pleasure, and even elation. Such a response may have occurred when you mastered a difficult skill, calmed an angry client, initiated an innovation in the agency, or received a hug from a child or older adult client. Joys are very personal experiences and important to recognize (even when you may have difficulty seeing your work as joyous!).

The Frustrations

Social work practice can also elicit feelings of frustration even in the educational phases. Again, recall those experiences that created a sense of tension for you. Do any of the items on the following list sound familiar? What would you add to the list? Do you have strategies for resolving or preventing these frustrations?

- **Changing practicum sites.** You may feel there is more to learn at your current site, you like this population, the agency feels comfortable and familiar, and this is the work you want to do in your social work career. The social work program's requirement that you have to complete practica at multiple sites feels like an impediment to your own predesigned professional development.
- **Transferring cases or projects.** You may feel no one else can understand your clients or projects as well as you can and you realize that you are not yet ready to part with these experiences.
- **Termination feelings.** You may be used to clients leaving you but had not anticipated your feelings associated with your departure.
- **Loyalty to the agency and clients.** Also perceived as a joy, you may have developed a strong sense of commitment and loyalty to the clients, agency, staff, and your field instructor. Your loyalties may have sprung from your passion for your work and now you feel frustration that you must remove yourself from these people and the mission.

Terminating from your practicum can bring joy *and* frustration—both of which are normal responses. The key to a successful termination is to recognize and explore your feelings and to move forward.

Lessons Learned

To begin to grasp the extent of learning that has occurred during your practicum, an essential task is the evaluation of *all* your learning experiences related to your skills and growth—even the experiences that you might deem to have been traumatic or unsuccessful. You may believe that negative experiences cannot serve as valuable learning, but these experiences tend to leave indelible impressions on us. You can use these to mold your approach to social work practice. To examine your learning, compare your knowledge, skills, and values as you began your practicum with your current knowledge, skills, and values by creating a pre- and postlist of these areas or using your learning plan as a guide for comparison. Engaging in a concerted effort to examine the learning you have experienced can help you to identify those social work skills you have mastered and to develop a plan.

You cannot change the way in which this experience has evolved, but you can use the insights gained from this experience to enhance your next learning experience, whether it will be in your next practicum, in the role of a new social work professional, or in the future as a field instructor. As you know by now, the practicum experience can be a significant learning experience and one that is often hard to capture in words. Without a formalized plan for identifying the lessons you have learned during this practicum experience, you may find yourself unable to describe your professional growth. The following practice applications may help integrate your learning as you prepare for terminations and articulate your learning.

Practice Application 10.2 **Termination through Journaling**

If you have been journaling during your practicum, shift your focus to include specific reflections about your feelings regarding termination. If you have not journaled during practicum, you can use this practice application to gain insight into your own termination process.

Utilizing the termination process as a focal point, journal on knowledge and skills learned; positive and negative feelings about your experience and leaving your clients, co-workers, and field instructor; and future directions for your learning. Two areas to add to your journal: (1) Utilize your individual or group supervisory sessions or integrative practice field seminar to discuss terminations and new knowledge and skills gained; and (2) utilize the formal and informal evaluation processes at your agency to review and assess your past, current, and future learning.

Practice Application 10.3 **Termination through Presentation**

Having to summarize and present information is a useful technique for identifying and gaining insight into your learning, outcomes, challenges, and future learning. Ask your field instructor or seminar instructor if you can present a case/project that entails a description of your practice with a client system with which you worked from assessment through termination and evaluation. After the presentation, ask for feedback.

Practice Application 10.4 **Termination through Illustration**

Develop an individual, group, or organizational eco-map with a future perspective—that is, depict the client or organizational system as you envision it may be in the future after the social work intervention has been implemented and terminated. This activity can help you identify the knowledge, competencies, and skills you have learned and mastered at each phase of the intervention as well as those of the client(s) or project. Share and discuss your eco-map with a member of your practicum team.

Practice Application 10.5 **Termination through Simulation**

Role-playing can be a useful exercise for simulating the dynamics involved in terminating the range of relationships that have evolved during your practicum. Practicing the termination experience can provide the confidence you need and allow you to complete the termination process in a professional and therapeutic manner. Do not be self-conscious or uncomfortable, but consider the exercise just another aspect of your learning experience.

Identify a partner for rehearsing terminations. Possibilities include a fellow student, field instructor, social work program faculty or staff member, or agency staff member. Select a specific situation that can be helpful to simulate. Suggestions include: termination session(s) with an individual client, family, or group; evaluation session(s) with your field instructor; exit interview with the dean or chair of your social work program; employment/graduate school interview; or meeting with supervisor on the first day of a new social work position.

Complete the role-play (carrying the situation out as far as you need or want to), and then engage in a debriefing with your partner. You may wish to audio- or videotape the role-play to aid you in the review process. During the debriefing discussion, you and your role-play partner should focus on your strengths and areas for growth.

Developed by Robert Sontag, LCSW

If permitted, videotape or audiotape termination encounters with clients or groups at your practicum setting. You may then review the tape(s) with clients, colleagues, your field instructor, and faculty members to identify your strengths and areas for growth in facilitating an effective termination.

In sum, your termination is as important for you to process as for your clients. Viewed from a strengths-based perspective, the termination phase of your social work education can be used to assess practice behaviors, competencies, strengths, gains, outcomes achieved, and possibilities. Having examined the educational, intellectual, and emotional facets of termination, we now shift our focus to more pragmatic aspects of terminating a practicum.

THE NUTS AND BOLTS OF TERMINATION WITH YOUR CLIENTS, AGENCY, FIELD INSTRUCTOR, AND SOCIAL WORK PROGRAM

As with any social work skill, there are appropriate and inappropriate methods for achieving closure. You are terminating at least three types of relationships, depending on your student status and situation. At a minimum, you are terminating from your clients, co-workers/agency, and field instructor. You may be ending your relationship with the social work program and the school you attend. Finishing your degree may mean transitions in your relationships with faculty, fellow students, family, friends, co-workers, or roommates. The following sections provide discussions of client, agency, and social work program terminations.

Terminating with Clients

Corina begins to plan for her departure from the adolescent group at her practicum. She has discussed the pending termination with her field instructor and developed a plan to transfer responsibility for the group to another practicum student, who will be continuing his practicum for the next semester. The teens had been informed at the outset that Corina was a student who would be leaving at the end of the semester. Corina implements her plan for terminating her involvement with the group by raising the issue several weeks prior to her departure. The week following this discussion, in which specific information was provided to the teens about the transition, Corina notes that Chad, a 15-year-old runaway with a history of truancy and burglary, is sullen and unresponsive and refuses to make eye contact with her. Corina had found Chad to be a challenge throughout his stay at the facility. She felt that he wanted to open up and turn his life around, but she had become frustrated by her unsuccessful (but persistent) efforts. Corina was mystified by Chad's behavior this week, and when she tried to talk with him after the group, he lashed out at her and stated that it did not matter that she was leaving. What is your assessment of this situation, and what strategies can you suggest to Corina regarding her interactions with Chad and the group?

What is appropriate client termination? How do you know you have achieved this elusive goal? When can you initiate termination, and how will you facilitate the process? How can you anticipate and handle clients' responses to your termination? These are important questions for a practicum student to raise, and they will be highlighted here.

Termination in direct practice situation should be planned, mutually agreed upon, and occur when goals are successfully achieved. This ideal situation does not always occur. In fact, 40–60 percent of cases may terminate unexpectedly due to social worker or student leaving the agency, client request, or agency constraints (Fortune, 2009). Terminations can also arise as a result of client withdrawal or noncompliance, cessation of eligibility for benefits, or agency policy. You can employ as many as possible of the skills for facilitating an appropriate termination.

Corina's challenge provides an example of a well-planned termination that becomes complicated by a client's unexpected reaction. Client reactions to termination are as varied as the clients themselves and will likely reflect the way in which the clients respond to other changes and terminations in their lives. Just as you may experience mixed feelings about your own termination, so, too, will your clients. Although most clients report positive feelings about termination, the worker must be prepared to deal with both positive and negative client responses (Fortune, 2009). Corina's client, Chad, presented her with a mixed-message response to termination. He is saying that her departure has no relevance for him, but the intensity of his response may suggest otherwise.

Termination of the worker–client relationship can evoke similar responses for both the worker and the client. Possibilities emerge as closure is pending and include pain, guilt, embarrassment, heightened emotions, awkwardness, or realization of an opportunity to engage in candid, mutual sharing (Shulman, 2009). Both the client and the social worker may experience these simultaneously and may revisit these feelings on multiple occasions before the actual termination of the relationship.

The nature and management of the termination process will influence the client's response. A planned termination may enable the client to anticipate his or her feelings, work through the transition, and view the termination as a positive experience in his or her life. As we see in Corina's case, even a planned termination can be troublesome. An unplanned, abrupt, or forced termination may leave the client (and you) feeling unfulfilled and lacking closure on the issues that had been the focus of the relationship.

As you know from your social work training, the topic of termination should be introduced at the outset of the professional relationship because the aim of any social work intervention is to successfully achieve the mutually established goals. Although anticipating termination can help you develop skills, you should resist having preconceived expectations regarding a particular client's reaction when you introduce and implement the termination. Compiled from the experiences of the authors and others, possible client responses to termination include (Fortune, 2009; Shulman, 2009):

Human behavior

Terminations are key to effective interventions. What conceptual frameworks guide your terminations with client systems?

- A sense of accomplishment that goals and outcomes have been met and increased autonomy.
- Feeling pleased that he or she no longer has to be involved with you or the agency—a common reaction of involuntary clients.

- Denial that you are leaving the agency or that the relationship must end—Clients may think that the relationship can continue even if you are no longer officially a part of the agency.
- Direct and indirect acting out (e.g., anger, regression, hostility toward you or others, lateness, absences, or the introduction of new problems intended to prevent your departure).
- Overemphasis of the positive contributions made by the worker.
- Ambivalence and a sense of loss and mourning.

In addition to gaining competency in engagement, assessment, and intervention, your practicum provides opportunity for learning skills for termination. An effective termination should encompass assessment of progress and process, generalizing and maintaining gains, and the transition itself, including client and worker responses to termination (Fortune, 2009). Gelman, Fernandez, Miller, and Weiner (2007) offer a range of practice strategies and behaviors to practicum students to facilitate an effective termination including:

- View and explore termination as an opportunity for growth.
- From the outset of the relationship, inform the client that you are a student and the length of your practicum.
- Preview termination by using breaks and vacations as rehearsals for the actual termination.
- Individualize termination plans to fit the specific and unique client situation (i.e., longer and more intense relationships will require a longer termination process).
- Utilize supervision to discuss your as well as clients' reactions to termination, including the positives, negatives, and connections to past terminations.
- Employ such strategies as review of progress, discussion of your own feelings about the termination, and plan for follow-up and contact (as appropriate).

Consider including a ritual to symbolize the termination of the social worker–client relationship. A ritual can help both the client and the worker acknowledge the work that has been completed and the bond that has been forged, and it can provide an outlet for the expression of feelings regarding the termination. A ritual can be in the form of a formal service evaluation, an expressive task (e.g., art, writing, music), or an exchange of gifts (if permitted by the agency) (Walsh, 2002).

When facilitating a termination with a client under less than optimal circumstances (i.e., the relationship was stressful or unproductive, goals remain unmet, or the worker and client did not develop a viable working relationship), honesty is the best policy. Share with the client your perceptions of the problems that occurred, and ask for his or her perceptions as well. You must examine your contribution to this situation, but do not allow yourself to feel the sole responsibility for the outcome.

Terminating with clients, particularly those with whom you have established solid working relationships, is challenging even when you have facilitated an appropriate termination. Consider that termination provides you with the opportunity to reflect on and evaluate your learning; bring closure to this chapter of your professional development; and process the issues of separation for you, your clients, and your field instructor (Baum, 2007).

Terminating with Your Field Instructor and Agency Staff

As Ben is preparing for the completion of his foundation practicum at the community center, he is offered a position made possible by a three-year grant awarded to the agency. Ben provided input into this project, so he feels very committed to seeing it come to fruition. If he accepts the position, he will have the opportunity to continue working with clients with whom he has established positive working relationships. The position is well funded, full time with benefits, and will provide Ben with additional social work experience and could mean a future for him with this agency and in this community. Two outcomes result if Ben accepts the position: (1) He will be unable to complete his MSW degree in the two-year period he had planned, and (2) he must delay his plans to develop more advanced clinical skills to enable him to realize his goal of becoming a family therapist. He is experiencing a dilemma because he would like the income and experience, but he feels that he has learned all he can learn at this agency. What would you do if you were Ben?

Termination skills learned for your practice can be useful for engaging in the termination process with your field instructor and agency staff. Just as you address your clients' feelings about change and loss, you, too, will benefit from tackling those issues of your own change and loss related to leaving the practicum. Termination from your field instructor and agency staff encompasses dual issues: (1) *formal termination,* which includes disposition of practicum responsibilities and the evaluation process, and (2) *informal termination,* which involves the personal farewells. An important aspect of a successful and gratifying termination is to achieve a balance between the attention and resources devoted to each of the areas involved in the termination process (i.e., emotional, educational, and practical tasks).

Formal Termination

Formal termination from your practicum site involves two primary tasks. You and your field instructor will review the status of your practicum assignments and determine the future of each case or project. Next comes the formal evaluation of your performance as well as of your perception of your practicum experience.

In achieving closure, you and your field instructor will address each individual activity in which you have been involved to determine if continued attention is required and, if so, the way in which this will be facilitated. You can and should begin this discussion well in advance (four to eight weeks, at least) of your actual completion date because planning and transitions can be timely and complicated. Specific issues to address during your supervisory sessions may include the following:

 ‣ **Closure or transfer of client cases.** You and your field instructor will review each case to evaluate if the goals and outcomes have been met and to determine if the case should be closed or continued. If the case will remain open, you and your field instructor can identify the worker/program who will assume responsibility and then facilitate the transfer process.

 ‣ **Projects.** Informing your field instructor of the status of any projects is the first step in terminating your involvement in grant proposals, research projects, educational materials, and program evaluations. Ideally, these projects will be completed as you are finishing your practicum. Realistically, this may not be the case. Projects, particularly those that involve collaborating with others, often take longer than expected. If you are in the midst of a project, present your suggestions for handling the remainder of the project requirements to your field instructor. Can another worker or practicum student assume responsibility for the project's completion? Might your field instructor take over the remainder of the project? Is this a situation in which you may consider continuing your relationship with the organization? These are all possibilities and should be considered carefully, based on the needs of the project and available resources.

▶ **Group activities.** If you have been involved with a group at your practicum, you will want to develop a plan for transitioning out of the group. If you have served as a co-facilitator, your departure from the group may not create a disruption or a need for disposition because your co-facilitator can carry on the group leadership responsibilities in your absence. If you have been the sole leader, you must determine if the group will continue after you leave and, if so, who will lead the group. A transition task such as a change in group leadership may require additional time for planning because a new facilitator must be identified and introduced to the group for at least one to two sessions prior to your departure.

▶ **Administrative issues related to termination.** End-of-practicum duties may include physically transferring cases/projects; completing final documentation; notifying agency staff and relevant community persons (including clients); and returning identification badges, parking permits, keys, and other agency supplies. Be certain to address the disposition of electronically stored information. If you have saved client- and agency-related information on an agency or personal computer (in documents, e-mails, or in databases/spreadsheets), discuss with your field instructor how this information should be accessed, deleted, or transferred.

The final activity required for your completion of your practicum experience is the twofold formal evaluation process: the field instructor's evaluation of the student and the student's evaluation of the field instructor. The field instructor's evaluation of your performance is used as the basis for your official grade, while the evaluation that you complete regarding your practicum perspective is typically used by the practicum faculty to evaluate the quality of field instruction at your site. Both documents are of critical importance to your and other students' social work education and should be given serious attention by all involved in their completion.

Being Evaluated

The formal and informal evaluation of your performance during this practicum is a significant task that culminates in your termination (and, of course, your grade). Being evaluated by your field instructor and other agency staff is likely to serve as the formal and official evaluation that is submitted to the social work program to serve as the basis for the grade you will receive. Regardless of the type or extent of your evaluation, you are encouraged to focus not on the grade that is assigned but on the feedback provided and identify ways in which you can incorporate that information into your growth as a social work professional.

Even a glowing and exemplary evaluation requires you to engage in critical-listening skills. We may assume that no change is needed if we are positively evaluated by supervisors and peers. To continue to grow and develop as a social work professional, change is essential. Some field instructors may have difficulty delivering feedback that they perceive as negative or harsh. If you have not received feedback regarding your areas for growth—and you may not welcome the receipt of such information—you may want to encourage your field instructor to provide such feedback for you to enable you to grow further.

Being the Evaluator

Your field instructor's evaluation of your practice behaviors, competencies, and practice skills and knowledge is one aspect of the evaluation and termination process. You will likely be asked to provide feedback to your social work program regarding your perspective of your experience. This evaluation may be a standardized quantitative evaluation form (anonymity may or may not be an option), an interview with your practicum liaison, or some combination.

Information provided by students about their practicum experiences may be used for several purposes. Your feedback may aid your field instructor in enhancing his or her supervisory skills and help the agency to create a stronger practicum experience. Your feedback may also assist the social work program to strengthen the curriculum, and fortify the connection between the agency and the social work program (Barretti, 2009). Information may also be made available to other students to aid them in selecting their practicum sites. Practicum faculty may use the information to determine the quality of field instruction provided by a site or field instructor.

Consider and be able to articulate your feelings about the practicum experience. Do you believe that the environment was amenable to student learning? In evaluating practica, students report that satisfaction with the practicum setting is based on agency and field instructor factors that include (1) a healthy work setting (i.e., high morale, activity, and staff commitment), (2) innovation in practicum tasks and activities, (3) clarity regarding roles and responsibilities, (4) field instructor support, and (5) orientation to the practicum (Giddings, Thompson, & Holland, 1997). Also important is the ability of the site to offer experiences that teach practice behaviors and competencies.

Ideally, you and your field instructor have provided each other with feedback from the outset of your practicum, thus making a formal feedback process simply a summarization of previous feedback sessions. If you have not had the opportunity to provide feedback to this or any other supervisor, you may begin by asking for clarification regarding the evaluation's purpose, process, and format, and the ways in which the information will be used. Giving your field instructor balanced feedback is important; balanced feedback means informing your field instructor of the positive and negative aspects of your learning experience in a professional manner without directing your comments to the field instructor's personal qualities.

Equally important is your recognition of your lack of objectivity regarding your experience. You do possess biased feelings (possibly positive *and* negative) about the practicum you are just about to complete. These feelings may involve the quality of the relationship you have established with your field instructor and other staff, your emotional state, and expectations regarding your evaluation. If you do have negative feelings about the experience or your field instructor, consider ways in which you can frame this feedback so that your field instructor can hear and use the information. Be cautious so that even if your experience was not ideal, you do not alienate your field instructor, other staff, or the agency. You may want your field instructor or another staff member to serve as a reference, or you may find yourself working with one of these professionals in the future.

When you are delivering evaluative feedback, adhering to several additional guidelines may enhance the quality of the experience for you and the recipient of the information. The following list is compiled from our experience as well as from suggestions from others (Munson, 2002):

- Take an active and invested role in the evaluation process; provide detailed, specific feedback.
- Focus your feedback on professional behavior(s) as they relate to the practicum supervisory role.
- Avoid offering personalized feedback regarding the field instructor or other staff.
- View your feedback as valuable and necessary for the practicum experience for you and your field instructor.

Providing feedback to your field instructor can be a valuable learning experience for you and your field instructor. You can each gain insights into your own styles and behaviors as well as learn skills related to evaluation.

Informal Termination

Like the formal termination process, the informal termination is important and necessary. Informally, termination rituals may include saying good-bye and thank-you to agency staff; writing notes of appreciation to all those who have been important parts of your learning experience; attending an event commemorating your farewell from the agency; and accepting gifts from staff or clients. (Check agency policy regarding accepting gifts from clients.)

Acknowledging your departure accomplishes several important milestones in your professional development. First, the ability to recognize endings brings closure to a situation. Should you leave the agency without recognition, you and the staff may feel as though you have unfinished business. Just as clients may distance themselves from you emotionally and physically, you, your field instructor, and the staff may experience similar feelings. Being able to say your farewells enables all to process feelings about your leaving the agency or program. Second, your field instructor and the agency staff have the opportunity to acknowledge your contributions and engage in an informal review of the work that you have completed during the practicum. Last, a ritual activity (e.g., a farewell party, a gift, or a card) that celebrates the completion of this phase of your professional training enables agency staff to begin to view you as a professional and a colleague.

A final part of the informal termination process is to discuss with your field instructor and agency staff the issue of recommendations and letters of reference. You may opt to obtain letters of recommendation (although generic letters are not as helpful as letters written for your application to a specific position) or at least to verify with your field instructor and other staff members that they are willing to provide references for you. Ensure that the reference they will provide will be a positive one. You obviously do not want any surprises.

Terminating with the Social Work Program

If you are graduating from the social work program following the completion of your current practicum, you have an additional termination issue to address. You have spent many hours with the faculty and students who compose your social work program. This group of people may have become a "family" for you as you have grown, learned, commiserated, and struggled with both your fellow students and faculty. You may be more than eager to move on from this phase of your life, but the faculty and student relationships you have established will shape and guide you as you enter your social work career.

Just as we have discussed the merits of attending to appropriate termination with clients, field instructor, and agency staff, graduation is an opportunity to reflect on your classroom termination as well. The chaos of completing coursework and practicum and preparing for graduation (which may involve relocation or an employment search) may not leave you the time or resources needed to explore your feelings about separating from your social work program. Graduation (or maybe the period after graduation) provides an opportunity to think about the knowledge and skills gained, relationships forged, personal changes experienced, and your visions for your personal and professional future. You may need time and emotional distance from the school experience to delve into your feelings. When you can, consider the contributions you have made and received through your social work education. Let the faculty and your student peers know that you valued the impact they made on your education, and provide balanced feedback regarding your experience with the social work curriculum.

Ethical Dilemma: When Is It OK to Let Go?

Rosa's practicum is coming to a close. She is engaged in closing and transferring cases and wrapping up projects. One case, in particular, is causing concern for her. Rosa has been very involved with a family from El Salvador. She and her field instructor have determined that the case should remain open and be transferred to another social work student who is arriving next semester. Rosa's concerns are centered on the fact that the other student's first language is not Spanish. In fact, the student, whose first language is English, speaks Castilian Spanish as his second language, while the family she has been involved with speaks the language of an indigenous group of people. Rosa is worried that communication will be a problem along with understanding the family's culture and undocumented immigrant status. The family has endured multiple traumas and is extremely needy. Rosa does not believe that the new social worker will be as competent in meeting the needs of this family as she has been. What is the source of Rosa's concerns? Are her concerns valid? Has Rosa overidentified with this client system? What steps should she take to assure the family that the new social worker will be effective? What steps should Rosa take to assure herself that the new social worker can be effective?

PROFESSIONAL DEVELOPMENT: WHERE DOES IT BEGIN AND WHERE DOES IT END?

As you contemplate joining the nearly 600,000 U.S. social workers, it is time to consider your ongoing professional development. Professional development begins with the first social work course you completed and does not end for the duration of your life. During your education, you have been exposed to a wide range of areas in which social workers are employed. As you plan for your own career progression, consider the expanding and emerging areas in which social workers are making a difference. For example, increasing numbers of social workers are needed in the following areas:

- Gerontological practice to serve the growing population of older adults and their families in such settings as hospital-based, outpatient medical, and residential facilities
- Community-based substance abuse treatment programs
- School social work at both the elementary and secondary levels
- Private sector, to respond to the privatization of social service, human resource management, and social welfare programs
- International practice, focusing on working with persons who have immigrated to the United States and providing social work services in an international arena
- Forensic social work in both institutional and community-based settings
- Interprofessional team comprised of health professionals

This segment highlights such professional development issues as the search for employment, strategies for succeeding in your first social work position, becoming involved in the professional social work community, and obtaining professional credentials.

Employment Search: A Needle in a Haystack?

Social workers learn in their training to establish goals and develop plans to achieve those goals. As a social work student, you established a goal to graduate, obtain a social work position, and become a social work professional. The search for employment is one step in that march toward your goal. Numerous resources are available to aid you in your search for employment. Take advantage of your university or college career services, using them early and often. Career counselors are invaluable resources for developing your résumé, identifying available positions, designing job search strategies, and preparing for interviews.

The Preparation

As you anticipate your employment search, consider developing a professional portfolio to present your competencies and skills in the best light. The professional social work portfolio typically includes personal and professional information and artifacts that provide evidence of your professional accomplishments, while it intends to help you integrate theory, action, self-reflection, learning, and assessment (Fitch, Peet, Reed, & Tolman, 2008). You may find that assembling examples of your accomplishments will help you articulate and demonstrate your social work competence to potential employers. Your self-confidence may be boosted when you are able to see examples of your work collected and organized in one place. Increased confidence in your abilities and assets can serve to enhance the impression you make during an interview. Items to consider adding to your portfolio are determined by the intended use and format of your portfolio. Portfolios developed for use in a capstone course or employment presentation can include, but are not limited to, examples of course and field work (e.g., papers, reports, evaluations, and client assessments), and philosophical/reflection statements in either paper or electronic forms (Fitch et al., 2008). Regardless of the format, a portfolio is your opportunity to showcase your competencies and achievements.

The Search

Networking with other social workers is an excellent means to securing employment. Let others know that you are "on the market." You may find networking with students and faculty in your social work program, staff at your practicum site(s), and members of professional social work organizations a particularly useful strategy to consider. Organizations that employ social workers may not participate in on-campus recruiting and hiring activities, so you cannot rely on the employer to seek you out. Alumni surveys suggest that many graduates find employment at their former practicum agencies. With this thought in mind, maintaining your ties with faculty, your former field instructor(s), and the staff at your practicum site(s) may be a professionally astute and meaningful endeavor. If you do receive an employment offer from your practicum site, treat it just as you would any other offer. You may feel tempted or obligated to accept such an offer because it is flattering or convenient or because you feel a sense of loyalty, but (like Ben in the earlier student scenario) you should weigh all the issues and options carefully.

While working with your career service office and professional networking will likely yield the best results for your job search, we would like to suggest some additional strategies for securing a social work position:

- **Informational interviewing.** There are two types of informational interviewing you may consider:
    - Meeting with agency personnel (who may be social work supervisors or human resource personnel) to discuss the types of social work positions for which they hire can provide you with insights regarding agency mission and culture, position type and scope, salary ranges, and frequency of openings. Although not all agencies are interested in conducting informational interviews when they do not have position vacancies, you should find that staff at many agencies are willing to meet you. Even if the agency does not have an opening at the time of the informational interview, you may be considered, should an opening occur, as a result of the initiative you have shown.
    - Interviewing social work practitioners who are employed in the type of position, agency, or setting in which you may be interested can provide you with a more realistic portrayal of employment options.

- **Internet resources.** Position vacancies are routinely posted on the websites of federal and state governmental agencies; some social service agencies (check United Way for a listing of agencies); college/university career service centers or schools of social work; local, regional, and national newspapers; and professional social work organizations. Also available are sites that provide not only specific position advertisements but career information as well. For example, www.monster.com provides interviews with social workers who describe career opportunities in gerontological social work.

- **Resources in other areas.** If you are thinking of relocating following graduation, consider checking the local newspaper's website or connecting with your school's alumni or the NASW chapter in the area for networking and job listings.

To help form your mindset about the employment search process, we have compiled the following list of suggested strategies (Doelling, 2004):

- Assess your strengths in the areas of knowledge, skills, and accomplishments.
- Identify your career objectives and preferences (including work setting, geographic location, and salary) and determine if your competencies and skills are applicable across populations, settings, and functional areas.
- Research opportunities and options (e.g., employment openings and requirements, credentials required, and salary data).
- Develop a plan for the employment search, including identifying professional associations, online directories, and contacts that can be helpful connections to employment opportunities.

Application/Interview Process

If you are prepared for your employment search, the application and interview process need not be daunting. Once you have identified the types and locations of positions that you will apply for, the application is the next step. Preparing your résumé and yourself are essential for a successful employment search. The career services office at your college or university can introduce you to the varied styles and formats that are appropriate for your résumé, but the key is that you present yourself as positively and accurately as possible. For example, your cover letter and résumé should be adapted for each position for which you apply. Similarly, you may want to have a list of persons who have agreed to provide references for you that can be utilized for various positions.

The ideal outcome from a well-written résumé is an invitation to interview. Following are tips for managing the interview process:

- Be on time. Being a few minutes early is even better.
- Greet the interviewer openly with a smile and a firm handshake.
- Smile frequently but always appropriately.
- Listen and speak with interest, enthusiasm, and intelligence.
- Allow the interviewer to assume and maintain control of the interview. Try to determine whether he or she wants to do most of the talking or expects that you will do most of the talking.
- Maintain a high level of enthusiasm, but do not convey overeagerness or desperation.
- Devote more time to the significant questions (e.g., practice approaches and experiences) that you are asked and less time to the insignificant questions (e.g., coursework and non–social work positions).
- Take brief notes so that you may refer to them later in the interview or following the interview.
- Remember the interviewer's name, and use his or her title.
- Do not speak negatively about your social work program, previous employers, former field instructor(s) or practicum site(s), social work agencies, or social workers.
- Make and maintain eye contact with all persons you meet during the interview. Attend to your posture, but appear relaxed. (Do not sit on the edge of your seat.)
- Ask for clarification if you are unsure about the meaning of the question you have been asked.

- Observe (or ask about) the pace and the feel of the agency and the work. (Do people seem frantically busy? Is staff idling at their desks? What is the appearance of the physical space? How does staff interact with one another and the clients?)
- Clearly annunciate your words and avoid fillers such as "you know," "like," and "um."
- Develop a list of questions to ask during the interview.
- Although you may not have an opportunity to present such a statement, have a summary statement to offer regarding your understanding of the position, timeframe, and your interests.
- Most of all, be honest and be yourself!

Follow up the interview with a letter, e-mail, or note thanking the staff at the agency for the interview. Reiterate your interest in the position and your availability.

The Negotiation

You may not yet have considered your response to an actual offer of employment. You may want to delay your response in order to allow yourself time to consider the offer, discuss it with others, or weigh it against other offers. As you begin a new career, you may not consider the way in which you can negotiate the details of the job being offered. As a social worker, you are by now well trained in the area of advocating for others. One area in which you are well advised to assert your advocacy skills is in the discussions that surround employment arrangements, including salary, benefits, and "tangibles" (e.g., job description, schedules, flexibility, and workspace issues).

You will want to thoroughly research salary-related issues before negotiating with a potential employer. Salaries are often an issue about which beginning professionals feel (and should feel) curious. Median salaries for social workers ranged from the upper $30,000s to the mid $40,000s. Median salaries and ranges by category were as follows (U.S. Department of Labor Bureau of Labor Statistics, 2008–2009):

	Median	Range
Child, family, and school social work (School social work is highest; residential care is lowest)	$37,480	$24,480–$62,530
Medical and public health social work (Hospital social work is highest; individual and family services is lowest)	$43,040	$27,280–$66,070
Mental health and substance abuse (State government social work is highest; individual and family services is lowest)	$35,410	$22,490–$57,630

NASW reports that nearly half (46 percent) of all social workers surveyed have annual earnings between $40,000 and $59,999 (Whitaker & Arrington, 2008). According to the U.S. Department of Labor Bureau of Labor Statistics (2008–2009), the number of social work positions is expected to increase 22 percent by 2016, which is faster than the average for other professions with the largest growth occurring in mental health and substance abuse treatment services (30 percent), followed by medical and public health (24 percent) and child, family, and school social work (19 percent). Growth is also expected in gerontological and rural social work practice. Half of all social workers are currently employed in health or social services, while 30 percent work in state or local government. Social workers with baccalaureate degrees typically earn approximately 70 percent of that earned by master's-level social workers (Center for Health Workforce Studies and Center for Workforce Studies, 2006).

Knowing average salary ranges for your degree and experience and the type of agency, position, and geographic area is an advantage in discussing a job offer. This information may be obtained from the career center at your college or university, NASW chapter offices, and informational interviewing with faculty, student colleagues, and practitioners. Once you are well informed about salaries, given your situation, determine a salary range that you find acceptable and be prepared to state it during the discussions that follow an offer of employment (Doelling, 2004). The benefits being offered to you may account for 25 to 30 percent of the total package being presented to you and you want to be certain you are clear about the benefits that your potential employer is offering you. Inquire about the following benefits typically included with a professional social work position (Doelling, 2004):

- Health/dental insurance (ask for information on type and extent of coverage and persons eligible for coverage).
- Professional insurance, life insurance, and retirement programs (again, ask for specific details).
- Leave policies (e.g., sick, family, vacation, and personal).
- Educational benefits (e.g., payments and time allocated for pursuit of a professional degree or credential [to include supervision] and continuing education).

Last, but not least, is the negotiation concerning the "tangibles." These may be the issues that make a job attractive or not attractive to an interviewee. Gaining insight into the specific expectations and options related to the job being offered is critical to your future quality of life and professional development. Be willing to ask questions and make requests regarding such issues as the following:

- **Job description.** How specifically defined is the current description, and is there room for current or future negotiation of job duties?
- **Work schedule.** Are the hours you work rigidly determined, or are there options for flexibility (i.e., permanent or intermittent "flex" time or compensatory time)? Is working from home an option?
- **Dress code.** What are you expected to wear in various work situations (and will this involve a major expenditure for a new wardrobe before you begin the new job)?
- **Flexibility.** Will you be able to determine your daily agenda/calendar, or will the position/agency dictate that?
- **Supervision.** Who will provide supervision? Is that person a licensed or certified social worker in the event that you want to pursue licensure or certification? If not, is there a qualified social worker available to provide supervision, or will the agency fund you to seek supervision outside the agency?
- **Workspace.** Will you be required to share an office, telephone, or computer, and, if so, is there space available for private interviews with clients? Will you have access to e-mail and Internet?
- **Travel requirements.** If your potential position involves travel, will an agency vehicle be provided for your use (and if so, what is the availability

of that vehicle), or will you be reimbursed for using your own vehicle (and if so, what is the rate of reimbursement)? If the position requires considerable travel, you must determine if your vehicle is adequate for that task, and if not, you must decide whether you can afford to purchase a new vehicle and/or insurance at this time.

▶ **Safety issues.** Does the agency provide training on safety issues, including HIPAA? If you will be seeing clients outside the office, what safety precautions (e.g., cellular telephones, pagers, or escorts in certain situations) are available? If the agency requires background checks, who is responsible for obtaining and paying for the checks, and how extensive are the checks required in terms of duration and geographical locations? Are staff allowed/encouraged to take co-worker(s) with them on a visit?

Landing your first job is an exciting end to your journey toward becoming a social worker, but we urge you to use the social work skills of communication and advocacy to secure a gratifying employment arrangement. Negotiating a mutually agreed-on employment situation can mean the difference between a positive first experience and an unsatisfactory one for both you and your new employer.

Involvement with the Professional Social Work Comunity

Your socialization as a social worker does not end with graduation or with your first social work position. Your career evolves as you move from student to practitioner and possibly on to supervisor or administrator. Many of the suggestions offered here to guide you through your student career have merit for the entirety of your professional life. To keep your passion and avoid stagnation and burnout, use the following strategies:

Professional Identity

▶ Regularly revisit and modify your professional goals, interests, and needs. You may find that you prefer to change positions more frequently than others you know, or you may find gratification in long-term employment with one organization. You may choose to relocate, work part time, return to school, or move into administration or private practice.

▶ Regardless of your career choices and directions, you will benefit from ongoing evaluation completed with your family and friends, professional mentor, or a career counseling service.

▶ Assess your interest in pursuing supervisory/administrative positions, private practice, consulting, or any one of the many opportunities available to social workers.

▶ Based on your ongoing evaluation, develop a multiyear plan for keeping your social work career exciting. This may involve planning for additional training, requesting a change of job duties, or taking a leave.

▶ Keep in mind the realities of the profession you have chosen and your life issues.

▶ Avoid reacting drastically to the myriad changes that confront the social work profession.

▶ Actively engage in self-care on a regular and frequent basis.

Your willingness to challenge yourself, ask the difficult questions, and confront the answers will help you establish your professional social work identity and respond to each new transition that comes your way. Joining professional social work organizations is one strategy for becoming and staying

---

Professional Identity

Career-long learning is important to competent practice. Identify areas of interest for your continuing professional education.

"Your willingness to challenge yourself, ask the difficult questions, and confront the answers will help you establish your professional social work identity and respond to each new transition that comes your way"

connected to your profession. For example, the National Association of Social Workers is the primary professional social work organization, and you may have taken the opportunity to join this organization as a student. Being an NASW member provides you with access to information through journals, newspapers, and websites. We encourage you to begin your involvement with such organizations by attending local or state meetings and volunteering to serve on committees, recruit new members, and present information to others at meetings.

As you immerse yourself in your new profession, you will learn there are many specialized international, national, regional, or local organizations that embrace social workers. You may find that social workers in your community with specialized interests (e.g., gerontology, home health, and volunteer management) are organized and meet regularly. You may also find that the area of service delivery in which you are involved has an affiliation to a larger professional organization that has a subgroup for social workers (e.g., elementary education associations with social work sections). We encourage you to explore what is out there or create something.

A final area of professional involvement to consider once you are an established practitioner is that of giving back to the social work profession by becoming a field instructor. Being a field instructor is a way to share your knowledge and skills and see the impact that mentorship can have on another social work professional. You may choose to volunteer your time and service to the local social work program(s) (which may or may not be your alma mater) through serving on committees or guest lecturing in social work classes. Practitioners provide linkages to social work programs from the service community and are invaluable in identifying directions for curriculum and school policy.

Social Work Credentials: To Get or Not to Get?

As a new professional, you may be overwhelmed at the number of options for national, state, and specialized licensures and certifications and uncertain which credentials are most critical for you to pursue. You are encouraged to explore the criteria for being awarded the range of credentials, the benefits of being credentialed in that area, and the requirements for maintaining the credential once you have received it. Presented here is a brief summary of available credentials that you may want to consider at some point in your career.

National Credentials

Academy of Certified Social Workers (ACSW)—offered by NASW, criteria includes: current NASW membership; MSW degree from a CSWE-accredited social work program; documented two years of postgraduate social work employment and professional supervision by an ACSW or DCSW credentialed supervisor; professional evaluations from an MSW supervisor and two social work colleagues to validate knowledge, understanding, and application of social work principles and values; 20 verified hours of relevant continuing education; and agreement to adhere to the NASW *Code of Ethics* and NASW *Standards for Continuing Professional Education.* Information is available at www.naswdc.org

Board Certified Diplomate in Clinical Social Work (BCD)—awarded by the American Board of Examiners (ABE) in Clinical Social Work, criteria includes: master or doctoral degree in social work with course and fieldwork in direct practice; state licensure at the highest clinical level available in the state(s) of practice; five years (7,500 hours) postgraduate clinical social work practice with 3,000 hours under supervision (1,500 hours for an advanced clinical social worker); 40 hours of continuing clinical education in past three years; successful completion of an application process with clinical peer evaluations; adherence to the ABE Code of Ethics and annual recertification (includes 20 hours of continuing clinical education). More information is available at http://www.abecsw.org. ABE also offers credentials in Practice with Children and their Families, Clinical Supervision, and Psychoanalysis.

State Licensure/Certifications

Each state in the United States has some form of legal regulation (i.e., licensure, certification, or registration) for professional social workers. To obtain information on the requirements in any state, visit the American Association of State Social Work Boards (AASSWB) at http://www.aswb.org or Social Work Examination Services (2009) at http://www.swes.net/home.html.

Applications for state licensure examinations can be obtained from the state licensure board office. Each office can provide information regarding application criteria and process, testing sites and times, passing rates, notification procedures, re-examination requirements, and cost. Most states grant multiple credentials (e.g., baccalaureate, master, advanced, and clinical). Upon determining the type and level of licensure you seek, ensure that you understand the requirements for obtaining the credential. In some states, you can sit for the examination immediately on completion of your degree, while in others, you must first fulfill the professional experience and supervision requirements. You may inquire about options for taking the examination—computer-delivered, available accommodations for special needs, and frequency and cost of retakes if you fail to pass the examination—and examination preparation materials, workshops, and study groups.

Specialized Credentials

If you find yourself interested in obtaining a credential in a specialized area, consult with colleagues, the state chapter of the NASW, or your alma mater regarding criteria and contact information. Although not typically required for receiving third-party reimbursements or obtaining employment, specialized credentials verify expertise in a particular area and that your knowledge and expertise are sanctioned by an accrediting body. Use caution, however, in seeking specialized credentials until you determine that the accrediting body is a credible entity that is recognized by social workers and the NASW or CSWE. Obtaining specialized credentials may entail significant costs in the application, examination, and renewal processes.

An exercise for you and your integrative practice field seminar colleagues to consider is an investigation of available general and specialized social work credentials. You and your fellow students can divide credentials by area of interest, gather and compile the information, and then share it with one another.

SUMMARY

This chapter has discussed termination with clients; field instructor; practicum site; and your social work program, school, and fellow students. Termination and evaluation have educational, emotional, and logistical components. Suggestions for evaluation of students and field instructors were highlighted along with professional development in employment searching, strategies for success in your first social work position, involvement with the professional social work community, and social work credentials for you to consider.

As you approach the termination of this practicum experience, take a moment and congratulate yourself on the completion of the beginning phases of becoming a professional social worker. Consider the legacy that you leave at your practicum. What have you contributed to the agency that will live on after you are gone? There have been many high points and some low points, but they have all resulted in learning and mark the beginning of your social work career. As a student of both authors wrote in a journal entry, "There is always something to learn" (Knapp, personal communication, 1998).

Cameron was able to hear the feedback from his fellow students regarding his "obsession" with working with addicts and consulted with his field instructor and a favorite faculty person. Admittedly, he did not want to consider the possibility that he was overly invested in his practicum and this area of his professional development. After considerable reflection, he concluded he may have crossed a boundary of his professionalism and lost the detached concern necessary for effective social work practice. Although painful, this process enabled Cameron to realize a need to broaden his experience base. He opted to complete a practicum in a different setting. He had not lost his enthusiasm or commitment for working in substance abuse treatment, but he realized that he could benefit from shifting his focus to include a wider range of skill areas.

Corina immediately shared her concerns with her field instructor. The field instructor, having seen this type of reaction from adolescents before, helped Corina to process her feelings about Chad and her work with him. The two discussed ways in which Corina could help Chad acknowledge his feelings, terminate appropriately with her, and feel positive about someone leaving him. As with her initial efforts to facilitate an effective termination, Corina mapped out her strategies and even rehearsed with her field instructor how she would approach Chad. Again, Chad provided Corina with an unexpected turn of events. He escaped from the facility! Corina was able to learn new skills even if she did not have the opportunity to apply them.

Ben struggled for several weeks with the dilemma of staying at the agency as an employee or moving on to other things. He processed this dilemma with everyone he knew, but ultimately, he alone had to make the decision. Although he knew that his day-to-day life would be made easier by having a full-time paid position with benefits, he weighed that against having to delay his goals of becoming a family therapist. In the end, he opted to leave the agency in pursuit of his original aspirations.

Succeed with **mysocialworklab**

Log onto **MySocialWorkLab** to access a wealth of case studies, videos, and assessment. (*If you did not receive an access code to* **MySocialWorkLab** *with this text and wish to purchase access online, please visit* www.mysocialworklab.com.)

1. Click on My Social Work Library. Select "Want a Social Work Career?: What You Need to Know: Salaries and Benefits: What to Expect, What to

Request." After reading this article, develop a list of questions that you can ask during an employment interview.

2. Click on Core Competency Videos. Select Engagement, Assessment, Intervention, and Evaluation. View the Evaluation video and document the evaluative methods depicted.

PRACTICE TEST The following questions will test your knowledge of the content found within this chapter. For additional assessment, including licensing-exam type questions on applying chapter content to practice, visit **MySocialWorkLab.**

Ethical Practice

1. Which of the following is not an inappropriate client termination strategy?
   a. Agree to be available for future services
   b. Inform client that she or he will be "ok" after you leave
   c. Agree to attend a social gathering together
   d. Provide information for future contact by client

Engage Assess Intervene Evaluate

2. Which of the following is the best response to a client who is reacting negatively to a social worker's departure?
   a. Introduce a ritual to formalize closure
   b. Refer client to your field instructor to discuss her or his feelings
   c. Assume client will adjust to termination
   d. Arrange for client to continue working with your co-worker

Professional Identity

3. Formal evaluations of practicum should include all of the following except:
   a. Review status of assignments
   b. Determine disposition of cases/projects
   c. Mutual feedback between student and field instructor
   d. Personalized feedback regarding agency staff members

4. The best strategy for ending a practicum that has not been a positive experience is to:
   a. Leave as soon as possible
   b. Provide balanced feedback to field instructor
   c. Inform field instructor of reasons for problems
   d. Suggest social work program discontinue agency as practicum site

Research Based Practice

5. Intervention evaluations include all of the following strategies except:
   a. Standardized tools to document behavior change
   b. Client satisfaction surveys
   c. Behavior change tool administered post-termination
   d. Case conference presentation

6. A professional portfolio may include all of the following items except:
   a. Writing sample
   b. Photograph of your family
   c. Recording of a presentation
   d. Power point slide presentation

7. Optimal interviewing strategies should not include:
   a. Summary of career goals
   b. Negative comments about practicum site/field instructor
   c. Research on agency history, mission, and funding
   d. Questions about employee benefits

8. Social work employment opportunities are increasing in all areas except:
   a. In-patient substance abuse treatment
   b. Gerontological practice
   c. International practice
   d. School settings

9. When offered employment, it is appropriate to ask about each of the following questions except:
   a. Employee benefits
   b. Racial and ethnic make-up of staff
   c. Criminal and background check
   d. Salary increases

10. Social work credentials (license/certification) typically require all of the following except:
    a. Social work practice experience
    b. Social work supervision
    c. Recommendation from a former client
    d. Criminal background investigation

Log onto **MySocialWorkLab** once you have completed the Practice Test above, to access additional study tools and assessment.

Answers:

Key: 1) d 2) a 3) d 4) b 5) c 6) b 7) b 8) a 9) b 10) c

References

Abram, F., Hartung, M., & Wernet, S. (2000). The non-MSW task supervisor, MSW field instructor, and the practicum student: A triad for high quality field education. *Journal of Teaching in Social Work, 20*(1–2), 171–185.

Albert, R. (2000). *Law and social work practice*. New York: Springer.

Aldgate, J., Healy, L., Malcolm, B., Pine, B., Rose, W., & Seden, J. (2007). *Enhancing social work management: Theory and best practice from the UK and USA*. Philadelphia and London: Jessica Kingsley Publishers.

Armour, M. P., Bain, B., & Rubio, R. (2004). An evaluation study of diversity training for field instructors: A collaborative approach to enhancing cultural competence. *Journal of Social Work Education, 40*(1), 27–37.

Arndt, J., King, S., Suter, E., Mazonde, J., Taylor, E., & Arthur, N. (2009). Socialization in health education: Encouraging an integrated interprofessional socialization process. *Journal of Allied Health, 38*(1), 18–23.

Aronoff, N. L. (2008). Interprofessional and partnered practice. In T. Mizrahi & L. E. Davis (Eds.), *Encyclopedia of social work* (20th ed., Vol. 2, pp. 533–536). Washington, DC and New York: National Association of Social Workers and Oxford University Press.

Arrington, P. (2008). *Stress at work: How do social workers cope? NASW Membership Workforce Study*. Washington, DC: National Association of Social Workers.

Arthur, G., Brende, J., & Quiroz, S. (2003). Violence: Incidence and frequency of physical and psychological assaults affecting mental health providers in Georgia. *Journal of General Psychology, 130*(1), 22.

Association for the Advancement of Social Work with Groups, Inc. (AASWG). (2006). *Standards for social work practice with groups*. Retrieved from www.aaswg.org

Association of Baccalaureate Program Directors. (2006). *Generalist practice*. Available at www.bpdonline.org/Content/NavigationMenu/ResourceCenter/Definitions/default.htm

Barker, R. L. (2003). *The social work dictionary* (5th ed.). Washington, DC: NASW Press.

Barker, R. L., & Branson, D. M. (2000). *Forensic social work: Legal aspects of professional practice*. New York: Haworth Press.

Barlow, C., & Hall. B. L. (2007). What about feelings?: A study of emotion and tension in social work field education. *Social Work Education, 26*(4), 399–413.

Barlow, C. A., Pelech, W., & Badry, D. (2005). The workplace practicum: A disquieting aspect of Canadian social work field education. *Canadian Social Work Review, 22*(1), 71–87.

Barretti, M. (2004). What do we know about the professional socialization of our students? *Journal of Social Work Education, 40*(2), 255–283.

Barretti, M. A. (2007). Teachers and field instructors as student role models: A neglected dimension in social work education. *Journal of Teaching in Social Work, 27*(3/4), 215–239.

Barretti, M. A. (2009). Ranking desirable field instructor characteristics: Viewing student preferences in context with field and class experience. *The Clinical Supervisor, 28*(1), 47–71.

Barton, H., Bell, K., & Bowles, W. (2005). Help or hindrance? Outcomes of social work student placements. *Australian Social Work, 58*(3), 301–312.

Baum, N. (2007). Field supervisors' feelings and concerns at the termination of the supervisory relationship. *British Journal of Social Work, 37*(7), 1095–1112.

Birkenmaier, J., Rubio, D. M., & Berg-Weger, M. (2002). Human service nonprofit agencies: Studying the impact of policy changes. *Journal of Social Work, 2*(2), 133–147.

Birkenmaier, J., & Timm, T. (2003). Feedback in practicum: Givin' it and takin' it. *The New Social Worker, 10*(1), 13–15.

Black, H. D. (2004). *Black's law dictionary with pronunciations* (8th ed.). St. Paul, MN: West Publishing.

Bobo, K., Kendall, J., & Max, S. (2001). *Organizing for social change*. New York: Seven Locks Press.

Boddie, S. (2008). Faith-based agencies and social work. In T. Mizrahi & L. E. Davis (Eds.), *Encyclopedia of Social Work* (Vol. 2, pp. 169–175). Washington DC and New York: National Association of Social Workers and Oxford University Press.

Bogo, M. (2005). Field instruction in social work: A review of the research literature. *The Clinical Supervisor, 24*(1–2), 163–193.

Bogo, M. (2006a). Field instruction in social work: A review of the research literature. *The Clinical Supervisor, 24*(1), 163–193.

Bogo, M. (2006b). *Social work practice: Concepts, processes, and interviewing*. New York: Columbia University Press.

Bogo, M., Regehr, C., Power, R., Hughes, J., Woodford, M., & Regehr, G. (2004). Toward new approaches for evaluating student field performance: Tapping the implicit criteria used by experienced field instructors. *Journal of Social Work Education, 40*(3), 417–426.

Bogo, M., Regehr, C., Woodford, M., Hughes, J., Power, R., & Regehr, G. (2006). Beyond competencies: Field instructors' descriptions of student performance. *Journal of Social Work Education, 42*(3), 579–593.

Bogo, M. & Vayda, E. (1998). *The practice of field instruction in social work: Theory and process* (2nd ed.). Toronto: University of Toronto Press.

Brown, T. M. & Waites, C. (2002). Mentorship: What it can do for you. *The New Social Worker, 9*(1), 4–5.

Burry, C. L. (2003). Working with potentially violent clients in their homes. *The Clinical Supervisor, 21*(1), 145–153.

California State University San Bernardino School of Social Work. (n.d.). Process recording micro forms. Available at http://socialwork.csusb.edu/majorsPrograms/BA/field-practicum.htm

Calloway-Graham, D., Mason, D. T., & Peak, T. (2004). Shaping your professional self in the practicum. *The New Social Worker, 11*(3), 6–7.

Cameron, M., Turkiewicz, R. M., Holdaway, B. A., Bill, J. S., Goodman, J., Bonner, A. (2009). Teaching organization theory and practice: An experiential and reflective approach. *Journal of Teaching in Social Work, 29*(1), 71–84.

Center for Health Workforce Studies & Center for Workforce Studies. (2006). *Licensed social workers in the US, 2004.* Rensselaer, NY and Washington, DC: University of Albany School of Public Health Center for Health Workforce Studies and NASW Center for Workforce Studies.

Chase, Y. (2008). Professional liability and malpractice. In T. Mizrahi & L. E. Davis (Eds.), *Encyclopedia of social work* (Vol. 3, pp. 425–429). Washington DC and New York: National Association of Social Workers and Oxford University Press.

Chu, W. & Tsui, M. (2008). The nature of practice wisdom in social work revisited. *International Social Work, 51*(1), 47–54.

Clements, J. A. (2008). Social work students' perceived knowledge of and preparation for group-work practice. *Social Work with Groups, 31*(3–4), 329–346.

Council on Social Work Education. (2008). *Educational policy and accreditation standards.* Alexandria, VA: Author.

Dettlaff, A. J., & Wallace, G. (2002). Promoting integration of theory and practice in field education: An instructional tool for field instructors and field educators. *The Clinical Supervisor, 21*(2), 145–160.

Dietz, C. & Thompson, J. (2004). Rethinking boundaries: Ethical dilemmas in the social worker–client relationship. *Journal of Progressive Human Services, 15*(2), 1–24.

Dill, K. (2007). Impact of stressors on front-line child welfare supervisors. *The Clinical Supervisor, 26*(1), 177–193.

Doelling, C. N. (2004). *Social work career development. A handbook for job hunting and career planning* (2nd ed.). Washington, DC: NASW Press.

Equal Employment Opportunity Commission (EEOC). (2009). *Sexual harassment.* Retrieved July 2, 2009, from www. eeoc.gov/types/sexual_harassment.html

Figley, C. R. (2002). Compassion fatigue: Psychotherapists' chronic lack of self care. *Journal of Clinical Psychology, 58*(11), 1433–1441.

Fitch, D., Peet, M., Reed, B. G., & Tolman. (2008). The use of e-portfolios in evaluating the curriculum and student learning. *Journal of Social Work Education, 44*(3), 37–54.

Fleming, N. D. & Mills, C. (1992). Not another inventory, rather a catalyst for reflection. *To Improve the Academy, 11*(137).

Floyd, C. (1995). Preparing for supervision. *The New Social Worker, 2*(2), 8–9.

Fogel, S. J. (2008). Sexual harassment. In T. Mizrahi & L. E Davis (Eds.), *Encyclopedia of Social Work* (Vol. 4, pp. 25–29). Washington, DC and New York: National Association of Social Workers and Oxford University Press.

Folaron, G. (2001). Understanding published research to enhance competent practice. *The New Social Worker, 8*(4), 8–10.

Fortune, A. E. (2009). Terminating with clients. In Roberts, A. R. *Social workers' desk reference* (2nd ed., pp. 627–631). New York: Oxford Press.

Fortune, A. E., Lee, M., & Cavazos, A. (2005). Achievement motivation and outcome in social work field education. *Journal of Social Work Education, 41*(1), 115–129.

Fortune, A. E., Lee, M., & Cavazos, A. (2007). Does practice make perfect? Practicing professional skills and outcomes in social work field education. *The Clinical Supervisor, 26*(1/2), 239–263.

Fox, R. (2004). Field instruction and the mature student. *Journal of Teaching in Social Work, 24*(3), 113–129.

Furman, R., Coyne, A., & Negi, N. J. (2008). An international experience for social work students: Self-reflection through poetry and journal writing exercises. *Journal of Teaching in Social Work, 28*(1/2), 71–85.

Gamble. D. N. & Weil, D. (2008). Community: Practice interventions. In T. Mizrahi & L. E. Davis (Eds.), *Encyclopedia of social work* (Vol. 1, pp. 355–368). Washington, DC and New York: National Association of Social Workers and Oxford University Press.

Garvin, C. D. & Galinsky, M. J. (2008). Groups. In T. Mizrahi & L. E Davis (Eds.), *Encyclopedia of Social Work* (Vol. 2, pp. 287–298). Washington, DC and New York: National Association of Social Workers and Oxford University Press.

Gelman, C. R. (2004). Anxiety experience by foundation-year MSW students entering field placement: Implications for admissions, curriculum, and field education. *Journal of Social Work Education, 40*(1), 39–54.

Gelman, C. R., Fernandez, N. H., Miller, S., & Weiner, M. (2007). Challenging endings: First year MSW interns' experiences with forced termination and discussion points for supervisory guidance. *Clinical Social Work Journal, 35*(2), 79–90.

Gelman, C. R. & Lloyd, C. M. (2008). Pre-placement anxiety among foundation-year MSW students: A follow-up study. *Journal of Social Work Education, 44*(1), 173–183.

General Accounting Office. (2003). *Child welfare: HHS could play a greater role in helping child welfare agencies recruit and retain staff* (GAO 03-357). Washington, DC: Author.

Giddings, M. M., Thompson, K. H., & Holland, T. P. (1997). The relationship between student assessments of agency work climate and satisfaction with practicum. *Areté, 21*(2), 25–35.

Giddings, M. M., Vodde, R., & Cleveland, P. (2003). Examining student–field instructor problems in practicum: Beyond student satisfaction measures. *The Clinical Supervisor, 22*(2), 191–214.

Globerman, J., & Bogo, M. (2003). Changing times: Understanding social workers' motivation to be field instructors. *Social Work, 48*(1), 65–73.

Golensky, M. & Mulder, C. A. (2006). Coping in a constrained economy: Survival strategies of nonprofit human service organizations. *Administration in Social Work, 39*(3), 5–24.

Gould, K. H. (2000). Beyond Jones v. Clinton: Sexual harassment law and social work. *Social Work, 45*(3), 237–248.

Gourdine, R. M. & Baffour, T. D. (2004). Maximizing learning: Evaluating a competency-based training program for field instructors. *The Clinical Supervisor, 23*(1), 33–53.

Green, G. P. & Haines, A. (2008). *Asset building and community development.* Thousand Oaks, CA: Sage Publications.

Green, R. G., Baskind, F. R., Mustian, B. E., Reed, L. N., & Taylor, H. R. (2007). Professional education and private practice. Is there a disconnect? *Social Work, 52*(2), 151–159.

Grise-Owens, E. (2008). Traveling toward a social work degree: Ten road-tested trip-tips. *The New Social Worker, 15*(2), 20–22.

Grobman, L. M. (2003). Lunch talk. *The New Social Worker, 10*(1), 9.

Groccia, J. E. (1997). The student as customer versus the student as learner. *About Campus,* 31–32.

Gronbjerg, K. (2008). Fundraising. In T. Mizrahi & L. E. Davis (Eds.), *Encyclopedia of social work* (Vol. 2, pp. 236–239). Washington, DC and New York: National Association of Social Workers and Oxford University Press.

Harkness, D. (2008). Consultation. In T. Mizrahi & L. E. Davis (Eds.), *Encyclopedia of social work* (Vol. 1, pp. 420–423). Washington, DC: National Association for Social Workers and Oxford University Press.

Haynes, K. S. & Mickelson, J. S. (2006). *Affecting change: Social workers in the political arena.* New York: Pearson and Allyn/Bacon.

Hodge J. G. Jr. (2004). *Advancing HIV prevention initiative: A limited legal analysis of state HIV statutes.* The Center for Law and the Public's Health at Georgetown and John Hopkins Universities. Retrieved November 15, 2009, from www.publichealthlaw.net/Research/PDF/AHP%20Report%20-%20Hodge.pdf

Holden, C. (2005). The internationalization of corporate healthcare: Extent and emerging trends. *Competitions and Change, 9*(2), 201–219.

Holland, T. (2008). Organizations and governance. In T. Mizrahi & L. E Davis (Eds.), *Encyclopedia of Social Work* (Vol. 3, pp. 331–333). Washington, DC and New York: National Association of Social Workers and Oxford University Press.

Holloway, S., Black, P., Hoffman, K., & Pierce, D. (2009). *Some considerations of the import of the 2008 EPAS for curriculum design.* Available at www.cswe.org/CSWE/accreditation/2009-06+CompetencyPractice+Behavior.htm

Homonoff, E. (2008). The heart of social work: Best practitioners rise to challenges in field instruction. *The Clinical Supervisor, 27*(2), 135–169.

Iatridis, D. S. (2008). Policy practice. In T. Mizrahi & L. E. Davis (Eds.), *Encyclopedia of social work* (Vol. 3, pp. 362–368). Washington, DC and New York: National Association of Social Workers and Oxford University Press.

Itzhaky, H. & Eliahou, A. (2001). The effect of learning styles and empathy on perceived effectiveness of social work student supervision. *The Clinical Supervisor, 20*(2), 19–29.

Jansson, B. S., Dempsey, D., McCroskey, J., & Schneider, R. (2005). Four models of policy practice: Local, state and national arenas. In M. Weil's (Ed.), *The handbook of community practice* (pp. 319–338). Thousand Oaks, CA: Sage Publications.

Jaskyte, K. (2005). The impact of organizational socialization tactics on role ambiguity and role conflict of newly hired social workers. *Administration in Social Work, 29*(4), 69–87.

Jaskyte, K. (2008). Management: Practice Interventions. In T. Mizrahi & L. E Davis (Eds.), *Encyclopedia of Social Work* (Vol. 3, pp. 158–162). Washington, DC and New York: National Association of Social Workers and Oxford University Press.

Jayaratne, S. & Faller, K. D. (2009). Commitment to private and public agency workers to child welfare: How long do they plan to stay? *Journal of Social Service Research, 35*(3), 251–261.

Jenson, J. M. & Howard, M. O. (2008). Evidence-based practice. In T. Mizrahi & L. E. Davis (Eds.), *Encyclopedia of social work* (20th ed.,Vol. 2, pp. 158–165). Washington, DC and

New York: National Association of Social Workers and Oxford University Press.

Johnson, A. K., Kreuger, L. W., & Stretch, J. J. (1989). A court-ordered consent decree for the homeless: Process, conflict and control. *Journal of Sociology and Social Welfare, 16*(3), 29–42.

Johnson, L. & Schwartz, C. L. (1997). *Social welfare: A response to human need.* Boston: Allyn & Bacon.

Johnson, W. B. (2007). Transformational supervision: When supervisors mentor. *Professional Psychology: Research and Practice, 38*(3), 259–267.

Kadushin, A. & Harkness, D. (2002). *Supervision in social work.* New York: Columbia University Press.

Kagle, J. D. (2009). Record-keeping. In A. R. Roberts (Ed.), *Social workers' desk reference* (2nd ed., pp. 28–32). New York: Oxford University Press.

Kagle, J. D. & Kopels, S. (2008). *Social work records* (3rd ed.). Long Grove, IL: Waveland Press, Inc.

Kane, M., Hamlin, E. R., & Hawkins, W. (2000). Perceptions of field instructors: What skills are critically important in managed care and privatized environments? *Advances in Social Work, 1*(2), 187–202.

Karger, H. & Stoesz, D. (2006). *American social welfare policy.* Boston, MA: Pearson and Allyn & Bacon.

Kayser, K. & Johnson, J. K. M. (2008). Divorce. In T. Mizrahi & L. E. Davis (Eds.), *Encyclopedia of social work* (Vol. 2, pp. 76–84). Washington, DC and New York: National Association of Social Workers and Oxford University Press.

Kirst-Ashman, K. K. & Hull, G. H. (1998). *The macro skills workbook. A generalist approach.* Chicago, IL: Nelson-Hall.

Kirst-Ashman, K. K. & Hull, G. H. (2009). *Generalist practice with organizations and communities.* Chicago, IL: Nelson-Hall.

Knight, C. (1996). A study of BSW students' perceptions of and experiences with risks to their personal safety in the field practicum. *The Journal of Baccalaureate Social Work, 2*(1), 91–108.

Knight, C. (2001). The process of field instruction: BSW and MSW students' views of effective field supervision. *Journal of Social Work Education, 37*(2), 357–379.

Knopf, R. (1979). *Surviving the BS (Bureaucratic System).* Wilminston, NC: Mandala Press.

Knowles, M. S., Holton, E. F., & Swanson, R. A. (2005). *The adult learner: The definitive classic in adult education and human resource development* (6th ed.). Burlington, MA: Elsevier.

Kolb, A. Y. & Kolb, D. A. (2005). Learning styles and learning spaces: Enhancing experiential learning in higher education. *Academy of Management Learning and Education, 4*(2), 193–212.

Kolb, D. A., Rubin, I. M., & McIntyre, J. M. (1971). *Organizational psychology: A book of readings.* Englewood Cliffs, NJ: Prentice-Hall.

Kong, E. (2007). The development of strategic management in the non-profit context: Intellectual capital in the social service non-profit organization. *International Journal of Management Reviews, 10*(3), 281–299.

Kretzman, J. & McKnight, J. (1993). *Building communities from the inside out: A path toward finding and mobilizing a community's assets.* Chicago, IL: ACTA.

Lager, P. B. & Robbins, V. C. (2004). Field education: Exploring the future, expanding the vision. *Journal of Social Work Education, 40*(1), 3–11.

Lawson, H. A. (2008). Collaborative practice. In T. Mizrahi & L. E. Davis (Eds.), *Encyclopedia of social work* (Vol. 1, pp. 341–347). Washington, DC and New York: National Association of Social Workers and Oxford University Press.

Ligon, J. & Ward, J. (2004). 10 tips to maximize the student–field instructor relationship. *The New Social Worker, 11*(2), 10–11.

Linsley, J. (1998). Self-disclosure: How much should I tell? *The New Social Worker, 5*(4), 4–6.

Lloyd, C., King, R., & Chenoweth, L. (2002). Social work, stress, and burnout: A review. *Journal of Mental Health, 11*(3), 255–265.

Lohman, R. A. & Lohman, N. (2008). Management: Financial. In T. Mizrahi & L. E. Davis (Eds.), *Encyclopedia of social work* (Vol. 3, pp. 163–173). Washington, DC and New York: National Association of Social Workers and Oxford University Press.

Lohmann, R. A. & McNutt, R. (2005). Practice in the electronic community. In M. Weil, M. Reisch, D. N. Gamble, L. Gutierrez, E. Mulroy, & R. A. Cnaan (Eds.), *Handbook of community practice* (pp. 636–646). Thousand Oaks, CA: Sage Publications.

Lynch, J. G. & Versen, G. R. (2003). Social work supervisor liability: Risk factors and strategies for risk reduction. *Administration in Social Work, 27*(2), 57–72.

Macdonald, G. & Sirotich, F. (2005). Violence in the social work workplace: The Canadian experience. *International Social Work, 48*(6), 772–781.

Madden, R. G. (2008). Legal system. In T. Mizrahi & L. E. Davis (Eds.), *Encyclopedia of social work* (Vol. 3, pp. 67–70). Washington, DC and New York: National Association of Social Workers and Oxford University Press.

Maidment, J. (2003). Problems experienced by students on field placement: Using research findings to inform curriculum design and content. *Australian Social Work, 56*(1), 50–60.

Mailloux, K. J. & Whitten, R. B. (2009). Social work intern logs: An effective learning Exercise for reflecting on a first hospice experience. *The New Social Worker, 16*(3), 8–10.

Mama, R. S. (2001). Violence in the field: Experiences of students and supervisors. *The Journal of Baccalaureate Social Work, 7*(1), 17–26.

Mayer, B. (2008). Conflict resolution. In T. Mizrahi & L. E. Davis (Eds.) *Encyclopedia of social work* (Vol. 1, pp. 415–420). Washington, DC and New York: National Association of Social Workers and Oxford University Press.

McBride, A. M., Hanson, S. L., Beverly, S., Schreiner, M., Sherraden, M., & Johnson, L. (2004). *Asset building: Increasing capacity for performance measurement and effects.* St. Louis MO: Center for Social Development, Washington University in St. Louis. Retrieved February 8, 2005, from www.gwbweb.wustl.edu/csd

McInnis-Dittrich, K. (1994). *Integrating social welfare policy and social work practice.* Pacific Grove, CA: Brooks/Cole.

McIntosh, D. (2004). Taking no action is an action. *The New Social Worker, 11*(2), 6–8.

Memmott, J. & Brennan, E. M. (1998). Learner–learning environment fit: An adult learning model for social work education. *Journal of Teaching in Social Work, 16*(1/2), 75–98.

Moniz, C. & Gorin, S. (2007). *Health and mental health care policy.* Boston, MA: Pearson.

Mort, G. S., Weerawardena, J., & Carnegie, K. (2002). Social entrepreneurship: Towards conceptualization. *International Journal of Nonprofit and Voluntary Sector Marketing, 8*(1), 76–88.

Moxley, D. P. (2008). Interdisciplinarity. In T. Mizrahi, & L. E. Davis (Eds.), *Encyclopedia of social work* (Vol. 2, pp. 468–472). Washington, DC and New York: National Association of Social Workers and Oxford University Press.

Munson, C. E. (2002). *Handbook of clinical social work supervision* (3rd ed.). New York: Haworth Press.

National Association of Social Workers (NASW). (2001). *NASW standards for cultural competence in social work practice.* Available at www.naswdc.org/pubs/standards/culture.htm

National Association of Social Workers (NASW). (2005). *National procedures for professional review.* Washington, DC: Author.

National Association of Social Workers (NASW). (2007). *Indicators for the achievement of the NASW standards for cultural competence in social work practice.* Available at www.socialworkers.org/practice/standards/NASWCulturalStandardsIndicators2006.pdf

National Association of Social Workers (NASW). (2008a). *Code of ethics.* Available at www.socialworkers.org/pubs/code/code.asp

National Association of Social Workers (NASW). (2008b). Professional self-care and social work. *Social Work Speaks (2009–2012).* Washington, DC: Author.

National Institute for Occupational Safety and Health. (2002). *Violence. Occupational hazards in hospitals.* Washington, DC: Author.

Netting, F. E. (2008). Macro social work practice. In T. Mizrahi & L. E. Davis (Eds.), *Encyclopedia of social work* (Vol. 3, pp. 139–144). Washington, DC and New York: National Association of Social Workers and Oxford University Press.

Netting, F. E., Kettner, P. M., & McMurtry, S. L. (2008). *Social work macro practice.* New York: Addison Wesley Longman.

Newhill, C. (2008). Client violence. In T. Mizrahi & L. E. Davis (Eds.), *Encyclopedia of Social Work* (Vol. 1, pp. 313–317). Washington, DC and New York: National Association of Social Workers and Oxford University Press.

Ngai, S. S. & Cheung, C. (2009). Idealism, altruism, career orientation, and emotional exhaustion among social work undergraduates. *Journal of Social Work Education, 45*(1), 105–121.

O'Neill, M. (2002). *Nonprofit nation: A new look at the third America.* San Francisco: Jossey-Bass.

Papadaki, V. & Nygren, L. (2006). 'I'll carry this experience with me throughout my studies and future career': Practice tutorials and students' views on social work in Iraklio, Greece. *Social Work Education, 25*(7), 710–722.

Patti, R. J. (2008). Management: Overview. In T. Mizrahi & L. E. Davis (Eds.), *Encyclopedia of social work* (3:148-158). Washington, DC and New York: National Association of Social Workers and Oxford University Press.

Polowy, C. I. & Gilbertson, J. (1997). *Social workers and subpoenas: Office of General Counsel law notes.* Washington, DC: NASW Press.

Reamer, F. G. (2003). *Social work malpractice and liability.* New York: Columbia University Press.

Reamer, F. G. (2006). *Ethical standards in social work: A review of the NASW Code of Ethics.* Washington, DC: NASW Press.

Reamer, F. G. (2009). Ethical issues in social work. In A. R. Roberts (Ed.), *Social workers' desk reference* (2nd ed., pp. 115–120). New York: Oxford Press.

Reeser, L. C. & Wertkin, R. (2001). Safety training in social work education: A national survey. *Journal of Teaching in Social Work, 21*(1/2), 95–113.

Reisch, M. (2005). Radical community organizing. In M. Weil, M. Reisch, D. N. Gamble, L. Gutierrez, E. Mulroy, & R. A. Cnaan (Eds.), *Handbook of community practice* (pp. 287–304). Thousand Oaks, CA: Sage Publications.

Respass, G. & Payne, B. K. (2008). Social services workers and workplace violence. *Journal of Aggression, Maltreatment & Trauma, 16*(2), 131–143.

Robert, H. M., Evans, W. J., Honemann, D. H., & Balch, T. J. (2004). *Robert's rules of order newly revised, in brief.* Cambridge, MA: Da Capo Press.

Ruggles, T. (2004). How to avoid the crash and burn. *The New Social Worker, 11*(3), 20–22.

Russo, R. (1993). *Serving and surviving as a human service worker.* Prospect Heights, IL: Waveland Press.

Saint Louis University. (2007). *Harassment policy.* Retrieved July 2, 2009, from www.slu .edu/services/HR/hrpolicies.html

Scalera, N. R. (1995). The critical need for specialized health and safety measures for child welfare workers. *Child Welfare, 74*(2), 337–350.

Shaffer, G. L. (2008). Field work. In T. Mizrahi & L. E. Davis (Eds.), *Encyclopedia of social work* (20th ed., Vol. 4, pp. 120–124). Washington, DC and New York: National Association of Social Workers and Oxford University Press.

Sheafor, B. W. & Horejsi, C. R. (2008). *Techniques and guidelines for social work practice* (8th ed.). Boston: Allyn & Bacon.

Shulman, L. (2008). *Supervision.* In T. Mizrahi & L. E. Davis (Eds.), *Encyclopedia of social work* (Vol. 4, pp. 186–190). Washington, DC: National Association for Social Workers and Oxford University Press.

Shulman, L. (2009). *The skills of helping individuals, families, groups, and communities* (6th ed.). Belmon, CA: Brooks/Cole.

Shulman, L. S. (1999). Signature pedagogies in the professions. *Daedalus, 134*(3), 52–59.

Simmons, C. S., Diaz, L., Jackson, V., & Takahashi, R. (2008). NASW cultural competence indicators: A new tool for the social work profession. *Journal of Ethnic and Cultural Diversity in Social Work, 17*(1), 4–20.

Simmons, W. J. & Enguidanos, S. (2006). Health maintenance organizations and managed care companies. In B. Berkman & S. D'Ambruoso (Eds.), *Handbook of social work in health and aging* (pp. 483–489). New York: Oxford Press.

Simpson, G. A., Williams, J. C., & Segall, A. B. (2007). Social work education and clinical learning. *Journal of Clinical Social Work, 35*, 3–14.

Social Work Examination Services. (2009). *State licensing boards.* Available at www.swes.net/home.html

Spencer, P. C. & Munch, S. (2003). Client violence toward social workers: The role of management in community mental health programs. *Social Work, 48*(4), 532–544.

Stein, T. J. (2004). *The role of law in social work practice and administration.* New York: Columbia University Press.

Streeter, C. (2008). Community: Overview. In T. Mizrahi & L. E. Davis (Eds.), *Encyclopedia of social work* (Vol. 1, pp. 348–355). Washington, DC and New York: National Association of Social Workers and Oxford University Press.

Teigiser, K. S. (2009). New approaches to generalist field education. *Journal of Social Work Education, 45*(1), 139–146.

Thyer, B. A. (2009). Evidence-based practice, science, and social work. In A. R. Roberts (Ed.), *Social workers' desk reference* (2nd ed., pp. 1115–1119). New York: Oxford Press.

Todd, S. & Schwartz, K. (2009). Thinking through quality in field education: Integrating alternative and traditional learning opportunities. *Social Work Education, 28*(4), 380–395.

Toseland, R. W. & Horton, H. (2008). Group work. In T. Mizrahi & L. E Davis (Eds.), *Encyclopedia of Social Work* (Vol. 2, pp. 298–308). Washington, DC and New York: National Association of Social Workers and Oxford University Press.

Tropman, J. E. (2003). *Making meetings work* (2nd ed.). Thousand Oaks, CA: Sage Publications.

Tully, C. T., Kropf, N. P., & Price, J. L. (1993). Is field a hard hat area? A study of violence in field placements. *Journal of Social Work Education, 29*(2), 191–199.

Tyuse, S. W. & Linhorst, D. M. (2005). Drug courts and mental health courts: Implications for social work. *Health & Social Work, 39*(3), 233–240.

Um, M. Y. & Brown-Standridge, M. D. (1993). Discovering organizational "rules" that contribute to student stress in social work field placements. *The Journal of Applied Social Sciences, 17*(2), 157–177.

U.S. Department of Labor. (2004). *Guidelines for preventing work place violence for health care & social service workers* (OSHA 3148-01R 2004). Retrieved June 18, 2009, from www.osha.gov/Publications/OSHA3148/osha3148.html

U.S. Department of Labor Bureau of Labor Statistics. (2008–2009). Social workers. In *Occupational outlook handbook, 2010–11 Edition.* Available at www.bls.gov/oco/ocos060.htm (visited August 22, 2009).

Vandiver, V. L. (2008). Managed care. In T. Mizrahi & L. E. Davis (Eds.), *Encyclopedia of social work* (Vol. 3, pp. 144–148). Washington, DC and New York: National Association of Social Workers and Oxford University Press.

Waites, C. (1998). Ode to a practicum student. *The New Social Worker, 5*(2), 23.

Walsh, J. (2002). Termination and your field placement. *The New Social Worker, 9*(2), 14–17.

Ward, K. & Mama, R. S. (2006). *Breaking out of the box: Adventure-based field instruction.* Chicago, IL: Lyceum Books, Inc.

Weil, M. (2005). Contexts and challenges for the 21st century communities. In M. Weil, M. Reisch, D. N. Gamble, L. Gutierrez, E. Mulroy, & R. A. Cnaan (Eds.), *Handbook of community practice* (pp. 3–22). Thousand Oaks, CA: Sage Publications.

Weinger, S. (2001). *Security risk: Preventing client violence against social workers.* Washington, DC: NASW Press.

Weisman, T. & Whitaker, T. (2008). Social work profession: Workforce. In T. Mizrahi and L. E. Davis (Eds.), *Encyclopedia of social work* (Vol. 4, pp. 165–168). Washington, DC and New York: National Association of Social Workers and Oxford University Press.

Wharton, T. C. (2008). Compassion fatigue: Being an ethical social worker. *The New Social Worker, 15*(1), 4–7.

Whitaker, T. & Arrington, P. (2008). *Social workers at work. NASW membership workforce study.* Washington, DC: National Association of Social Workers.

Wing, K. T., Pollak, T. H., & Blackwood, A. (2008). *The non-profit almanac*. Washington, DC: The Urban Institute.

Whitaker, T., Weismiller, T., & Clark, E. (2006). *Assuring the sufficiency of frontline workforce: A national study of licensed social workers*. Washington, DC: NASW

Yalom, I. D. & Leszcz, M. (2005). *The theory and practice of group psychotherapy* (5th ed.). New York: Basic Books.

Younes, M. N. (2003). Coming full circle: Putting advocacy ethics into action. *The New Social Worker, 10*(2), 8–9.

Zastrow, C. & Petracchi, H. (2009). *An interpretation for incorporating EPAS 2008 into social work baccalaureate and masters curriculum in CSWE-accredited programs: Recommendation from the Field*. Alexandria, VA: Baccalaureate Program Directors Listserv.

Photo Credits

Index